NATIONAL IDENTITIES &
BILATERAL
RELATIONS

NATIONAL IDENTITIES &
BILATERAL
RELATIONS

WIDENING GAPS IN EAST ASIA AND
CHINESE DEMONIZATION OF
THE UNITED STATES

Edited by
GILBERT ROZMAN

Woodrow Wilson Center Press
WASHINGTON, D.C.

Stanford University Press
STANFORD, CALIFORNIA

CONTENTS

ACKNOWLEDGMENTS

This second volume on East Asian national identities, which treats bilateral dyads rather than comparisons, progressed through two stages. The first stage, in the years 2009–10, was marked by workshops to discuss drafts of papers. They were supported by the Mercer Fund of the East Asian Studies Program at Princeton University. The second stage, in 2010–11, was an academic year at the Woodrow Wilson International Center for Scholars, when I worked with the authors on revising their papers while centering my research on Chinese-language materials, writing the final chapters of the book. The collegial atmosphere of the Center as well as research assistance from Jing Jing and Nay Min Oo were conducive to maximizing the opportunity for research and reflection.

The United States–Japan Foundation provided primary support. Its generous assistance enabled the project to go forward as the authors prepared their papers and reworked them in order to meet the overall objective of a tightly cohesive volume.

The final product benefited from comments by two anonymous readers and fellowship support from the Woodrow Wilson Center as well as backing from Joe Brinley, director of the Woodrow Wilson Center Press, and the Center's Publishing Committee. I thank the contributors and others who assisted this project for their unstinting support.

Gilbert Rozman
August 2011

NATIONAL IDENTITIES &
BILATERAL
RELATIONS

PART I

BILATERAL RELATIONS AND NATIONAL IDENTITIES WITHIN EAST ASIA

INTRODUCTION:

CONCEPTUALIZING NATIONAL IDENTITY GAPS WITHIN EAST ASIA

Gilbert Rozman

National identities are existential and relational. They celebrate the existence of a nation-state, explaining why it is exceptional and is worthy of a better future. At the same time, they are built on contrasts, showing why one's state is different from and superior to other states deemed most relevant. Discourse on national identity is concerned with drawing sharp distinctions, in contrast to the diplomatic pursuit of the national interest, which often is aimed at resolving problems by narrowing divides. To concentrate on national identities is to highlight divergence and how it affects the way problems are conceptualized. That is the objective here, without in any way denying the value of also examining national interests as they figure in bilateral ties.

In explaining how national identities change, one needs to stress leadership changes. A revolution, unconditional surrender in a war, and a democratic shakeup due to a resounding electoral defeat are examples of far-reaching changes—each of which has occurred in East Asia—with profound consequences. However, another possibility is for leaders influenced by identity challenges to turn to foreign relations in order to affect a transformation in national identity. Driven by concern over the impact of bilateral relations on the existing national identity and

seeking relief by altering a relationship in a substantial manner in anticipation of its useful impact on the way national identity is constructed,
leaders may weigh their options in demonizing a rival. This is more
likely to happen in the course of a spike in national identity.

National identities change through diplomacy. Mere intentions of setting a new course do not suffice without joint accommodation and a
framework for boldly reconstructing how the new relationship trans-
forms international relations and domestic aspirations. The shift in diplomatic identity advances in stages. A critical step is envisioning why
reconceptualization of this bilateral relationship matters. Another step is
devising a new strategy for improving ties or reconstructing the framework that serves the intended national identity objective. The third and
most difficult step is finding a way to achieve this immediate objective
and to demonstrate its salience for the desired transformation of national
identity. However uncertain the prospects for diplomacy and identity, the
very pursuit of such a transformation is informative about a state's identity aspirations and how they remain in dispute. East Asian diplomacy can
be viewed through the lens of one or another normalization of relations,
in each case with a significant impact on national identity, and after the
reestablishment of formal relations, through the lens of how diplomacy
faces the challenge of transforming relations that still weigh heavily on
national identity because they are still seen as abnormal.

Japan, South Korea, and China have each sought diplomatic breakthroughs to achieve a major shift in national identity. In each case,
the search we discuss below is a reflection of discomfort with excess
dependence on the United States and the pressure that puts on national
identity and of widespread sentiment that the nation's identity is in
need of major adjustment. Here, the concept of identity gaps—which
is explored in detail in part II, where the identity gap with the world's
superpower is discussed—comes into play. At this point, it suffices to
simply note that an identity gap is an indicator of how substantial and
sensitive is the difference in national identity between two nations. The
focus of part I is how Japan, South Korea, and China consider ways
to change their diplomatic environment in Asia in order to transform
their national identities. Japan began this postwar quest as early as the

mid-1950s, whereas China's quest accelerated in the decade of the 2000s. The three bilateral cases of Japanese–South Korean, Sino–South Korean, and Sino-Japanese relations in the shadow of U.S. reliance offer striking examples of this quest over extended periods from the Cold War era to the present.

NATIONAL IDENTITIES AND UNREALIZED OPTIONS

In about 1990, Japan anticipated unprecedented diplomatic breakthroughs as the gateway to the normalization in relations with its neighbors that it had been missing since 1945. A decade later, it was South Korea that was hopeful that Asian diplomacy would transform the sense of abnormality that it had endured since 1945. The greatest optimism arose in China in 2010, which recalled a much longer period of humiliation and unrealized expectations. Eventually, however, all three countries overreached after succumbing to excessive optimism about their prospects in Asia. Their aspirations are revealed in their most meaningful bilateral relations over an extended period of time. Diplomacy became focused on meeting a national identity objective.

Japan's two primary options to resolve its unrealized quest for a national identity breakthrough were convergence with the United States and diplomatic diversification with powerful identity implications. The former was rejected in the 1960s, and only recent shocks have revived interest. Foreign Minister Aso Taro's "arc of freedom and prosperity" in the years 2006–7 and Foreign Minister Maehara Seiji's wholehearted embrace of a values-based alliance in 2010–11 may be limited to ideas proposed by a foreign minister, but they indicate a trend.

A debate about Japanese modernization proceeded in the 1960s as Japan achieved more than a decade of double-digit economic growth and thrust itself into the forefront of developed capitalist states with democratic systems. Although the most widely noted contributors were in the United States, especially social scientists taking a long-term historical perspective, the debate reverberated in Japan after the conclusion in 1960 of the U.S.-Japan Security Alliance drew the two allies closer.

The crux of the debate centered on four questions: (1) By siding with the United States in the Cold War, were national interests converging, especially in foreign policy toward East Asia? (2) By expanding economic ties as part of the free market system with the United States, was Japan succumbing to a quest for integration that left no scope for a separate economic system and leadership in organizing an Asian division of labor? (3) By accepting the logic of social transformation based on ideals of democracy and the free market, was Japan losing its distinctiveness in the way its society and polity were organized? (4) By recognizing itself as part of the West while reducing barriers to cultural diffusion, was Japan in danger of jettisoning its unique thinking about history and Japanese culture?

It is important to briefly put these four questions in historical context. In the aftermath of World War II, the United States had occupied Japan for six years and had rewritten its Constitution. It had left Japan defenseless, dependent on U.S. power for security and international relations more broadly. Japan's economic growth rested on U.S.–led institutions and the U.S. market. Finally, the flow of culture came from the West, inundating Japan with new ideals, which Western opinion leaders assumed would result in rapid convergence. Thus, for Japan to preserve its national identity, clear answers to the four questions had to reassure the Japanese people that convergence would not occur.

For progressives and conservative revisionists, convergence threatened cherished beliefs. The sizable leftist population, notably in the cultural and academic fields, claimed to be repulsed by the mainstream of Japanese history; yet that did not endear them to U.S. values. Influenced by a strain of socialism, they distanced themselves from U.S. foreign policy in favor of pacifism and an independent course and from the capitalist system in favor of a compact between state and society and modified communal values. The thought of convergence alienated them. A resolute corps of staunch conservatives, in turn, found the U.S. alliance expedient, but they were eager to revive justifications for Japan's conduct of foreign policy until 1945 and could not countenance the U.S. worldview. The center was very weak, and many moderate conservatives or potential centrists were discouraged by educational and media

4

socialization from analyzing Japan through the prism of general principles or comparative study. No serious debate on convergence arose in these circumstances.

In spite of the Yoshida Doctrine, which stipulated that Japan's foreign policy would rely on the United States, Japanese leaders, beginning with Hatoyama Ichiro and Kishi Nobusuke in the mid-1950s, pursued a national identity shift through diplomatic diversification. They needed a breakthrough with a state or cluster of states whose identity significance was distinct from the United States. The Ministry of Foreign Affairs, working in conjunction with the prime minister's office, identified the diplomatic targets and explored how a breakthrough could occur. In the 1950s, two options held some promise: the Islamic world and the Soviet Union. The former could reinvigorate a form of Asianism that did not appear to be blocked by the postwar repudiation of past conduct, and the latter could give Japan an independent role in shaping the international system. Both choices would mean reduced dependency on the United States, a vital objective in changing national identity. Japan's quest, as discussed by Kazuhiko Togo in this book, has persisted for at least half a century, even without resolving the national identity dilemma introduced by Yuichi Hosoya in the companion volume to this book.[1]

Starting in the 1960s, Japan's normalization of its relations with South Korea held the most hope for a shift in its national identity; but starting in the 1970s, its reconciliation with China had eclipsed South Korea as the pathway to Asianism. In the 1980s, the end of the Cold War combined with a spike in national identity confidence offered many possibilities, even if none came to fruition. This was the time of confidence that Moscow would return four islands and vindicate one quest for normalization, China would accept Japan as a bridge to the West and as leader in Asia, and South Korea would rely on Japan's economic clout in pursuing North Korea. Increasingly, since the late 1990s, Japan's options have narrowed to a partnership with China in establishing an East Asian community or reinforcing its alliance ties to the United States, linked to a sweeping embrace of universal values. Only in 2010 did opposition to the latter choice decline significantly as the China option lost appeal.

In chapter 1, Kazuhiko Togo explores how individual Japanese diplomats pursued a breakthrough strategy with the Islamic states, the Soviet Union and then Russia, and China. In each case, they sought to open more space for Japan distinct from the U.S. alliance, with often-unstated implications for how this would affect the six dimensions of national identity (i.e., ideological, temporal, sectoral, vertical, horizontal, and intensity; see part II[2]): (1) the potential for overcoming the left/right split in ideology that was heavily centered on views of bilateral ties with the United States; (2) the importance in opening the door to a reconsideration of the temporal dimension by resuscitating Asianism as a valid objective; (3) the vitality of political national identity as a sectoral goal that had not been achieved; (4) reinforcement of Japan's vertical distinctiveness as a separate model of development from that of the United States; (5) the significance, above all, of rebalancing Japan's horizontal identity by diminishing its dependence on the United States; and (6) the intensification of Japan's national identity through pride in the long-awaited breakthrough. If these efforts failed, that would not mean that they had been in vain. They would pave the way to further efforts driven by the same quest for a breakthrough in Japan's national identity through diplomacy.

In chapters 2 and 3, respectively, Cheol Hee Park and Ming Wan reflect on more sustained pursuits of benefits to national identity from Japan's relations with South Korea and China after the normalization of their relations. Apart from the United States, these two countries were foremost in Japanese minds because they associated history with national identity and considered the implications of the ups and downs of relations with Asian states. Clearly, they deserve emphasis in our exploration of how national identities influenced East Asian bilateral relations. In both instances, Japan failed to build on diplomatic normalization with a sustained narrowing of the gap in national identity. Preference for historical revisionism made this difficult, and especially China's Sinocentric aspirations became a rising barrier.

South Korea's options were essentially the same, assuming that North Korea was in no mood to indulge its aspirations for reconciliation, apart from symbolic gestures aimed at economic assistance and negotiations with the United States. South Korea was not at all ready for convergence with the United States, although its conservatives eventually were more favorably inclined than were Japanese conservatives, and it was limited to China as a serious partner for diplomatic diversification. As South Korea's national identity gap with China widened and that with Japan was painfully slow to narrow, the appeal of shared values with the United States rose, as reflected in the policies and rhetoric of Lee Myung-bak. After striving from the time of the Sino-U.S. breakthrough to gain an edge over North Korea through ties to Beijing and also Moscow, Seoul awakened to the need to turn back to its Cold War ally.

In chapter 2, Park also looks closely at the national identity implications of the Japanese–South Korean relationship from the Korean perspective. South Korean diplomacy had fewer options. There was scant prospect for an independent approach to the Soviet Union or a breakthrough with the Islamic world, apart from economic ties of meager national identity value. Yet, as Park explains, the relationship with Japan was of such identity significance that it severely tested diplomacy as it revealed the power of national identity in influencing how diplomacy is interpreted.

For South Koreans, China's importance for national identity kept rising in the 1990s and 2000s, with changing consequences. Pursuit of China had already proven to be a factor in the decline of anticommunism in South Korean identity. Both before and after the normalization of relations in 1992, China held considerable promise for national identity. It offered South Koreans hope of a breakthrough with North Korea, reduced reliance on the United States, and a path to Asian regionalism. All three objectives were critical to a shift in national identity. Over time, China's relations with North Korea and the United States, the two states with most significance for South Korean identity, cast a shadow on how it was perceived. This shadow darkened in the years 2009–10, when North Korea opted for threats and aggression as its means of revival and was supported by China, which put the onus for tensions on South Korea and also the United States. In chapter 4, Scott Snyder and See-Won Byun unravel the evolving impact of China for South Korean national identity, pointing to far-reaching changes in twenty years.

Japan and China figured in each dimension of South Korean identity: (1) the ideological struggle, as conservatives fretted when progressives tilted toward China, above all in the years 2003–5, and progressives were critical of the growing tilt toward Japan in 2009–11; (2) the temporal dimension, as the premodern and colonial periods were viewed through the lens of revived Japanese militarism and, increasingly, reasserted Sinocentric regional ambitions, whereas China's Korean War role as military adversary was not totally forgotten when its leadership in 2010, at the sixtieth-anniversary commemoration of China's entry into the war, referred to the war's glorious nature; (3) the sectoral dimension, as a shift was also occurring in which Japan's challenge to cultural and economic identity faded as China's challenge grew, including to political national identity because of resurgent Sino–North Korean ties; (4) the vertical dimension, when the initial promise of South Korea being a model for China yielded to China setting itself up as a model, leaving South Korea more aware of similarities with Japan; (5) the horizontal dimension, as the appeal of Asian regionalism for balancing U.S. dependency was limited, due first to concern about Japan's unwelcome leadership and then to alarm about an assertive push for an East Asian community under China's leadership; and (6) the intensity dimension, as national identity responded to Japan on many occasions, especially in 2005, and to China, first in 2004 and again in 2008–11. Diplomacy toward these states kept vacillating under the sway of deep-seated national identity concerns.

China's leaders were never tempted by the prospect of convergence with the United States, although they did give the impression for a time that China would accept the international system much as it was, and embraced the construction of an East Asian community before insisting that this must be Sinocentric in character. Approaches to Japan and South Korea changed abruptly as a reflection of shifting approaches to internationalism focused on the United States as well as regionalism. Unlike the other two states, China was guided by a consistent top-down strategy for national identity manipulation with no possibility of dissent, just indirect hints of alternative ways of thinking on matters that were considered of lower sensitivity.

Indicative of the way sensitive matters are being handled was the speech by Chinese president Hu Jintao at the Central Party School on February 19, 2011, which followed a secret Politburo meeting on the ongoing tumultuous events in North Africa and the Middle East. Concerned that mass demonstrations could spread to China and target another dictatorship, Hu called for further strengthening control over information on the Internet, regulating the "virtual society" that it had spawned, and guiding public opinion in "healthy directions."[3] The national identity discussed in this book is that which is constructed in a top-down manner by China's leadership in ways that would be unimaginable in Japan and South Korea.

Naturally, China had the most diplomatic options for adjusting its national identity. It proved this in the strategic triangle by breaking sharply from the Soviet Union and then reconciling with the United States. South Korea also had importance for its identity, leading China to handle normalization and its aftermath with great care, as is explained by Snyder and Byun in chapter 4. Japan had greater importance. In chapter 3, Wan discusses how China's identity was affected. Yet the treatment of its changing diplomacy also requires a delineation of the context for how it reenvisioned Asia within a different international system. This occurred with the rediscovery of Tianxia (All-under-Heaven), the old model of China's relations with the outside world, which acquired new meaning as an alternative to the Western system under which China had operated since the nineteenth century. In chapter 5, Yongnian Zheng assesses this rediscovery as a factor in national identity.

China had an opportunity to promote an East Asian identity. At various times, the Japanese and South Koreans welcomed this notion—not only in the 1990s, when they were confident of their own position relative to China's, but even in the second half of the 2000s, when first Roh Moo-hyun sought a balance in the region less dependent on the United States and then Hatoyama Yukio highlighted his desire to advance the East Asian community. Welcoming progressive partners in South Korea and the loss of the conservative Liberal Democratic Party in Japan, China's leaders praised new thinking about regionalism, but they failed to provide the necessary encouragement of their own support for a shared community with a meaningful identity. For instance, one journal article written in response to Hatoyama noted his view that Japan must not forget its identity as part of Asia, approvingly reporting that "the East Asian region must be recognized as Japan's basic sphere of being" and insisting that China is working for realization of an East Asian community, as are many East Asian states. Yet no mention is made of what China should do to reassure Japan and forge a shared sense of community. Instead, the article repeats increasingly strident demands that Japan trust China and distance itself from the United States by forging an equidistant triangle as well as a new mentality of rejecting U.S. leadership, including Obama's November 2009 call in Tokyo for an inclusive region. Only a community excluding the United States and also India, Australia, and New Zealand is possible based on what is called a "real and irreversible trend" of "equal" relations between the United States and Japan.[4] Self-serving appeals for geopolitical realignment ignore the need for community building.

In 1987 and 1998, with the Reagan-Gorbachev breakthrough and the Asian financial crisis, respectively, Japanese concerns about the United States had intensified. If usually blamed on U.S. passing, as in direct negotiations with Moscow, or bashing, as in trade disputes, an alternative explanation is that they originated largely within Japan in the stormy years of striving for an escape from the identity grip attributed to the United States. Similarly, from 1997 to 2008 South Korean thinking about the United States, under progressive leaders, reached new intensity and kept surprising most observers. Finally, Chinese distaste for the United States intensified starting in 2008 for reasons internal to China, although it blamed the other side. These cases reflect an unbalanced dyad, in which emboldened and frustrated states become even more obsessed with their most significant other. The national identity significance of key partners in Northeast Asia evolved in the shadow of perceptions of U.S. relations.

NATIONAL IDENTITY AND DIPLOMACY

When diplomacy centers on national interests, it usually proceeds normally, with ample feedback from the other side; however, values-centered advocacy results in a higher likelihood of misperceiving the other side and ignoring what may give offense. Claims to superior values both embolden one state to set aside pragmatism for supposed principle and arouse the other state to see greater threats toward its own basic values. The impact may be enlarged in countries where values play a large role and loss of face can pose a serious problem. East Asian states base their legitimacy heavily on a mix of nationalism rooted in their history of relations with the outside world and state guidance of society centered on supposedly beneficial and moral objectives. They are especially sensitive to the sorts of pressure applied in the name of another's national identity, notably when it comes with assumptions about a moral divide that casts the other side in a most unfavorable light.

Foreign policy challenges in the 1990s and 2000s called for compromises, to which pragmatic diplomats and experts aware of the conflicting claims in East Asia were often inclined. The balance of power had been shifting with unusual rapidity. Problems of divided nations had risen anew amid the conflicting approaches of the great powers. Major actors differed in their assessments of how the Cold War had ended, what should be the nature of regionalism, and what role the United States and China should best play in new regional institutions. In these circumstances, the unresolved disputes over national identity easily reverberated as warnings against compromise. Disagreements in the United States set the stage for regional discord. This was the case when U.S. Republicans took Bill Clinton to task during the first North Korean nuclear crisis in 1993–94 and during the effort to establish a strategic partnership with China in 1997–98, as well as for tolerance of South Korea's Sunshine Policy and of emerging regionalism through the ASEAN + 3 allowing no role for the United States in 1999–2000 of unprincipled, weak policies inconsistent with what the world's lone superpower and victor over Communism should do in line with its historical mandate and identity. Similar accusations arose in Japan aimed at some politicians, and especially at the Ministry of Foreign Affairs, for weakness in the face of China (almost yearly, events occurred that refueled these charges), Russia (in 2001 this put an end to a diplomatic initiative), North Korea (in 2002–4 this was a rallying cry), and even South Korea (notably in 2005). Inside South Korea, compromise with the United States and Japan drove progressives to rebuke leaders as compromise with North Korea increasingly rallied conservatives against Roh Moo-hyun through 2007. Although in China there were no electoral politics to expose similar claims to defend the national identity, Internet nationalism and bursts of public outrage with apparent backing within the leadership over excessively soft policy toward Japan and the United States (e.g., there were demonstrations in 1999 and 2005) testify to parallel phenomena. Each country has a reservoir of "purists" who appeal to the "true" national identity against pragmatists who are inclined to compromise. In China they are most unfettered.

Symbols evoking a country's national identity play a large role in post–Cold War international relations, notably in Northeast Asia, where there are no status quo powers. Of the six states shaping the region, four are bona fide great powers (the United States, China, Russia, and Japan), each of which has entertained superpower hopes during the past quarter century, and two behave in the manner of middle powers (South Korea and North Korea), with unusual aspirations to manipulate the great powers. The symbols selected to guide the foreign policies of these six states provide striking indications of their claims to a distinctive role in the region and to the justness of their aspirations to exert more power in the future. In a series of bilateral relationships, they express national identity as a driving force in foreign policy. China, Japan, and South Korea exist in this context, and thus they are closely attentive to issues of identity.

The record of China, Japan, and South Korea in narrowing their national identity gaps is not commendable. Opportunities have been repeatedly missed to build on diplomatic ties and economic cooperation. When the identity gap has appeared to narrow for a time, it has widened sharply again due to insensitivity or deliberate demonization. The nature of the East Asian National Identity Syndrome discussed in the companion volume to this book is a factor,[5] as are the legacy of Communism in China and militarism in Japan, which are highlighted in the chapters that follow as factors that led leaders to ignore moves useful for narrowing national identity gaps. Most important, the determination of China's Communist leaders to construct an identity that would preserve their power and ease the need for coercion became the driving force in reshaping national identity gaps, especially starting in 2008, when an emboldened China envisioned an opportunity to gain ascendancy in the regional order. Whereas earlier identity gaps opened in the shadow of U.S. ascendancy, the new environment called that into question as China envisioned itself as an all-around challenger able to pose an unprecedented alternative to Western civilization. For that reason, this book devotes most attention to China's widening of national identity gaps in 2010.

In the first months of 2012, the same widened gap remained. After the Arab Spring of 2011, China was in no mood to loosen controls at home or even to narrow the identity gaps with other states. Joining Russia in vetoing a February 2012 resolution in the UN Security Council intended to stop the Syrian government's bloody repression, it showed no indication in a year of leadership transition to find common cause with those it had been demonizing. Thus China's strong support for the new North Korean leader Kim Jong-un, as China focused on drawing that country closer, not on a shared agenda with other states, reflected its firm identity.

In part I, we observe that national identities are a driving force for a sporadic pursuit of diplomatic breakthroughs. They involve a search for national esteem that begins by looking back in a nation's history for an alternative model of international relations. Over time, they are manifested in sensitive bilateral relations. If Japan and South Korea aspired to limited adjustments in balancing regionalism and globalization, the case for China's challenge to both these orders is more compelling. By rediscovering an alternative order known as Tianxia, China was able to reconstruct its national identity in a far-reaching manner, which anticipated a newly assertive foreign policy in 2010. Only by comprehending its shift in identity can we begin to clearly see the motives for its policies.

NOTES

1   Yuichi Hosoya, "Japan's National Identity in Postwar Diplomacy: The Three Basic Principles," chap. 6 in *East Asian National Identities: Common Roots and Chinese Exceptionalism*, edited by Gilbert Rozman (Washington, D.C., and Stanford, Calif.: Woodrow Wilson Center Press and Stanford University Press, 2012).

2   More fully, these are (1) the *ideological* dimension, revealing contestation between the right, the left, and centrist advocates; (2) the *temporal* dimension, in three stages: prewar, postwar, and post–Cold War; (3) the *sectoral* dimension, whereby cultural, economic, and political identities each rise to the forefront, even as the balance shifts; (4) the *vertical* dimension, reflecting three levels: a family-community micro level; middle-level administrative, electoral, or abstract identities such as social class, ethnicity, religious affiliation, gender, and social movements; and a macro-level state identity; (5) the *horizontal* dimension, where a three-way division captures the main variations: the critical inner circle is the U.S. dyad, next are regional relations apart from the United States, and last is the international community, inclusive of the United States; and (6) the *intensity* of national identity, which can reflect the acute emotionalism over identity. For more on these dimensions, see Rozman, *East Asian National Identities*.

3   Perry Link, "The Secret Politburo Meeting behind China's New Democracy Crackdown," *New York Review of Books* blog, February 20, 2011, http://www.nybooks.com/blogs/nyrblog/2011/feb/20/secret-politburo-meeting-behind-chinas-crackdown/?printpage=true.

4   Wang Yusheng, "Some Thoughts on 'East Asian Community' and the Japan and U.S. Factors," *Foreign Affairs Journal*, Spring 2010, 31–38.

5   Rozman, *East Asian National Identities*, esp. the introduction to part I.

CHAPTER 1

THE SEARCH FOR A JAPANESE NATIONAL IDENTITY BY FOREIGN SERVICE OFFICIALS

Kazuhiko Togo

Foreign policy is an important arena of national identity formation, because a nation's search for the meaning of its existence requires the presence of one or more "others." A state, similar to an individual, comes to understand what makes it unique by identifying the distance between itself and others. In implementing foreign policy, one inevitably measures the distance between one's own country and other countries. The agents of foreign policy implementation—politicians, diplomats, other government officials, and in recent years, nongovernmental civil organizations— are expected to consider national interests, but at the same time they are well situated to reflect on and even influence the identity formation of the country to which they belong. Since 1945, the United States has dominated Japanese discussions of national identity, because America has become the most important object of Japan's foreign policy. But at the same time, America has also cast a shadow on Japan's diplomats at the front line who are engaged in efforts to redefine Japan's identity and thus gain some distance from this dominant partner. At various times, Japan's approaches to China, Russia, and even the Islamic world have opened a window on how Japan has been searching for a balancing force both in its diplomacy and in its quest for a more satisfying national identity. In none of these cases were serious attempts made to end the United States–Japan alliance or to identify Japan in opposition to the United States, but each case added to the picture of dissatisfaction with the existing state of national identity and revealed signs of an answer.

Japan's relationship with the United States has important implications for national identity. In post–World War II Japanese foreign policy, relations with the United States had vital importance. This situation originated in the simple facts that the United States primarily fought Japan in the Pacific front of the war starting in 1941, the United States defeated Japan, and the United States occupied Japan for seven years and set its direction in the Cold War era. The Japanese government adjusted well, and with the Yoshida Doctrine it concentrated on economic development, maintaining minimum Self-Defense Forces, and relying on the United States to fill in the power vacuum to ensure Japan's security. Among ordinary people and mainstream intellectuals, strong pacifism led in some instances to "anti-Americanism," but the country's concentration on economic development and improvements in material life resulted in what may loosely be defined as Japan's "Americanization." Throughout the Cold War, Japan defined itself as an ally supportive of U.S. leadership, as a competitor catching up and establishing its own economic model, and as an independent state anxious to confirm its own identity through foreign policy. The diplomatic initiatives discussed in this chapter illustrate the search for proof that Japan's aspirations for identity were being pursued through its foreign relations.

This fundamental structure continued throughout the Cold War and two decades later has not been fully replaced. The fact that Japan and America share values and interests as industrial countries and as members of the "Western world" meant that Japan's "Americanization" always outweighed the appeal of Asia. Yet Asia was important for Japan, both economically and geopolitically, and gradually its ties expanded to Southeast Asia, South Korea, and finally China, while the Islamic world and the Soviet Union / Russia had sufficient global significance to play a meaningful role in Japan's search for relief from what was perceived as its excessive dependency on the United States for its national identity. Particularly after the end of the Cold War, with the Japanese-U.S.

dyad in the forefront, Japanese diplomats strove to realize a more well-rounded foreign policy that would satisfy a yearning for a balanced national identity. However, as is shown in this chapter, these quests were made more challenging by the complexity of what was sought to make national identity more "normal" and by targets that failed to meet Japanese expectations.

This chapter focuses on the political thought of three Japanese diplomats who are known for original thinking about national identity as shaped through foreign relations. Ogura Kazuo, Sato Masaru, and Kato Jumpei were among many distinguished Japanese diplomats trained in the language of their area of specialization and recognized for their area expertise. However, not only did they make significant contributions to diplomatic ties through effective foreign policy implementation, they also had the ability to develop and express original ideas on the key issue of how Japan's relations with the country of concern should be understood from the point of view of Japan's identity formation. They are singular individuals whose quest reflects a broader search for identity across the nation.

THE GENERAL PICTURE: CHINA, RUSSIA, AND THE ISLAMIC WORLD IN THE UNITED STATES' SHADOW

Only after the end of the Cold War were Japan's international environment and its sense of identity shaken, albeit not abruptly. Despite recurrent tensions in Northeast Asia that kept the importance of the U.S. alliance from diminishing, Japan's dyadic relations with China, Russia, and the Islamic world acquired newfound significance. Although none of these three relationships surpassed Japanese-U.S. ties, each for a time attracted attention as a potential counterweight in Japan's quest for national identity. After all, the Soviet Union occupied the primary spot in the United States' global strategy and identity formation during the Cold War era, especially in the second half of the 1980s, when relations were filled with expectations. After the September 11, 2001, terrorist attacks on America, the Islamic world became the preoccupation of the

United States. Subsequently, as China continued its rapid rise, it stood in the forefront of U.S. concern. Each of these states had previously drawn Japan's interest, and in the post–Cold War period each, in its own way, elicited renewed interest as the search for clarity in national identity intensified.

China was most important, becoming associated with the popular objective of Asianism. As early in the Cold War as 1957, "Asia" was designated, along with "member of the West" and "United Nations–centered diplomacy," as one of three pillars of Japan's foreign policy. When the United States led in imposing sanctions on China in reaction to the Tiananmen Square massacre on June 4, 1989, China acquired added weight in Japan's foreign policy and search for an identity adjustment—just as the Cold War ended. And China's significance kept growing. Now that China has surpassed Japan in gross domestic product and become much more assertive in establishing its economic, political, and military position, Japan is at a crossroads not only in its relationship with China but also in its assessment of China's significance for its national identity. With Sino-U.S. relations regaining the national identity gap that followed the Tiananmen massacre, Japan is again being tested as to whether its quest for distance from the United States takes priority over factors arousing concern about China and leaving doubt about it as a gateway to Asianism.

Until the end of the Cold War, Japan had almost no room for autonomy toward the Soviet Union and, despite the idealism of some pacifists, it had no cause to anticipate a benefit to national identity from an initiative to boost relations. Not only was the impact of the East/West rivalry paramount; historical memories of Soviet conduct in August 1945 also worked against optimism about a new relationship. Starting in the late 1980s, aspirations grew. Japan began to look at Russia in a wider geopolitical and economic context, and this culminated in the strategic and diplomatic initiative toward Russia launched by Prime Minister Hashimoto Ryutaro in 1997. The role of identity in this dyad gained relevance in a new international environment, and the challenges continued as Russian president Vladimir Putin pursued a more assertive foreign policy and more autocratic style of governance.

The possibility of Japan experiencing a breakthrough with the Islamic world unfolded differently. When the brief reprisal of prewar Asianist interest in Arab Islamic countries from a few enthusiastic diplomats in the 1950s was over, Japan sided with the West on the Arab-Israel issue under the conditions of the Cold War, despite its shift to the Arab side after the oil crisis in 1973. Only in 2001 did Foreign Minister Kono Yohei launch a new approach by conducting a civilizational dialogue with these countries, starting just eight months before 9/11. This represented an attempt to better understand these countries, including their identity implications, but the context changed dramatically with the terrorist attack on the United States and its retaliation in the "war on terrorism." The pressure on Japan to side with its ally continued in 2010 as U.S. diplomacy focused on sanctions against Iran over its nuclear weapons program. In the pursuit of an independent way of dealing with the Islamic world, Japan was again revealing aspirations to find a new scope for its national identity while also confronting severe limitations in its choices.

The Soviet Union, the Islamic world, and China have loomed as rivals of the United States during the past quarter century. Achieving a breakthrough with any one of them would not only transform Japan's relationship with its sole ally but also fuel new thinking about its national identity as separate from the West and its capability of serving as a bridge in the post–Cold War global transformation. Yet Japanese aspirations do not extend to opposing U.S. global leadership or striving to lead a resistant bloc of states. As long as Russia, China, and key Islamic states were basically cooperating with the United States while also seeking to affirm their distance, Japanese diplomacy could find openings to seek a breakthrough. Yet when anti-Americanism spiked and the identity gap with the United States widened, Japan had much less room to maneuver. Its efforts to use diplomatic gains in each of these arenas to refocus its national identity have failed, but that does not mean they will not continue, given current driving forces.

ASIA AND CHINA: THE THINKING OF OGURA KAZUO

Many postwar Japanese diplomats were known to be specialists on Asia through China. In 1972, Hashimoto Hiroshi, who was then the director of the China Division of Japan's Ministry of Foreign Affairs (MOFA), led Prime Minister Tanaka Kakuei's policy to establish diplomatic relations with the People's Republic of China. Successive ambassadors to China in the era of Heisei (this era, starting in 1989, began with the death of Emperor Hirohito and the succession of Emperor Akihito)—starting with Hashimoto and continuing with Kunihoro Michihiko, Sato Yoshiyasu, Tanino Sakutaro, Anamai Koreshige, and Miyamoto Yuji—were generally perceived in the MOFA as able diplomats with well-established views on China and Japan-China relations. But from the point of view of an extended perspective on Japan's identity formation in relation to China, Ogura Kazuo was by far the most conspicuous diplomat who developed original thinking and writing.

Ogura was born in 1938, joined MOFA in 1962, specialized in French, and assumed two key posts as the deputy director of MOFA's China Division at the time of Japan's establishing diplomatic relations with the People's Republic of China and director of the Korea Division when Nakasone Yasuhiro substantially consolidated the country's relationship with Chun Doo-hwan. In July 1993, Ogura published an article in *Chuo koron* titled "For the Resurrection of Asia," which became a sensation.[1] Some hailed it as the appearance of new thinking that could lead Japan to adopt an independent policy from the United States. Some interpreted it as a straightforward expression of anti-American policy and severely criticized it as dangerously attacking the alliance. It was also attacked because the article was perceived to be too conciliatory toward China. Ogura's main logic was as follows:

1.   For a long time, Asia was an Asia "made" by Europe and America. Europe and America perceived Asia as a threat, so they made it an object of deprivation, or it became a place where lessons had to be taught. Some Asians accepted this situation and saw Asia through European spectacles.

2. In the last few years, Asia has begun to appear as an entity with substance and values, economically, politically, and culturally. It is time to listen once again to the words of Tagor and Sun Yat-sen, who advocated Asian values, and also to today's advocates such as Mahathir and Lee Kwan Yew, who advance contemporary Asian values.

3. "One of the key ideas which Asia should convey to the world is how to control human desires, in particular to create harmony between human beings and nature. At the same time, the way to improve relations among human beings, in particular in family ties or in the way groups and individuals interact, is to seek Asian wisdom."[2] Asia should increase the free flow of investments, trade, information, and ideas both within and outside its boundaries, while also drastically increasing Asian study centers, not relying on Asian studies in America or Europe.

4. "The biggest obstacle which hampers the advancement of Asian values is the psychological scar which was created by past history. As for Japan, naturally there is a need for history education and remorse to transform the scar created by past history from a minus symbol to a plus symbol."[3]

5. The United States' role in Asia should not be limited to its military presence. America needs to be accepted in Asia. For this purpose, in conjunction with the process of Americanization in Asia, America should become Asianized, learn to understand Asia, and take a posture of identifying with Asia.

Ogura's article appeared in the media at a time when Japan–United States relations were quite tense. The Cold War ended in the years 1989–91, and the United States appeared as the victor. While the Soviet Union relinquished the position as archenemy, Japan appeared as the greatest rival or possible threat to the United States because of its perceived economic might. Japan's growth for forty years, starting in the

1950s, resulted in a bubble economy in the later 1980s. The bursting of the bubble in 1991 was treated as a passing event, and the Bill Clinton administration pressured Japan to open its markets, with measurable results. Japan's inability to offer any troop support in the first Gulf War not only disappointed the Americans but also angered them. In the years 1992–94, Ogura assumed the post of director-general for economic affairs, the position specifically responsible for Japan–United States trade frictions.

The unstated message in Ogura's article was that he did not consider the U.S. approach to "liberalize the Japanese market" justified or fair. Yet, instead of stating his view based on the language of trade negotiations, he astonishingly based his entire logic on the civilizational debate on what Asia is, how Asians should advance their values and identity, and how the United States should adjust to these rising Asian values. In fact, reading his previous works, we can trace Ogura's serious reflections on the righteousness of the Asian approach back several years, if not earlier. Ogura became the director for cultural exchanges from 1989 to 1992. In the June 1991 edition of *Gaiko Forum*, he wrote an article titled "Split between the 'Empire of Ideas' and 'Lost People,'" in which he asked: "Why did the U.S. pressure Japan so much in the Gulf War not only on financial assistance but also on *human* assistance? The hidden psychological background was that by doing so, America did not need to bow to Japan's *money*. The United States wanted to think that Japan assisted it because Japan shared values with it…. But for many in Japan, U.S. values just sounded like a vision for spiritually colonizing Japan."[4] He apparently wrote this article because he thought that Japan–United States frictions had reached the stage where cultural differences were rising to the surface and that mere usage of the "alliance first slogan" could increase the Japanese people's detachment from the United States. Be that as it may, the straightforwardness of the language he used in the article shocked many, and a Japanese newspaper reported that major U.S. media had branded it the most striking criticism of the United States in recent times.[5]

Ogura's assertion that something was definitely wrong in the way the West treated Asia, or Japan, had already appeared in November 1990 in his book titled *East-West Cultural Friction*.[6] He selected fifteen Westerners who stayed in Japan, ranging from Philipp Franz von Siebold, a medical doctor from the Netherlands, and Minister Rutherford Alcock from Great Britain, in the pre-Meiji era; to Ambassador Joseph Grue from the United States, who was stationed in Japan in the years leading up to the Pacific war, and General Douglas Macarthur. Ogura cited many examples where these Westerners were exclusively attached to their own values. They wanted to teach a lesson to Japan. Alcock was often irritated by the petty government bureaucracy of the Tokugawa Bakufu and argued that it worked against the real interests of the Japanese people: "But to argue that the Japanese government obstructed the real interests of the Japanese people in reality despised the Japanese people. Because it implied that the Japanese people did not have the courage or ability to do more than just follow a government which contradicted their own interests."[7] William Griffis, who was adviser to Echizen han just before it became Fukui Prefecture, found that the Japanese were doing something that went beyond their normal ability, and that this overstretching produced something abnormal. Those who arrived in Japan to expand knowledge emphasized the country's backwardness and displayed the missionary need to correct the Japanese and teach them the right way. Behind their missionary spirit, there was prejudice that modern Japanese success was underpinned by something unfair, unnatural, and unjust. It is well known that General Macarthur saw the Japanese as twelve-year-old boys and implemented the U.S. occupation policy so that the Japanese people would be led to higher principles, ideals, and objectives. To achieve the spiritual revolution of the Japanese was his mission.

In some cases, such a missionary spirit was accompanied by fear that Japanese modernization was producing a country so deeply divided between two opposing values that it was tantamount to schizophrenic. Grue described this dualism between a state increasingly hostile to the United States, which could develop into a dangerous challenger of the West, and the fundamentally friendly Japanese people. The well-known anthropologist Ruth Benedict is noted for describing Japan's dualism. According to Ogura, "the more this duality and contradiction are revealed, the more the

West takes an advantageous position in the international imagery warfare. Whether those writers recognized it or not, it was purposeful and useful to emphasize the duality and contradiction of the Japanese because it could damage the Japanese, who challenged the West."[8]

For Ogura, disagreement with the Western countries' way of enforcing their values and way of life was not limited to the pending negotiations on U.S. president Clinton's numerical trade targets. Civilizational analysis starting from the pre-Meiji period was the foundation of his thinking about Japan versus the West, and it remained deeply entrenched. In contrast, Ogura saw Asia in a more favorable light. His 1993 article postulated a commonality in Asia, linking the views of Tagor and Sun Yat-sen, and creating a foundation for a modern Asian way of life. Ogura expanded his views on Asia, first as ambassador to Vietnam in 1994–95, and then after two years working in Tokyo as the vice minister on economic affairs, as ambassador to South Korea in 1997–99. Recently, when I queried him on his view of Asia, he responded, "Asia is what we are going to make of it. There have been many views on Asia that it is a diversified world; Japan aimed to create a Great East Asia Co-Prosperity Sphere, and now there is a lot of debate on the creation of an East Asian community. But the most important essence is that Asia is in the process of formation and Japan is a part of it and a part of its formation. There is no static Asia."[9]

In 2001, Ogura published a book titled *China's Authority and Japanese Dignity*, which examined relations between China, on the one hand, and Japan, Korea, and Vietnam, on the other.[10] He went through a comparative history of Japan, Korea, and Vietnam from the times of their formation, and in the last two chapters concluded his analysis as follows:

1. China, Japan, Korea, and Vietnam all lived in the Sinocentric world until the middle of the nineteenth century.

2. Japan lived outside the narrow boundary of the Sinocentric world. China never ruled Japan directly, nor did it play a decisive role in its domestic policymaking. China was used as a symbol for power in domestic politics.

3. Korea and Vietnam lived inside the narrow boundary of the Sinocentric world, at times subjected to Chinese colonial ruling through direct rule (the same as inside China), investiture of their kings by the Chinese ruler, or a looser form of tributary ties. Even if these countries were independent, in domestic politics "Chinese acknowledgment was almost indispensable to legitimize their authority."[11]

4. In the middle of the nineteenth century, when the Euro-American powers began invading Asia, both Korea and Vietnam sought refuge in the power and authority of China. By consolidating the Sinocentric world order, they sought to protect their own power and failed. Japan took a different path, entering into the international order of the West and pursuing modernization. It eventually chose to leave Asia and enter Europe.

5. Having made the analysis above, Ogura added that in the long range of history, "in reality China and surrounding countries shared a common philosophy, religion, and values. Depending on the time or power, it could have been Taoism, Buddhism, or Confucianism, but the fact that surrounding countries shared these values was one of the fundamental reasons why an order centered around China was constructed in East Asia."[12] In this Sinocentric order, state formation did not necessarily follow territorial boundaries. Spiritual space sometimes played a decisive role: "How to face America or Europe as a spiritual space and China as another spiritual space required Japan to have historical perspectives which went beyond simple foreign policy strategy."[13]

Ogura proceeded to stress differences between Japan and the West, suggesting that the Japanese concept could be shared with Asia, given that both were in the formative stage. He asserted,

In the process of making Asia, naturally Japan needs to explore its own identity. This may not be entirely the same with other countries' identity. But they may well be compatible. The concept of right and wrong is different in Japan from that of Europe and America. Right and wrong are rigorously defined in the West, whereas in Japan it is more amorphous. The concept of happiness may be different in Japan than in the West. Long life, environment, harmonious relations with nature—all these factors are more closely associated in traditional Japanese society. Rapid modernization, or Westernization, is destroying them, but we still have a lot of these factors left in the society. The concept of social order may also be different in Japan. Japan has maintained some kind of social discipline, which distinguishes itself. Chinese youth who come and study in Japan are generally impressed by the politeness, cleanliness, and strict social order maintained in Japan.[14]

Ogura terminated his diplomatic career as ambassador to France in the period 1999–2002, but he continues to expand his intellectual activities.[15] He began writing a series of articles on Asia in *Asahi shimbun*. In December 2003, he proposed to establish an Asian Charter so that Japan, China, South Korea, the members of the Association of Southeast Asian Nations (ASEAN), and other Asian countries can promulgate their shared values and common principles of action.[16] In July 2006, commenting on the Japan-U.S. Joint Document of that year, Ogura questioned: "It is said in that Joint Document that Asia was transforming into a region, where it stood more firmly on such universal values as democracy, freedom, human rights, market economy, and rule of law. But is it really so?"[17] Ogura argued that there were still many factors that fundamentally distinguish Asia, such as Korean youths' preference for North Korea over the United States, China being a stakeholder but not a values-sharing country, and a persistent split between Japan and China and Korea on historical memory issues. He urged that much greater effort should be made to develop shared values and consciousness among these countries, while calling for Japan and the United States to do much more to deepen democracy, freedom, and other shared values in their countries.

Ogura is far from alone. The fact that Hatoyama Yukio made the creation of an East Asian community his foremost foreign policy initiative in 2009 is indicative of the power of this ideal, which is of course linked to Asianism. Elements of Ogura's thinking were also accepted in the Cold War period, but there was no obvious way to advance them. In the 1990s, they gained popularity, and some diplomats strove to develop relations with China that could realize this ideal. However, more remarkable than the progress in diplomatic relations was the thinking associated with national identity that shaped aspirations for them. To understand it, further attention is needed on three questions. First, what resentments of the United States drove this dogged pursuit of an alternative external focus of national identity? After all, Japan's postwar development—which, at least until the end of the Cold War, was based on a peaceful economic rise, democratization, and Americanization— led Japan to unprecedented success. The place of the United States in Japanese national identity needs clarification. Second, why, after repeated disappointments from China, have experienced Japanese officials revived such hopes for shared values? After all, after the emperor's visit in 1992, after the establishment of an annual summit of the ASEAN + 3 in 1999, and after the victory of the Democratic Party of Japan, bringing Hatoyama to power in 2009, a more assertive Chinese approach to Asia marginalized Japan rather than drawing it closer. Third and finally, what is the gist of Japanese identity, which Ogura optimistically claims is compatible with Asian identity? After all, if the Japanese themselves cannot prove the domestic and universal validity of Japan's identity formation in its relations with both the rest of Asia and the West, it would lose significance on matters critical to the international order in an era of momentous shifts.

RUSSIA: THE THINKING OF SATO MASARU

In the early Cold War period, idealism toward the Soviet Union had the benefit of confirming the pacifist worldview that Japan could do without the U.S. alliance while forging a third way to bridge the East/West divide.

However, the conservatives in power and the bureaucrats who exercised that power did not share this thinking, and even among the progressives such optimism faded as the public became extremely critical of Soviet policies. The Ministry of Foreign Affairs in the latter part of the Cold War was considered to be a bastion of pessimism about Japanese-Soviet relations. In these years, Japan's policy was heavily concentrated on the issue of the Northern Territories, the last issue from World War II profoundly reflecting victim consciousness and amplified by the Cold War rivalry between the West, with which Japan was solidly integrated, and the East, where the Soviet Union was the leading country. National identity was bolstered by taking a negative view of Soviet behavior from 1945 to the present, not by imagining a promising future.

After the Cold War, when the East/West rivalry mostly disappeared, the Japanese kept their focus on the territorial issue, but now it became a serious object of negotiations between the two countries. In conjunction with the activation of negotiations, endeavors began on the Japanese side to look at Japan-Russia relations from a broader perspective than the territorial issue. On a political level, Hashimoto Ryutaro was probably the first prime minister who looked at Japan-Russia relations in strategic terms, reflecting Japan's overall interests in Northeast Asia and beyond. Not only resolution of the territorial issue but also mutually beneficial economic cooperation and the strategic value of improving Japan-Russian relations in the era of a rising China were taken into account. In the view of some, a real hope for a breakthrough in relations was to minimize all national identity concerns in order to maximize the pursuit of common interests. But the idea that Japanese interest in Russia would be boosted by aspirations other than the territorial issue linked to national identity has drawn scant attention.

Tamba Minoru, vice minister for political affairs in the years 1997–99, was the leading MOFA official to have supported Hashimoto and his successor, Obuchi Keizo. He was, perhaps, the first to have begun speaking about the issue of Russian identity against the background of Japan's strategic thinking. In his memoirs, published in 2004, Tamba quoted an analytical policy paper he wrote upon his visit to Moscow at the beginning of 1999,[18] the period when Russia was trying to recover just after it was struck by an economic crisis in the summer of 1998. Tamba wrote, "Russia was searching for its identity in a time of crisis. Doubts were raised that there may not be a future for Russia in the Euro-American oriented democracy and market mechanism. That was an extension of the debate between the Slavophiles and Westernizers starting from the nineteenth century. It may well be possible that out of this debate would emerge a uniquely Russian, autocratic, and national-istic direction."[19] Tamba observed that there was not much perspective that the so-called liberal-reformist politicians—such as Yegor Gaidar, Sergei Kirienko, or Boris Nemtsov—would return to power, but some Russian opinion leaders were suggesting that it was at an important turning point to seek enhanced cooperation with countries in the East such as China or Japan, and the importance of the United Sates was declining. Tamba saw the importance of the identity issue for Russia, hinting in his article that just dwelling on shared values with the West might not be sufficient to bring relations between the two countries closer. Finding hope in the shift of Russian identity, he foresaw how it might serve Japan's national interest to negotiate with the conserva-tive-nationalists, whose power was growing. This position was at vari-ance from the earlier approach to Moscow of just following Western/American values in implementing foreign policy. Yet Tamba did not propose any additional ideas for better understanding Russian identity or linking it to Japanese national identity.

I assumed the post of MOFA's director-general of European affairs in 1999–2001 and virtually replaced Tamba in guiding MOFA's pol-icy toward Russia. In this capacity, I took some interest in analyzing Russian identity connected with Japanese identity. Like Tamba before me, I directed attention to the identity legacy between the Slavophiles and Westernizers, but I connected this issue more directly to the issue of Japan's identity. In my memoir, I recalled a conversation with Anatolyi Lukyanov in 1995 during my stay at the Japanese Embassy in Moscow, when intense debates flared between contemporary Westernizers and Slavophiles. I observed that this modern debate took the geographical shape of West (Euro-American supporters) and East (Asian or Eurasian supporters). Lukyanov was originally an ally of Mikhail Gorbachev. He had sided with the conservatives who waged the coup of August 1991 and was jailed after the coup failed, but Boris Yeltsin rehabilitated him, and he had become a deputy of the Communist Party by the time I met him. I recalled that he insisted that the

rapid process of Americanization and Europeanization is making the Russian people so angry. The Russian people strongly reject individualism and materialism imposed on Russia by the West and assert a different civilization based on collectivism and spiritualism. Russia aims at Eurasianism from there. Relations with Japan are important from the point of view of anti-Europeanism and pro-Eurasianism. There are many features that Japan can offer to Russia in the spiritual, economic, and political arena. Similar to Russia, Japan was also torn apart between the dualism of the Orient (tradition) and the Occident (Americanization) but succeeded in creating a unique society based on traditional culture. The state-led planned economy and a company-oriented welfare system have similarity with Russian collectivism. The importance of consensus and a parliamentary system to select the prime minister better fits Russian society than the French-American presidential system. There must be large potential for cooperation between Russia and Japan based on these commonalities between the two countries.[20]

Given my responsibilities for leading government policy toward Russia through the March 2001 meeting of Mori Yoshiro and Vladimir Putin, I did not pursue this logic. Among MOFA officials, the person who most deeply analyzed issues of Russian identity while deepening his thinking on Japan's identity is Sato Masaru, who joined the ministry as a specialist in the Russian language and spent the years 1987–88 at Moscow State University and then seven years at the Japanese Embassy. He experienced some of the most turbulent years in Russian history before returning to Tokyo in March 1995 to work extensively on Russian affairs and Japan-Russia relations. He made an extraordinary contribution to enhancing peace treaty negotiations before becoming the object of criticism for his close relations with Suzuki Muneo, a parliamentarian who gained considerable influence over Japan's foreign policy toward Russia.

In 2002, Sato fell from grace in MOFA and was arrested for the misuse of money, and in 2009 the Supreme Court issued a guilty verdict with four years of probation. In 2005, he published *Kokka no wana* (*A Trap Laid by the Nation*), which described his arrest and fight against the prosecution.[21] This book became a runaway bestseller, rehabilitated Sato in Japanese society, and launched him on a new career as a prolific writer and opinion leader. In 2006, he published *Jikaisuru teikoku* (*Empire in Self-Eclipse*), which gives a detailed account of the fall of the Soviet Union as he personally experienced it.[22]

Empire in Self-Eclipse is an extraordinary account of Sato's experience seeing the fall of the Soviet Union from the inside through his web of networks, which he established both with the Russian conservatives who waged the coup and the Russian reformers who gathered around Boris Yeltsin. Seen as an effort to grasp the essence of the Russian identity debate and gauge its implications for contemporary Russian politics, the most revealing part of the book is about his year at the university, when he befriended a Latvian student, Alexander (Sasha) Kazakov, in the Department of Philosophy. Nikolai Berdyaev, the religious philosopher who was exiled in 1922, was very popular and became the center of the identity debate among the students. Sato noted, "At the time I started my Moscow life, it was clear that Marxism-Leninism could not attract Russians' soul. Berdyaev split Marxism from Leninism, and he considered Leninism a heresy of the Russian Orthodox Church. If the Russians rediscovered God and returned to Russian Orthodoxy, the Soviet Union might gain another possibility for development."[23] Early in the country's phenomenal transformation, the search was under way for a creative combination of the essence of Russian "traditional" thinking and some residue of "modern" thinking. Sasha voiced the opinion that Berdyaev was a Bolshevik because he too supported elitist rule over the passive masses, while he also drew on Ivan Ilin, who had rejected Nazism and Bolshevism as two diseases but recognized in fascism a way to resolve social problems that capitalism had created while underlining the need to overcome it to ensure material wealth and freedom. When, in April 2005, Putin referred to Ilin in a presidential speech and stated that the way freedom and democracy would be implemented would depend on the way each state makes decisions, Sato recalled his talk with Sasha and his opinion that Ilin's thought derived from a reformed fascism.[24]

With Communism discredited, Russians had refocused their debates on what makes their national identity distinct from identities found in the West. Sato credited Putin with success in restructuring Russia in eight years, explaining that it was because he drew on Russia's history and tradition: "Having learned from history and tradition, he took such measures as enlarging libraries, allocating resources from oil and natural gas to pensions, and creating a society where elders can live safely."[25] However, Sato's message was tempered by warnings that Russia has all the aspects of a new empire, with its power and autocracy: "As a Russian specialist, I feel threatened by a Russia which is turning into an imperial state."[26] Extending his discussion to Japan, Sato drew parallels with Russia's experience in Japan's need to look back to history for guidance, seeking to establish its new direction in the world of rising new imperialisms, about which he was deeply concerned.

Sato became deeply troubled that the basis of Japanese society had begun to be shaken, particularly after Koizumi Junichiro's new liberalism was introduced, and explored the prospect that the ultimate way to overcome this problem would be to return to Japan's best spiritual tradition, which developed around the emperor. Sato suggested that the *Jinno shotoki*, which was written by Kitabatake Chikafusa at the time of the North/South split of the imperial system during the Muromachi era to show the historical legitimacy of the Southern dynasty, might provide clues on how to retain tradition while adjusting to new circumstances.[27] He urged Japanese to study well-known figures from the prewar period on—among them Gondo Seikyo, Okawa Shumei, and Kita Ikki, who all fought intensely to find a way to preserve Japan's tradition under a wave of modernization.[28] He emphasized that the Japanese polity is ensured by the imperial tradition, and it is absolutely essential to protect articles 1 to 8 of the current Constitution.[29] Sato is embarking on a search for a national philosophy equivalent to what he found in Russia.

In the case of Russia, the collapse of the Soviet Union and of Communist rule created a vacuum that led briefly to an attempt to emulate the West and then to rejecting, or supplementing, its influence, in search of a unique Russian approach rooted in tradition. The Japanese motivation for a comparable quest might be considered as analogous. Are the two countries, whose modernizing reforms began in a parallel fashion in the 1860s and whose catch-up strategies each ended in defeat, similar in their aspirations for a national identity less beholden to the West? If so, does Japan share the goal of distancing itself from the United States, perhaps in a manner that could boost its relations with Russia? I, too, have lately begun writing about Japan's shift toward some kind of "Japanization," discussing the dichotomy between the West and tradition and posing the direction of a new "open Edo" as distinct from Western or Chinese identity.[30]

In 2011, Japanese-Russian relations were still stymied by differences centering on the territorial dispute that has continuously plagued the two countries' ties. Any sense of a shared identity is overwhelmed by the identity implications of this dispute. Russia and Japan each views China as far more important than each other in the search for balance versus the West or the United States. However, forging normal relations that overcome the territorial dispute has promise for each nation's identity, offering Japan some closure on one of the foremost symbols of its abnormal postwar status and a measure of confidence in dealing with the other great powers, particularly China. To a certain extent, Japan's search for a parallel identity depends on what kind of Russia Japan may select as a partner. At this point in time, Russia is awaiting a presidential election, which most likely will bring back Vladimir Putin back to the presidency. Though Putin's popularity has declined, he aims for a strong and stable Russia based on the creation of a Eurasian space, at the center of which lies Russia and some former Soviet republics. If Russia develops a stance of perpetual opposition to the West under the sway of authoritarianism and assertiveness, then the nature of Japan's synthesis may raise questions, the same as those that would be raised about Russia. Although Japan's search for a shared identity with China as part of the East Asian community keeps being revived, it is much less clear that any search for commonality with Russia will proceed beyond occasional speculation. Nevertheless, if the Japanese leadership behaves with sufficient flexibility over the Northern Territories and Putin sees an opportunity to create normal ties with Japan, the possibility of finding a fundamentally upgraded relationship with Russia might emerge.

THE ISLAMIC WORLD: THE THINKING OF KATO JUMPEI

The history of Japanese diplomats specialized on Arab countries and the Islamic world is not extensive. Katakura Kunio, who joined MOFA in 1960 as the first postwar career diplomat specializing in Arabic, recalled in his memoir that "my knowledge on Arab/Islam themes was rather limited before joining the ministry. I knew that before the war Okawa Shumei, who was the leading ideologue of the Great East Asia War, became seriously interested in Islam and translated the Koran into Japanese, and in the years leading to the Pacific war there was also an Islam Study Forum established inside MOFA to improve understanding on Islamic civilization among bureaucrats, scholars, and the business community. When the Pacific war started, special efforts were made to befriend the indigenous Muslims in Indonesia, eventually to support such educated nationalists as Sukarno."[31] Katakura listed the names of Arabist diplomats of prewar and postwar origin, whose number amounted to 110 at the time of the writing of his memoir in 2005.[32] Among those who accumulated special knowledge and experience of the Arab/Islam world, there were some who did not specialize on it at the beginning of their career. Kato Jumpei, Japan's ambassador to Oman and Belgium, was one of them, and he left many insightful writings on Japanese diplomats' views, from the point of view of not only diplomacy but also Japan's identity formation. Two main themes permeate Kato's writing. First, he highly praises Japan's foreign policy toward the Middle East in the 1950s and the 1960s as assertive and observes that one of the key dynamos of this active diplomacy was the idea of Asianism, which remained alive from prewar years. Second, he is very critical of the trend of identifying Japan's interests with U.S. foreign policy alone and laments the weakening of active policy toward the Middle East underpinned by Japan's originality and identity. In particular, he does not hide his indignation that Japan cannot take a more independent position on the righteousness of the Palestine people facing the enormity of Israel's power accumulation.

With reference to the immediate postwar Japanese foreign policy, Kato wrote in 2003:

> Under the Hatoyama and Kishi cabinets, former Prime Minister Yoshida's influence remained strong and leading Foreign Ministry officials tended to direct their attention exclusively toward the United States. But in the Middle East area, the situation was different. After the San Francisco Peace Treaty came into force, the Japanese government established its embassy in Cairo and appointed Tsuchida Yutaka, one of the leading Asianist diplomats during the war, as ambassador, concurrently accredited to other Arab countries, including the United Arab Republic incorporating Syria, and Saudi Arabia and Libya. Tanetani Seizo and Odaka Masano were two leading experts at the embassy. I had the fortune to serve at the Japanese Embassy in Cairo then, and throughout my service in the Foreign Ministry I have never seen such an honorable, selfless, and creative diplomat as Ambassador Tsuchida and never experienced an embassy where all members were united in working so closely with a sense of solidarity.[33]

Because Tsuchida was convinced that foreign policy should not be monopolized by diplomats, he created a vast network with leading politicians in Tokyo and succeeded in influencing them directly and, through this networking, implemented concrete projects. Gaining excavation rights in collaboration with Yamashita Taro of the Arabian Oil Company from Saudi Arabia and Kuwait for the Kafuji oilfield in the years 1957–58 was a dramatic achievement. The decision to give private companies loans for the importing of Japanese capital goods with the collaboration of a leading businessman of that era, Takasaki Tatsunosuke, was another achievement. Major Japanese scholars of Islamic studies—such as Izutsu Toshihiko, Itagaki Yuzo, and Mutaguchi

Yoshiro—all had close contacts with the embassy. Nakasone Yasuhiro, Tsuji Masanobu, Nakatani Takeyo, and other politicians visited Cairo. In the 1950s, historical linkage with the war and the prewar period had not yet been cut off. On the Arab side, there was admiration for the Japanese who dared to fight against the United States and Britain, and this turned into a favorable feeling toward Japan backed up by Arab nationalism. On the Japanese side, the ideas of Asianism were still alive, and this resulted in sympathy toward Arab nationalism.34

In a recent interview, Kato Jumpei emphasized two points:

First, at the higher political level, Ambassador Tsuchida composed a formidable network. He was one of the three leading prewar Asianist diplomats, together with Okazaki Katsuo and Sugihara Arata. After the war Okazaki became very close to Prime Minister Yoshida Shigeru and eventually became foreign minister, but Sugihara became a deputy to the House of Councilors and, as one of the main advisers of Prime Minister Hatoyama on foreign policy, he exerted political influence in Tokyo with his Asianist thinking. Tsuchida succeeded in communicating his message from Cairo through Sugihara. At that time Mitsubishi had maintained a Cairo office with a formidable network in the Arab world, and Tsuchida became well connected to business circles through Mitsubishi. Second, the 1950s and early 1960s were a different period for the Arab side. In general, there was resentment toward British rule in the Middle East. Japanese initial victories in World War II were basically remembered with great sympathy. After the war, when Korea and China criticized Japan for colonialism and aggression, in the Arab world it was better remembered as a fighter against Euro-American imperialists. This memory naturally dovetailed with memories of their own fighting against European imperialism. Immediate post-war Japanese foreign policy was conducted based on goodwill from both sides and, therefore, resulted in substantial success.[35]

Kato proceeded to turn his review into strong criticism of the fact that Japan's foreign policy had just drifted into the orbit of Western values and thinking. He wrote, "After the 'golden period' of the 1950s, Japan lost its sense of identity as an Asian nation, and defined its identity solely based on its position as a member of the 'advanced world.' This one-sided approach to international relations deprived Japan of the sense of realism of living in the world where interests clash with each other, and by way of losing its sense of realism, Japan increasingly lost its ability to apprehend reality in the Middle East."[36] He made his criticism of recent Japanese policy toward the Middle East with an even sharper edge in a coauthored book. After asserting unambiguously that the fundamental cause of instability in the Middle East is the deprivation of the right of the Palestinians to live in their homeland, Kato depicted Japan's policy as follows:

Traditionally, people in the region had warm feelings toward Japan. This is because they sympathized with Japan's steps from the Meiji Restoration. As the sole power from the non-Western peoples, its history of fighting against world governance in Europe and Asia drew the sympathy of people in the region. After the end of World War II, many Japanese tried to respond to the warm feelings of the people in the region and supported Iranian or Arab nationalism. But when the "North/South" issue began to be debated at the United Nations and Japan became a part of the "North," it began to feel separated from the developing countries in the "South." Relations between Japan and the Middle East grew further apart. In 1973 Japan recognized the importance of the countries in the region from an economic point of view, but that did not last long. From around the 1980s, Japan became unable to see countries in this region through its own eyes and became heavily influenced by Euro-American media. In the cessation of the Iran-Iraq war, Japan was expected by both countries to play a concrete role but could not. In the first Gulf War, Japan made huge financial contributions but was not appreciated either by the West or by the Arab countries. After 9/11, Japan began to shift its relations with the United States. It fully supported U.S. policy in the Afghan and Iraqi wars and maximized cooperation with the United States within the limits of its Constitution. The leadership considered cooperation with the United States indispensable because Japan needed U.S. cooperation in East Asia, where the situation was tense. Japanese public opinion was more doubtful of the U.S. position, but the government increasingly lost its power to look at the Middle East with original eyes and became, by and large, influenced by Euro-American views. Threads between the hearts of the Japanese and Middle Eastern people, which had developed from Meiji onward, seem to have been ultimately cut off. But if the Japanese may revive an independent position with even and fair eyes, they should be able to understand the cause and result of events taking place in the Middle East, in particular on the Israeli issue.[37]

A common criticism of postwar Arabist diplomats is that they lacked the integrity of having original thinking detached from European values. Katakura explains such hesitation, reproducing his nuanced view expressed in a parliamentary debate, on how it was difficult to define terrorism, how terrorism emerged from the complex political situation in the Middle East, how the terrorist threat began to emerge in real terms after the Iranian Revolution of 1979, and how it was exacerbated in the wake of the Cold War. Katakura continued to publicly state just before President George W. Bush attacked Iraq in 2003 that Japan should follow the United Nations' decision, distancing Japan from its ally, the United States.[38]

In addition, MOFA diplomats for a decade kept contributing to a civilizational dialogue, which Foreign Minister Kono Yohei took the initiative to hold in 2001:

In January 2001, Foreign Minister Kono Yohei made a future-oriented speech at Doha, in the United Arab Emirates. While acknowledging the importance of the oil connection with the Gulf countries, Minister Kono emphasized that future relations between Japan and these countries should develop on a multilayered basis. He underlined the need to deepen Japan's understanding of this world through direct and close contact and exchanges.

The time of relying on the images Japan has accumulated over the years in such romantic novels as the "Tales of Thousand and One Nights" is over. He referred to serious works on Islamic civilization made by Japanese scholars in a study group conducted under the minister's auspices and advanced several proposals; inter alia, to enact a new dialogue with the Islamic world. As an incarnation of his ideas, a seminar-dialogue with the Islamic world began in Bahrain in March 2002.[39]

Since then, eight rounds of dialogue have taken place—three in Tokyo, and five in Islamic countries, including Bahrain, Iran, Tunisia, Saudi Arabia, and Kuwait. The most prominent round was perhaps the sixth, held in Riyadh in 2008, when King Abdullah invited all participants in the dialogue, thirteen from Japan and about ninety from thirty Islamic countries, to his residence and enunciated his proposal to hold a dialogue among the three revelational religions (Judaism, Christianity, and Islam) and among different civilizations. Kono's initiative to hold the civilizational dialogue in 2001 was remembered as the trigger for such new initiatives.[40]

The eighth round of the dialogue took place in Tokyo on February 23–24, 2010, with eighteen intellectuals from Japan and twenty-three from Islamic countries, twenty-six student representatives, and members of the general public.[41] MOFA officials put a lot of effort into convening this meeting. The deputy director-general for Middle Eastern affairs attended the symposium and gave a speech. One official stated that it was really regrettable that MOFA's political leadership from the Democratic Party of Japan did not allow the Liberal Democratic Party politician Kono to attend this round, even the luncheon speech. Given the purpose, history, and composition of this forum, it was still one of the best possible places where Japan and Islamic countries could have a dialogue on Islam and Japanese identity, in two main ways.

First, in terms of Japan learning about Islam, one focal point of the debate was this issue: "How should we consider terrorist activities, just criminals who should be punished by the domestic and international penal code, or is there anything that we should

learn from their allegation that they are fighting for a 'just cause?'"
Presentations by Islamic countries were unanimous in emphasizing the noncoercive and fundamentally peaceful character of Islam.
Some of their responses were very clear in emphasizing that terrorist activities have nothing to do with genuine Islamic beliefs. It
was more the Japanese participants who raised such questions as
the following: "But some Islamic believers maintain that there are
good terrorists and bad terrorists. How do you differentiate them?"
or "Killing innocent citizens, women, and children by bus explo-
sions in Israel cannot be compatible with Islam's peaceful image. But
some Islamic believers maintain that they were doing this for a 'just
cause.' How could it be explained?"

Second, in terms of the Islamic people studying Japan's identity,
an intellectual from Southeast Asia raised the following question:
"Postwar Japan was perceived in Southeast Asia as an example of success with its rising economic power and its ability to blend the historical tradition and modern technological and economic development.
But recently there have been some doubts or uncertainty concerning
this postwar Japanese development. Is Japan maintaining economic
success with its blending with the past?" An answer was given by a
Japanese participant that "precisely Japan has lost its direction in the
last twenty years after the end of the Cold War, but people's frustration
that things just cannot go like this is the fundamental reason why the
[Liberal Democratic Party] lost its majority and was replaced by the
[Democratic Party of Japan] in the August 2009 elections. Japan is at
a crossroads in search of its new identity in the twenty-first century."
But no further deepening of the debates took place at this round of
the dialogue in February 2010.

Kato Jumpei told the author in his concluding remarks on Japanese
foreign policy and identity,

> The overwhelming trend of current Japan is to identity Japan's
> interest with that of the United States and structure its foreign
> policy on that basis. There are reasons that for Japan's safety
> and prosperity it is important to harmonize its interests with

those of the United States, but identifying entirely obviously goes too far. It is not conducive to Japan's interests. Ultimate national interests are more holistic. Diverging foreign policy interests naturally make Japanese think more of its broad and profound identity. In that context, it is important to question the issue of civilization and identity in the Islamic world and give thought to Japan's identity in that context. Efforts to continue for ten years the civilizational dialogue with the Islamic world are complementing efforts in search of deeper identity issues in both that world and Japan.[42]

Kato's articulation that the root cause of Islamic–Arab issues is the Israel issue raises a serious foreign policy as well as identity issue. Whether there is a margin for Japan to take an independent position somewhat deviating from the U.S. position on Israel, even hypothetically, is an issue that is totally untested, although Kato claims that a slightly different approach to this issue may ultimately be beneficial to both the United States and Israel. In addition to putting aside this root-cause consideration, more is involved in this search for an independent approach to the Middle East and Islamic states than national interests that have been judged to differ from those that lead the United States to support Israel. With Pakistan at the center of U.S. concerns about the spread of weapons of mass destruction and terrorism and with a showdown looming over the Iranian nuclear weapons program, Japan needs to clarify how it stands on urgent security matters. Whereas, in the 1950s, sympathy for Japan's war efforts may have provided some sort of bond, it is less clear what the identity bond may be in the second decade of the twenty-first century or how it may differ across the Islamic world. How the long-term issue of a civilizational search for a common identity might affect these fundamental and immediate international issues is totally unclear. Looking ahead to the challenges of a troubled world, it is not certain at all whether the search for a national identity will draw the two sides closer.

CONCLUSION

Having considered above the thinking on national identity of three key MOFA officials who have been closely involved in Asian, Russian, and Islamic policy, one can observe the following three characteristics. First, for all of them, Japan's foreign policy interests do not entirely converge with U.S. interests. None of them is specifically anti-American, but all of them seek a policy that may diverge from American policy. Detachment from American policy objectives means that all of them seek a foreign policy that serves Japan's own interests from a wider perspective than just identifying with U.S. interests. Second, all of them seek something more than foreign policy implementation. Their thinking invariably extends to the key question of Japan's identity, which is related to foreign policy implementation but goes beyond it. How clearly and in what form each of them perceives Japan's identity differs. Ogura, Sato, and Kato each has his own approach. Third, as a key factor for each to formulate his own thinking on identity, the issue of identity formation in the particular country or region where each of them was focused plays an essential role. One way or another, that country or region usefully works as the "other." In Ogura's case, he is trying hard to find a format in which Japanese values and identity merge well with Asian values and identity. Sato does not intend to find a way for Japanese identity to merge with Russian values or identity, but there is an inherent search for parallelism in Japanese and Russian identity formation in Sato's thinking, which has not yet been fully explored. For Kato, given his uncompromising thinking about the causality of the creation of Israel for Middle Eastern issues and his search for some kind of political settlement to bring justice to the Palestine side, his foreign policy and identity search faces much greater difficulty. His support for long-term efforts for a civilizational search vis-à-vis identity formation is not well connected to the realities of dealing with the current foreign policy agenda.

NOTES

1   Ogura Kazuo, "Ajia no fukken no tameni," in *Sengo Nihon gaiko ronshu,* edited by Kitaoka Shinichi (Tokyo: Chuo koron, 1995), 483–505.
2   Ibid., 496.
3   Ibid., 502.
4   Ogura Kazuo, "Rinen no teikoku to soshitsu no tamito no kiretsu," *Gaiko Forum,* June 1991.
5   *Asahi shimbun,* January 23, 1992.
6   Ogura Kazuo, *Tozai bunka masatsu: Obei vs Nihon no 15 no ruikei* (Tokyo: Chuo koron, 1990).
7   Ibid., 202.
8   Ibid., 180.
9   Author's meeting with Ogura Kazuo, August 26, 2010.
10 Ogura Kazuo, *Chugoku no ishin, Nihon no kini: Higashi Ajia no kokusai kankei no saikochiku ni mukete* (Tokyo: Chuo koron, 2001).
11 Ibid., 255.
12 Ibid., 262.
13 Ibid., 272.
14 Author's meeting with Ogura Kazuo.
15 Ogura became a professor at Aoyama Gakuin, and starting in 2003 was president of the Japan Foundation.
16 *Asahi shimbun,* December 9, 2003.
17 *Asahi shimbun,* July 19, 2006.
18 Tamba Minoru, *Nichiro gaiko hiwa* (Tokyo: Chuo koron, 2004).
19 Ibid., 220.
20 Kazuhiko Togo, *Hoppo ryodo kosho hiroku* (Tokyo: Shinchosha, 2007), 199.
21 Sato Masaru, *Kokka no wana* (Tokyo: Shinchosha, 2005).
22 Sato Masaru, *Jikaisuru teikoku* (Tokyo: Shinchosha, 2006 and 2008).
23 Ibid., 536–38.
24 Ibid., 557–58.
25 Murakami Masakuni and Masaru Sato, *Yamato gokoro nyumon* (Tokyo: Fusosha, 2008), 118.
26 Ibid., 268.
27 Ibid., 118.
28 Ibid., 102–3.
29 Ibid., 109–10.
30 Kazuhiko Togo, *Sengo Nihon ga ushinatta mono: Fukei, ningen, kokka* (Tokyo: Kadokawa shinsho, 2010).
31 Katakura Kunio, *Arabisuto gaikokan no Chuto kaisoroku* (Tokyo: Akashi shoten, 2005), 26.
32 Ibid., 239–44.

33   Kato Jumpei, "Nishiajia to Arabu shokoku nitaisuru Nihon gaiko: Bandon kaigi kara Iran/Iraku senso made," *Tokiwa kokusai kiyo*, no. 7 (March 2003): 134.
34   Ibid., 134–35.
35   Author's meeting with Kato Jumpei, August 6, 2010.
36   Kato Jumpei, "Nishiajia to Arabu shokoku nitaisuru Nihon gaiko," 137.
37   To Jyodo (Kato's pen name), "Gendai Chuto no kokusai seiji," in *Iraku senso e no hyakunen*, edited by Kuroda Toshio (Tokyo: Shoritsu shinsui, 2005), 136–38.
38   Katakura Kunio, *Arabisuto gaikokan no Chuto kaisoroku*, 195–96, 206–7.
39   Kazuhiko Togo, *Japan's Foreign Policy 1945–2003: The Quest for a Proactive Policy* (Leiden: Brill, 2005), 314–15.
40   See http://www.mofa.go.jp/mofaj/area/islam/seminar6_gh.html.
41   See http://www.mofa.go.jp/mofaj/area/islam/seminar8_gh.html.
42   Author's meeting with Kato Jumpei.

CHAPTER 2

NATIONAL IDENTITIES AND SOUTH KOREA–JAPAN RELATIONS

Cheol Hee Park

How a nation defines its identity affects its interactions with other countries. The South Korea–Japan relationship has been deeply influenced by shifting national identities, above all due to contrasting historical memories. Complicating this clash are frictions between progressives and conservatives within each country. After reviewing national identities in the colonial and Cold War periods and their impact on relations, this chapter concentrates on how refreshed identities and different combinations of identities in the two countries have affected relations since the Cold War. It supports the conclusion that cooperation is more likely when the two countries share a similar outlook on national identity, while a diverging composition of identities is prone to lead to conflicts. Furthermore, the chapter looks at how the political framing of national identity affects the nature of cooperation and conflict between two countries. What is unusual in the case of South Korea and Japan is the extent to which the national identities that are important to their relations remain contested in the post–Cold War era. This dyadic relationship is at issue in domestic struggles under way over national identity.

Recalling thirty-five years of Japanese colonial rule, South Koreans have developed a strong anti-Japanese identity, which serves as fertile ground for Korean nationalism and as a cause of setbacks in relations even decades after liberation. During the Cold War, the United States facilitated cooperation between its two allies,[1] mediating security cooperation and economic linkages that laid the foundation for a rapprochement, as South Korea and Japan stood together against the socialist bloc, sharing an identity as defenders of the free world. Both also made economic growth within the global free market system a priority. However, despite pursuing comparable national goals, they failed to overcome animosity, to the extent that preoccupation with each other left realistic adjustments to regional challenges out of reach. Revisionist conservatives in Japan and progressives in South Korea pressured leaders even during the Cold War not to draw close to the other state, and after the Cold War they gained more clout that seriously interfered with promising opportunities to boost relations.

The end of the Cold War set the stage for South Korea and Japan to redefine their national identities. In Japan, it meant the weakening of the progressive camp while the conservatives awakened to the need for international contributions in proportion to the size of Japan's economy.[2] A sense of humiliation resulting from criticism of Japan's past behavior expedited the rise of what I call neoconservatism, which refused to continue the country's "apology" diplomacy and even welcomed confrontations with its neighbors as a way to bolster Japan's national identity. South Korea also began to redefine its national identity, as progressives, who had long been oppressed, gained legitimacy, frontloading the desire for embracing North Korea through engagement while resurrecting historical issues deemed relevant to national legitimacy. Rivalry between progressives and conservatives in South Korea prevailed, unlike the predominantly conservative era that had preceded.[3] While neoconservatives emerged as a force that tried to redefine Japanese national identity differently from the liberals or moderate conservatives, progressives began redefining Korean national identity differently from conservatives. Interactions between South Korea and Japan have been strongly affected by these new political streams that were determined to reshape national identities.

REFLECTIONS ON NATIONAL IDENTITIES

National identity has often been perceived as static, monolithic, and apolitical. These biases stem from subjectively defining national identities rather than putting national identity formation in an interactive setting in a globalized world. If regarded as a constant, national identities have difficulty in accounting for the varying quality of interaction between countries. Instead, it behooves us to pay attention to three aspects of national identity: historical change, plural contention, and complex interaction. First, national identities are not stagnant but changeable, as they are constructed and redefined in the global-local nexus.[4] Definitions of national identity reflect not only historical experiences and debates within a country but also interaction among countries in a changing structural context. In a venue where global and local spheres intersect, national identities are transformed in a sticky, path-dependent way.[5] Historical experiences such as war, colonization, or even a critical national election open a window of opportunity to redefine national identity. This may reflect an externally driven identity transformation. For example, a nation that is exposed to a regional economic crisis or hit by an unprecedented attack from terrorists may redefine the way it organizes or views national security. National identities also can be reconceptualized in a self-reflective way. As a country's status shifts, either upward or downward, in the hierarchy of nations, a movement to renew the national identity can emerge.[6] A national identity developed when a country is economically vital and militarily strong would not be the same as a conception agreed on when it is small and weak.

Second, national identities should be understood as being contested, not uniform, particularly in a democratic political setting.[7] The political risk may be excessive to suggest an alternative national identity under an authoritarian regime; so, even though people may be inclined to a different conception of identity, outside watchers could hardly recognize it. However, in a democratic setting, plural conceptions may compete. Not all the people living in a country share the same national identity at a specific historical moment. Also, structural conditions do not dictate only one specific conception of identity. For example, Korean national identity can be defined as ethnic, with people expected to share a similar identity regardless of their location. Alternatively, South Korean identity can also be defined in terms of shared values. In other words, when national identities are defined, different concentric circles can be drawn to identify who "we" are and who "they" are.[8] As neighbors with intersecting histories on matters vital to identity in the formative transition to new regimes in the 1940s, Japan and South Korea are inclined to place each other in the first such circle.

Third, a predominant national identity reflects the thinking of ideologues and strategists in the political elite, who are often involved in the mobilization of biases.[9] Ideational contestation constitutes a major element of competing plural conceptions of identities. A redefinition of national identities contains an element of fluctuation and uncertainty, where plural conceptions are competing.[10] Out of politically activated competition, a certain conception of identity prevails over others and establishes itself as hegemonic. Still, counterhegemonic national identities do not fade away. Interaction between alternative notions of national identity is an ongoing process, especially in a democratic setting, where public support ultimately decides and hegemonic status has an element of contingency.

Though two countries may share structurally driven interests, perceptions can block progress in relations. Table 2.1 summarizes the analytical possibilities regarding the nature of interactions among countries affected by national identity conceptions. It offers a prism through which to view South Korea–Japan relations.

Table 2.1. Analytical Possibilities for Interactions among Countries Affected by National Identity Conceptions

Dispositional Dimension of National Identity	Qualitative Dimension of National Identity	
	Converging	Diverging
Congeniality	Amity	Accommodation
Confrontation	Friction	Clash

textbook controversy in 1982 and Nakasone's Yasukuni Shrine visit in 1985 reminded South Koreans of the past just as the burgeoning democratic movement was challenging the way dictators had been constructing national identity and paving the way for progressive influence.

Throughout the 1980s, South Korea achieved rapid economic growth, introducing a measure of controlled liberalization in the economy while also giving more room for overcoming a narrow, beleaguered national identity.[17] After gaining oil dollars through construction projects in the Middle East starting in the late 1970s, South Korea began to establish its global presence as firms performed well in such sectors as electronics, shipbuilding, automobiles, and construction. An expanded middle class with an active participatory orientation contributed to democratization, as students and the labor movement stood on the front line of the struggle for political freedom as critical to national identity. Democratization was facilitated by the active participation of white-collar workers.[18] The country's successful hosting of the Seoul Olympic Games in 1988, just as the Cold War was ending, fueled a surge in confidence. Ordinary South Koreans acquired a sense that North Korea was no longer a competitor or even much of a threat. Economic growth combined with political democratization aroused an elevated sense of confidence, enabling leaders to pursue diplomacy to normalize frozen ties with former enemies, the Soviet Union and China,[19] while striving to isolate North Korea.[20] Japan lost much of its importance as South Korea focused on states that could help to win over North Korea. Also, Japan was never a problem economically, because its rise helped to widen business opportunities for South Korea as part of the flying geese formation, or militarily, because its resilient U.S. alliance reduced concerns about an independent military buildup. In this time of national identity transformation in the late 1980s and early 1990s, a new momentum arose for changing relations with Japan.

First, South Korea's economic growth combined with democratization eliminated the "Red complex" among South Koreans. Though anticommunism persisted, South Koreans acquired a sense of confidence to cope with North Korea and, in the midst of the normalization of relations with Moscow and Beijing, Seoul in 1991 made its first bold gesture for reconciliation and peaceful reintegration.[21] At the same time, an inferiority complex against Japan was receding. Until the mid-1980s, the South Korean economy may have been growing, but authoritarian rule remained a source of disgrace. However, after South Korea accomplished democratic rule through a popular struggle, regime incongruence ended, leading to a shared democratic consciousness.[22] Anti-Japanese sentiment persisted, but the inferiority complex as a factor in national identity weakened sharply.

Second, South Korea's perimeter of action expanded rapidly to the global market. Until the late 1970s, the South Korean vision was limited geographically. Some attention was directed at Vietnam, where South Korea dispatched troops, and the Middle East, where South Korean workers gained oil dollars. However, in the 1980s, business and diplomacy expanded immensely, covering almost all corners of the world and awakening a globalized spirit. Establishing diplomatic ties with former socialist countries filled the remaining gap. If the strategic presence of the United States and Japan was not greatly changed, their role in national identity was subject to more contention.

BETWEEN AMITY AND FRICTION: POST–COLD WAR RELATIONS

Relations between South Korea and Japan in the post–Cold War era can be viewed through the prism of combinations of national identities newly defined in a changing domestic and international context. Japan's national identity was redefined after the end of the Cold War era. One cause of change came from engagement in the Gulf War, when a large monetary contribution was not much appreciated and "one-country pacifism" drew criticism. This shameful experience galvanized the public, which led to a debate on Japan becoming a normal country.[23] Acknowledging the dispatch of Self-Defense Forces overseas for peacekeeping operations, the Japanese reengaged in international security affairs, elevating a politico-military role in the country's national identity. Progressives were critical. Arguing that Ozawa Ichiro's call for Japan to become "normal" was actually a radical desire to become a great power in defiance of its postwar national identity, Takemura Masayoshi suggested that it instead should become a small but sparkling country.[24] Funabashi Yoichi took a somewhat different tack, rejecting a strong military tone in favor of becoming a "global civilian state."[25] With concern that Ozawa's move would redefine Japan as a militarily active state, the South Korean media were critical of the normal country discourse. In the eyes of those who still were suspicious of Japan's military intentions, a normal country orientation raised fears of Japan becoming a militaristic country potentially threatening to its neighbors.

Starting in 1989, South Korean civil movement activists raised a long-hidden agenda between the two nations: the issue of comfort women (i.e., Korean women who had been sex slaves of the Japanese military during World War II). Progressives showed strong interest in using this and other themes linked to Japan to resurrect the esteem of the South Korean people. Instead of appealing to Japan directly, they brought the issue to international attention. In 1992, Japan issued an apology, first by Chief Cabinet Secretary Kono Yohei and later by Prime Minister Miyazawa Kiichi's declaration. After the Liberal Democratic Party (LDP) lost power, Prime Minister Hosokawa Morihiro again expressed repentance on the issue. When Murayama Tomiichi took office in 1994, he went further, announcing the Murayama Declaration, seeking a Diet resolution in 1995 repenting the war, and establishing an Asian Women's Fund as a way to compensate for past wrongdoing. This stance, which was later labeled "apology diplomacy," contributed to the amelioration of South Korea–Japan relations. No single Japanese national identity seemed to prevail in the ensuing years. Even as the United States–Japan alliance was strengthened and "normal country" was perceived as positive to that relationship, South Koreans did not necessarily detect a challenge to their own national identity. Yet both Japanese and South Korean national identities were being steered in a direction that complicated and, at times, jeopardized bilateral relations.

A perilous collision of new national identity between Japan and South Korea emerged in the mid-1990s. In reaction to the apology expressed by Murayama and confident that progressives were at last marginalized in Japan, LDP neoconservatives argued for resurrecting pride in the nation. For them, history education should be revised to prevent shameful wrongdoings from being taught. This search for a new national identity, embodied in the Society for Making New History Textbooks (Atarashii kyokasho o tsukuru kai),[26] claimed that the existence of comfort women has not been empirically founded, and if they did exist, it was due to commercial benefit seekers, not the coercive mobilization of innocent victims by the Japanese government.[27] This argument was diametrically opposed to the claims of South Korean civic organizations, which were gaining influence as fears of North Korea further faded. With comfort women in the foreground as a divisive issue rooted in national identity debates, spillover to bilateral relations was unavoidable, especially for South Koreans.

Neoconservatives in Japan remained extremely critical of North Korea. To block any move toward a normalization of relations, neoconservative groups kept the abductee issue in the forefront, seeing this as a way to turn attention away from shame to self-esteem as a victim of a crime against humanity committed by a rogue neighbor. Their efforts gained momentum during the era of Koizumi Junichiro and Abe Shinzo, from 2001 to 2007. North Korea drew intense attention from the time of the first nuclear crisis, and in 1998 its launching of a Taepodong missile shocked the Japanese security community. Japan actively upgraded its military preparedness to deal with the North Korean threat, which gradually turned security policy from exclusive defense to active defense.[28] In addition to this realist move against a potential threat, some went further to argue that Japan should have an independent defense capability to counter any potential enemy without the help of the United States. Ishihara Shintaro suggested that Japan become an "independent defense state."[29] Later, this kind of argument developed into a call for Japan's nuclear armament, raised for instance by a high-ranking Self-Defense Forces officer.[30]

Although, in Japan, the year 1998 saw a negative shift toward North Korea, the same year marked the start of rule in South Korea by progressives, who were determined to assuage the security concerns of North Korean leaders by helping them open up and reform a malfunctioning system as a long-term strategy to end the threat.[31] This new strategic posture toward North Korea also reflected a sober assessment after the Asian economic crisis of the costs of applying the German unification formula. Kim Dae-jung, an opposition leader who served as the South Korean president between 1998 and 2003, defined his country's identity differently than did his conservative predecessors, highlighting ethnic reintegration rather than peace and prosperity in South Korea alone.[32] He treated North Korea not as an enemy but as a brother to be embraced in the long run. This had implications for thinking about the United States, opening the door to a wave of anti-Americanism, and also for Japan, toward which restraints that remained could be dropped. Confident progressives were inclined to react sharply to perceived new Japanese provocations, even amid lingering caution toward others.

The Roh Moo-hyun administration (2003–8) inherited this national identity conception. Extreme progressives went so far as to argue that autonomous decisions should be made concerning peace on the Korean Peninsula and that, on matters of unification, the United States might not be a facilitator. Roh was elected amid massive candlelight demonstrations against the United States over the deaths of two schoolgirls accidentally run over by an American tank, and he took advantage of this anti-Americanism. His thinking, which reflected ethnic nationalism, invited suspicion from the United States and Japan.[33]

Roh also resurrected the legitimacy of resistant nationalism and the struggle against injustice. As a part of political endeavors to criticize conservative mainstream political forces in South Korea,[34] progressives raised the question of identifying both pro-Japanese collaborators and those who cooperated with authoritarian governments. While resurrecting the dignity of the anti-Japanese independence fighters, they called for remembering the shameful acts of the past and punishing those who had benefited from them and remained privileged.[35] They made this a focus of national identity.

South Korean progressives for a time did not directly challenge Japanese national identity. They intentionally targeted conservatives at home, not those in Japan. However, there was potential for a collision because their conception of national identity was primarily past oriented. This finally sparked an active conflict between South Korea and Japan when Koizumi repeatedly paid visits to the Yasukuni Shrine, condoned a textbook review in favor of right-wing arguments, and, most important, presided as tensions surfaced after Shimane Prefecture initiated a resolution to celebrate the hundredth anniversary of Japan's annexing of Dokdo/Takeshima Island. In the eyes of South Koreans, the controversy concerning Dokdo is not simply a territorial dispute but a history issue.[36] This annexation has long been viewed as the first serious attempt to colonize South Korea. Thus, it resonates in South Korean discussions about national identity.

For Japanese conservatives, the Yasukuni Shrine is a symbol for paying respects to the dead who sacrificed their lives for the country, whereas from the Chinese and South Korean perspective, it symbolizes the past war and colonialism, especially because fourteen war criminals are enshrined there.[37] When Japanese government officials visit it, they discern an intention to glorify the war and colonialism. Koizumi's annual visits to the shrine may have drawn applause from conservative supporters as a way to give Japan a more assertive national identity, but they became a source of tension in bilateral relations when South Koreans perceived them as a direct challenge to their national identity.

The Roh-Koizumi era, which largely continued in the Roh-Abe period, saw a head-to-head collision of redefined national identities. South Korea embraced North Korea with the long-term goal of ethnic South Korean reintegration while turbulently attempting to manage security ties with the United States. Also, building a peaceful and prosperous Northeast Asian community was an ideal for the Roh regime, which suggested a soft policy toward China as well as North Korea. A historical orientation introduced for the purpose of legitimizing South Korean national identity eventually became fertile soil for escalating tensions with Japan. In contrast, Japan under the Koizumi administration pursued a strategy of strengthening the United States–Japan alliance while enhancing military preparedness against a potential North Korean threat and also growing more suspicious of China's intentions.[38] Elevating Japanese pride came at the expense of attentiveness to South Korean concerns, along with interest in finding common ground with China, reflecting the neoconservative quest for national identity.

Both South Korea and Japan learned a lesson from the collision course between the two countries.[39] Even though Abe was known to be intent on transforming Japan's identity as a "beautiful country," he chose to visit Beijing and Seoul first after his inauguration in order to calm down tensions. This did little to ameliorate the clash of identities. Only when Fukuda Yasuo became prime minister in 2007, putting an emphasis on Asian diplomacy to balance the U.S. focus, did the identity gap narrow. Aso Taro also strove to diminish tensions with South Korea, looking hopefully to the return of conservative rule as critical to reviving a positive image of South Korea, which had haltingly been emerging in Japan before the Roh era.

Lee Myung-bak, who assumed the presidency in 2008, pursued a different conception of national identity, with foreign policy in the forefront. Instead of appeasing North Korea, he favored principled engagement linked to the North's abandonment of nuclear weapons while boosting ties with the United States and also Japan. In place of Roh's Korean Peninsula identity, Lee aspired to a global Korea, including proactive contributions on such issues as climate change, green growth, official development assistance, and peacekeeping forces.[40] Lee emphasized constructing a future-oriented, strategic partnership with Japan, a sharp contrast with Roh's past-oriented way of thinking. Not even mentioning Japan in his speeches on March 1 and August 15, in both 2008 and 2009, two national holidays associated with Japanese rule, Lee met Japanese prime ministers at least seven times in 2009 alone, a contrast to Roh in 2007 never meeting the Japanese leader. Aspirations for global South Korea made it easy for the two countries to work together because they largely have the same concerns. A reframed national identity from a new administration gave an opening to Japan, which it was more inclined to seize given its own rethinking.

In August 2009, Japan experienced its first power change popularly endorsed by the voters following longtime LDP rule. The Democratic Party of Japan (DPJ) chose Hatoyama Yukio as prime minister, and he promised priority for public welfare,[41] while also boldly supporting the formation of an East Asian community, in contrast to the LDP's stress on the United States–Japan alliance. Hatoyama made it clear that East

Asian community building would not be possible without establishing firm and amicable ties with the United States.[42] Yet, by leaving doubt about the implementation of the existing bilateral agreement on a base relocation in Okinawa with an emphasis on lessening the burden on the Okinawa people, Hatoyama aroused confusion about the direction of Japanese foreign policy at a time of growing tension in the region. In bilateral ties, Hatoyama's approach to South Korea was quite comforting. After all, it also favored more active Japanese-Asian diplomacy and the long-term goal of an East Asian community. At the end of December 2009, the Hatoyama Cabinet took a silent but strong measure not to include the name Takeshima in the teaching guidelines for high school history textbooks, avoiding controversy with South Korea, when the latter is committed to building a future-oriented, constructive relationship. Also, the Hatoyama Cabinet remained sympathetic to bestowing the right to participate in local politics on South Korean special permanent residents.[43] Kan Naoto, who succeeded Hatoyama, was further committed to narrowing the gap with South Korea. He was worried about potential repercussions with the South Korean public, so his administration delayed publication of the Defense White Paper, which was assumed to contain a clause on Dokdo/Takeshima, until after sensitive dates in August.[44] On August 9, 2010, a few days before the hundredth anniversary of Japan's annexation of South Korea, it issued an apology that was welcomed in South Korea as a step forward. Having become aware of the danger of mismanaging national identity issues, Japan was proceeding positively.

Under Lee's conservatism and the DPJ's rejection of neoconservatism, there are no peculiar points of controversy deepening the national identity gap between South Korea and Japan. This is a result of the redefinition of national identities that has been accomplished through regime changes in each country. South Korea is focusing on the future, not the past. Amid tense relations with North Korea, it is taking a proactive stance toward global issues. Although the potential remains for Japan to reemerge as an object of political criticism if issues linked to the past are raised by the Japanese side, it has become a partner of South Korea.[45] Meanwhile, the DPJ is not inclined to evoke history issues, as it

too prioritizes a global agenda, raising the prospect of deeper collaboration. Given uncertainties about the recovery of the world economy from
the financial crisis that began in 2008 and dangers from security threats,
above all from North Korea, the international and regional environment is reinforcing the political trends toward a narrower national identity gap, although the potential remains for a return to political pressure
on both sides to widen the gap and for insensitive moves in Japan to
incite deeply rooted emotions linked to South Korean national identity. After Japan's March 2011 earthquake, tsunami, and nuclear disaster,
Japanese leaders welcomed the heartfelt South Korean humanitarian
aid to the victims. However, South Korean sympathy did not put a hold
on the Japanese textbook review that approved controversial clauses on
Dokdo/Takeshima. Growing political instability in the DPJ Cabinet is
closely associated with the failure to marginalize national identity divisions. Uncertainty also arose in advance of the 2012 presidential election in South Korea. After the island dispute had flared again and conservatives were on the defensive due to domestic issues, in December
2011 Lee Myung-bak spent much of a summit meeting with Japanese
prime minister Noda Yoshihiko criticizing Japan. Clearly, recent progress in narrowing the national identity gap was far from sufficient to
prevent such sharp setbacks to mutual understanding.

CONCLUSION

The analysis given here of Korea-Japan relations through a prism of
national identities leads to hope for the future mixed with caution for
unresolved barriers still deeply rooted in the way many people in each
country think about national identity. During the last one hundred years,
national identities have shifted from being mutually irreconcilable to
becoming potentially compatible. By forcibly annexing Korea against
the will of its people and later pressuring South Koreans to assimilate
and obliterate their national identity, Japan left a legacy of great bitter-
ness with scant interest in overcoming it in the Cold War era. Though
South Korea normalized diplomatic ties with Japan after twenty years

of decolonization, there remained a gap between compromising power elites and recalcitrant grassroots elements. Although Cold War logic bound the two nations together and allowed anti-Japanese feelings to remain in the background, friction between South Korea and Japan never faded away. With the emergence of progressive forces in South Korea, which prompted a reorientation of national identity to embrace North Korea while delegitimizing the colonial and authoritarian past, confrontation with Japan became more salient to national identity. In turn, neoconservatives, who advocated a revisionist conception of national identity, negating apologies for Japan's past aggression while condemning North Korea and China as a source of threat, left little room for reconciliation with South Korea. Yet the advent of Lee Myung-bak's government combined with the retreat from Koizumi's hard-line position, especially the rise of the DPJ, led to signs of compatibility.

Despite the two countries' increasingly compatible national identities, plural identity conceptions give mixed signals. No single conception of national identity permanently prevails. Comforting to many are signs that extremist versions of national identities have less chance of winning majority support today. Clashes based on conflicting national identities between South Korea and Japan are not inevitable. It is not yet certain whether the Japanese leaders learned the lesson from the frictions with neighboring countries that historical controversies do not serve Japan's national interest. Also, whether Japan now is on track to persistently define its national identity on the basis of a consensus among competing political forces is uncertain. However, after the turbulent Koizumi administration, Japanese political leaders are showing a spirit of moderation in handling bilateral relations with South Korea, and South Korean leaders are reciprocating with goodwill, reviving friendly ties between the two countries. Still, the neoconservatives remain adamant in Japan, and the South Korean progressives will not fade away. The lesson from the peak of clashes between the two is that a collision of national identities brings about turbulent times.

NOTES

1   Victor Cha, *Alignment Despite Antagonism* (Stanford, Calif.: Stanford University Press, 1999). Cha concludes that due to fear of abandonment, a gradual withdrawal of the United States would facilitate cooperation between South Korea and Japan. For the contrasting view—that U.S. engagement is critically important to cooperation between South Korea and Japan—see Tae Ryong Yoon, "Fragile Cooperation" (Ph.D. diss., Columbia University, 2006).

2   Cheol Hee Park, "Ilbon shin bosukjueui seryok eui songjang kwa Hankook e eui hameui," in *Geullobolhwa sidae eui Ilbon*, edited by Young Jak Kim and Jinho Jeon (Seoul: Hanul, 2006).

3   Haesook Chae and Steve Kim, "Conservatives and Progressives in South Korea," *Washington Quarterly* 3, no. 4 (Autumn 2008): 77–95.

4   Samuel Kim, "Korea's Democratization in the Global-Local Nexus," in *Korea's Democratization*, edited by Samuel Kim (New York: Cambridge University Press, 2003), 3–44; Ian Aart Scholte, "Globalization and Collective Identities," in *Identities in International Relations*, edited by Jill Kruase and Neil Renwick (Oxford: Saint Anthony's College, 1996).

5   National identity does not change abruptly or instantaneously; nor does it change in a vacuum.

6   Robert Gilpin, *War and Change in World Politics* (New York: Cambridge University Press, 1981).

7   Peter Katzenstein points out the importance of understanding national identities in a plural way. Peter Katzenstein, "A World of Plural and Pluralist Civilizations," in *Civilizations in World Politics*, edited by Peter Katzenstein (New York: Routledge, 2010), 1–40.

8   Carl Schmidt, *The Concept of the Political* (Chicago: University of Chicago Press, 1995).

9   On politics as mobilization of bias, see E. E. Schattschneider, *Party Government* (Westport, Conn.: Greenwood Press, 1977).

10 Multiple sovereignties may compete within one territory, suggesting that multiple national identities can, too. Charles Tilly, *From Mobilization to Revolution* (Reading, Mass.: Addison-Wesley, 1978).

11 Chong Sik Lee, *Japan and Korea: The Political Dimension* (Stanford, Calif.: Hoover Institution Press, 1985).

12 Bruce Cumings, *The Origins of the Korean War* (Princeton, N.J.: Princeton University Press, 1981).

13 Jang Jip Choi, "Political Cleavages in South Korea," in *State and Society in Contemporary Korea*, edited by Hagen Koo (Ithaca, N.Y.: Cornell University Press, 1993), 13–50.

14 In 1972, when Park forcefully extended his political rule, he called his move the October Restoration, reminding many of the Meiji Restoration in Japan, as he

appealed to make South Korea economically rich and militarily strong.

15 In the 1970s, two incidents led to crises in South Korean–Japan relations: the assassination of the first lady by a South Korean–Japanese, Se Kwang Moon; and the kidnapping of Kim Dae-jung, the former opposition leader, from a hotel in Japan. Neither directly targeted the Japanese people or government.

16 Katherine Moon, "Korean Nationalism, Anti-Americanism and Democratic Consolidation," in *Korea's Democratization*, ed. Samuel Kim, 135–58.

17 Stephan Haggard and Chung In Moon, "Institution and Economic Growth: Theory and the South Korean Case," *World Politics*, January 1990, 210–37.

18 Sung Joo Han, "Korean Experiment," *Journal of Democracy* 2, no. 2 (Spring 1991): 92–104; Sunhyuk Kim, *The Politics of Democratization in South Korea: The Role of Civil Society* (Pittsburgh: University of Pittsburgh Press, 2000).

19 The Seoul Olympic Games showed the way to linking the countries.

20 It is important to note that South Korea's move toward establishing diplomatic ties with the socialist countries preceded the end of the Cold War.

21 The then–Unification Church minister Hong Koo Lee called for a Korean national community as a signal for reintegrating with North Korea. Dong Won Im strongly pushed reconciliation between 1990 and 1992.

22 Okonogi Masao, "Chejemachal eseo euisik kongyu ro," in *Hankook kwa Ilbon*, edited by Young Jak Kim (Seoul: Hanul, 2006).

23 Ichiro Ozawa took the lead in this initiative; see Ichiro Ozawa, *A New Blueprint for Japan* (Tokyo: Kodansha, 1993).

24 Takemura Masayoshi, *Chiisakute kirari to hikaru Nihon* (Tokyo, 1994).

25 Funabashi Yoichi, *Nihon no taiagi koso: Reisengo no bijon o kaku* (Tokyo: Iwanami shoten, 1993).

26 For a study of the Tsukurukai, see Yoo Jin Koo, "Atarashii kyokasho o tsukurukai o toshite miru rekishi ninshiki no Nihon seiji" (M.A. thesis, Seoul National University, 2006).

27 In March 2007, Abe commented on the comfort women issue, wildly accepting the claims of the right-wing group's argument. His remarks surprised not only the South Korean public but also U.S. leaders. Representative Michael Honda led Congress in a resolution admonishing the Japanese government.

28 Cheol Hee Park, "Junsubangwi eseo jokgeuk bangwi ro," in *Kukje chongchi noncong* (Seoul, 2004).

29 Cheol Hee Park, "Japanese Conservatives' Conception of a Normal State: Comparing Nakasone, Ozawa, and Ishihara," in *Japan as a Normal State*, edited by David Welch, Masayuki Tadokoro, and Yoshihide Soeya (Toronto: University of Toronto Press, 2011).

30 Tamogami Toshio, *Soredemo wakaru Nihon kaku busoron* (Tokyo: Hicho shincha, 2009).

31 In the eyes of progressive political forces in South Korea, North Korea was in deep trouble after the floods in 1995 and 1996 and did not pose an imminent military threat to South Korea.

32   Kang Won-taek differentiates South Korean ethnic nationalism, or *hanminjokjueui*, from South Korean nationalism, or *daehanminkook minjokjueui*.

33   Gi Wook Shin, *Ethnic Nationalism in Korea* (Stanford, Calif.: Stanford University Press, 2006).

34   Jang Jip Choi, *Democracy after Democratization* (Seoul: Humanitas, 2005).

35   Though their ideological orientation was totally different from the Japanese neoconservatives, progressives in South Korea shared a similar ideal: that South Korea should be a country of pride and self-esteem.

36   The Northeast Asia History Foundation clarifies the link between territorial and historical issues in the homepage of the Foundation; see http://www.historyfoundation.or.kr.

37   On the complexity of the Yasukuni issue from a progressive Japanese intellectual perspective, see Takahashi Tetsuya, *Yasukuni mondai* (Tokyo: Chikuma shobo, 2005).

38   Yomiuri shimbun, *Gaiko wo kenka ni shita otoko* (Tokyo: Yomiuri shimbunsha, 2008).

39   During the Roh-Koizumi era, South Korean and Japanese diplomats stationed in the counterpart nations said, almost in despair, that there is nothing they could do to control the situation. It was up to the president and prime minister.

40   Lee Myung-bak, "The Path to Green Growth," *Global Asia* 4, no. 4 (Winter 2010).

41   Cheol Hee Park, "Bloodless Revolution: How the DPH's Win Will Change Japan," *Global Asia* 4, no. 4 (Winter 2010).

42   *Asahi shimbun*, January 29, 2010.

43   Opposition by the coalition partner and intraparty dissidents delayed the process, but Hatoyama and Ozawa repeatedly committed to this agenda.

44   *Asahi shimbun*, July 28, 2010.

45   Cheol Hee Park, "Hanil galdeung eui baneungjok chokbal kwa wonronjok daeeung eui guzo," in *Hankook jongchi oegyosa nonchong* (Seoul, 2008), 323–48.

CHAPTER 3

NATIONAL IDENTITIES AND
SINO-JAPANESE RELATIONS

Ming Wan

National identities often take precedence over national interests in Sino-Japanese relations, and, in turn, these identities are influenced by the two countries' interactions. These identities explain why the ties between China and Japan seem peculiarly emotional relative to their relations with other countries. Affinity or arrogance resulting from a long history of cultural exchange, contempt and victimization from wars or aggression since the 1890s, and confidence in superior modernization shape how the Chinese and Japanese view each other. In particular, both China and Japan have acquired a great power identity that is partially contingent on exclusivity with each other, which underlies their current tensions.

Three features of national identity deserve to be emphasized for influencing the Sino-Japanese relationship. First, once formed, they have a degree of stickiness even if the relationship has moved in a different direction. For example, the ugly mood that in the years 2002–6 reinforced mutually negative identities continued to limit relations, despite official warmth in the following years. Second, identities evolve, particularly in relative saliency in the overall identity complex. Third, with relations compartmentalized from each state's overall foreign policy, such porousness damages bilateral ties when the two countries

exhibit their worst tendencies toward each other, despite a calmer orientation overall.

This chapter examines the post–Cold War period in Sino-Japanese
relations after reviewing the pre-1945 and Cold War periods for insights
on how the bilateral identity gap took shape. I need to provide substan-
tive discussion of the prewar and postwar periods because what happened
in the past has a crucial impact on relations today. I have previously discussed how Chinese and Japanese national identities, particularly how
they played out in interactions, have affected the bilateral relationship
and have been shaped by it.[1] Here I deepen the analysis with specific
attention to how these identities have been transformed through recent
interactions and are complicating the cooperation that is understood
to be in each country's national interest as China's rise reverberates in
Japan's identity debate and, at the same time, fuels a more assertive outlook toward Japan as part of China's evolving national identity.

National identity is a complex and contested concept.[2] It is often
reinvented to serve specific purposes.[3] In this volume, we are concerned with how national identity relates closely to interaction, which
involves watching with strong interest developments in the other country, particularly the attitudes of the other toward one's own country.
Samuel Huntington noted in his study of American national identity
that "identities are defined by the self, but they are the product of the
interaction between the self and others. How others perceive an individual or group affects the self-definition of that individual or group."[4]
National identity has a strong component of exclusivity. Interaction
often reinforces or creates perceptions that one side is indeed different. Familiarity can breed contempt. Identities are typically sticky; once
they are formed, they take time to change. This emerges clearly over
the long history of Sino-Japanese interactions and mutual perceptions.

PRE-1945 INTERACTIONS

Historically, China had a strong cultural influence on Japan, as seen in
the conscious and organized cultural borrowing from China at the turn

of the seventh century, which lasted for the next two centuries. Chinese culture affected mainly Japanese ruling elites and scholars at this early stage. The China factor is also reflected in the narrow world horizon for Japan at this time, which was largely limited to China, Korea, and India, with China being particularly important. This history shaped a strong Japanese sense of cultural affinity with China, which was based more on reading Chinese classics than on actual human interaction. The Japanese absorbed Chinese culture and developed their own distinct culture. A millennium after the massive wave of borrowing, Japanese officials again turned to Confucianism, as they strove to legitimize their political dominance, often by combining Neo-Confucianism with Shintoism. They differentiated cultural China from political China, which was made easier by the fact that there was no state-to-state relationship. More broadly, the Japanese sought to define Japaneseness against what they imagined to be Chineseness, as revealed in their literature starting in the tenth century,[5] while remaining within the Chinese world order by sharing the values and expectations that made East Asia different from the Western international system, whose impact was drawing closer.[6] In the late Tokugawa period, a school of national learning emerged to emphasize Japan's unique imperial institution and values as superior to Chinese culture. With China's defeat in the Opium War and inability to resist the West, this contrast became increasingly appealing.

The Chinese were aware of Japan's presence and provided the earliest written records of the ancestors of the modern Japanese.[7] The first Chinese studies of Japan began in the fourteenth century due to the threat of "Japanese pirates" with blurred national origins. However, the Chinese did not conduct research in Japan,[8] and they were largely ignorant of what the Japanese wrote about China without concern for possible counterarguments from the Chinese.[9] In an asymmetrical relationship, Japan was less central for China, which had established a sense of itself as the center of the world and largely focused on its relations with steppe peoples to the northwest and north.[10] The Chinese Middle Kingdom mentality is now one of the analytical lenses used for studying Sino-Japanese tensions. Some say that cultural arrogance and contempt of Japan provoked resentment that such attitudes revealed a

Chinese intention to dominate the country, which endures. Although such a psychological dynamic does exist, one needs to scrutinize the validity of such claims. Cultural arrogance per se does not necessarily lead to political efforts to dominate and subjugate. It is often the consequence rather than the root cause of political domination, although it may be a powerful enabling factor. The Chinese sense of cultural superiority, which does exist, was arguably superficial when it comes to Japan due to limited direct contact before the mid–nineteenth century.

In the Sino-Japanese War of 1894–95, the Chinese and Japanese threw racist insults at each other with abandon, with the Chinese digging up ancient derogative terms for the Japanese and the Japanese creating their own insulting epithets.[11] But one does not need centuries of interaction to exhibit cultural hatred in a time of war, as seen in the Pacific front of World War II between Japan and the United States in 1941–45.[12] Japan's delegation to the Chinese capital in AD 702 requested that their country be called Nihon (Riben in Chinese) instead of Wa (Wo in Chinese), which the Chinese had used for their country until then. The Chinese accepted this request and have used Riben ever since.[13] There has been a controversy over whether the name "Wo" was derogatory. Similarly, early Chinese rulers called agricultural peoples Koreans, Japanese, and Vietnamese "Eastern Barbarians" and "Southern Barbarians," but they subsequently called these countries as they preferred to be called and did not treat them as barbarians throughout history. Yet this does not mean that the Chinese came to appreciate Japanese culture or even to show much awareness of it.

Having had little exposure to Japanese culture before the late nineteenth century, the Chinese have needed to overcome a strong negative association of Japanese culture with the militaristic Japanese state. The import of Japanese culture coincided with, first, a clear sense of Japanese superiority, and then with outright aggression against China. If, at times, leaders appealed to cultural similarities in an effort to improve relations, resting their case on firm historical grounds, this message was repeatedly overwhelmed by the populist preoccupation with Japanese culture serving as the source of jingoism.

In the 1860s, China and Japan began to perceive each other in the context of the Western international system. By 1862, the Chinese had basically accepted this system after the British and French sacked Beijing for violating the treaties imposed after the Opium War. The Japanese no longer treated China as the Middle Kingdom. They were cordial and deferential because they wanted the right to trade and to have a consulate in Shanghai. During the next several decades, Japanese confidence grew as the gap between the two countries' reforms and modernization widened. In the midst of fervent Westernization, Japan began to reject Asia, culturally sharpening differences with it while drawing closer to the West. Fukuzawa Yukichi famously called for Japan to leave Asia and join the West and seek civilization, pointing to a divide between enlightened Japan and unenlightened China. He made it clear that China was a negative "other" to be rejected, whereas the West was a positive "other" to be emulated. Along with Nishi Amane, he had a tremendous impact in contrasting the Enlightenment and progress to Neo-Confucianism and stagnation.[14] By contrast, China initially sought in vain to maintain the traditional East Asian international system,[15] incurring Japanese contempt and laying the basis for its adventurism in Asia.

Japan's psychological attempt to break from China and to adopt a Western lens to the world was reflected in its use of the name "Shina" rather than "Chugoku" (the Middle Kingdom) for China after the Meiji Restoration.[16] This departed from the past practice of using the same characters, even though they were pronounced differently in China, Japan, and Korea, such as in the case of China accepting the characters for Nihon, pronounced Riben. Because "Shina" consists of two Chinese characters that capture the Western pronunciation of China but otherwise have no intrinsic meaning and was imposed by Japan for discourse between the two countries, it conveyed Japan's superiority over China and was seen as derogatory. This is the reason that it was no longer used after Japan lost the war, and its revival by a few right-wing Japanese politicians would be reported resentfully in China.

Japan regained confidence in the late 1880s and the 1890s, particularly after winning the war with China. Chinese learning was part of Japanese tradition, which now drew more support. This would be the first period of a well-articulated identity of Japan as the most civilized country in Asia and the tutor for others. But the Western influence was felt in this process. Leading Asianists such as Okakura Tenshin framed their discussion based on an imported European discourse about Asia.[17] Japanese thinkers talked about pan-Asianism as a way to fend off Western pressure and viewed Japan's progress as tied to Asia's progress.[18] This was based on an identity of superiority in Asia while keeping a distance from the West. The Sino-Japanese War of 1894–95 partly resulted from clashing national identities, as recalled by Mutsu Munemitsu, the Japanese foreign minister at the time.[19] The war put Japan on the world map and won the country a large indemnity from China that helped stabilize its finance and monetary system. Its decisive victory had a great impact on its self-image. Equally important, the West came to view Japan as a modern power and China as a backward country, an easy target for imperialist powers.[20] Such perceptions led to different attitudes and policies toward the two, which contributed to self-images. Increased pressure from Japan focused China's emerging nationalism on it.

In the 1920s, the Japanese government turned to cultural diplomacy toward China. This was due to a confluence of factors. Japan's own internationalists were responding to democracy, disarmament, and peace. They were also concerned about increasing Chinese nationalism and Chinese's negative image of Japan, amid cultural rivalry with the United States and Europe. Some Japanese were asking questions one would hear today, namely, why Chinese students who have studied in Japan seem to dislike Japan while students who have studied in the United States seem pro-American. This awareness did not lead to any soul-searching about Japanese identity, although it did bring more money and better treatment of Chinese students. The Japanese government took the center stage, and took an approach that was different from the American one but similar to those of some European countries. It wanted to shape Chinese thinking. Some may see this as a case of cultural imperialism, but there was a degree of idealism and internationalism for many who were enthusiastic about this endeavor, and there was an attempt to elicit Chinese participation in some of the cultural projects.[21]

In the 1930s, some Japanese thinkers, particularly military officers, wanted Japan to unify Asia under its leadership in an epic battle against the Western powers.[22] Japan descended into a period of heightened racist identity and military conquests, which ended in its own destruction. This period of militarized interaction, with the large presence of the Japanese military and the Japanese nationals in China who counted on the military for protection, furthered the Chinese association of the Japanese with the Japanese military.[23]

The Japanese national identity of superiority and contempt for the Chinese contributed to the start of the Second Sino-Japanese War of 1937–45. As later research shows, the hawks within the Japanese army for expanding the war in 1937 were centered in the China Section of the General Staff Intelligence Division. Though they were considered second rate in the army because more promising officers developed expertise on Europe and the United States, the division's old China hands had acquired their expertise through service with the field units and special service organs in China, focusing on espionage and subversion to keep China weak and divided. Not surprisingly, they did not acquire a deep knowledge of China, particularly the meaning of rising Chinese nationalism. Their contempt for Chinese military capabilities, shared by the army and the country, resulted in their limited knowledge of China and Japan's sinking ever deeper into a prolonged war on the continent.[24]

Japan's invasion and atrocities, particularly the Nanjing Massacre, have defined contemporary Chinese nationalism. The personal suffering and humiliation experienced by many Chinese were passed down from generation to generation, forming a societal basis for anger toward Japan. However, there were some "good Japanese" from the Chinese perspective. Some worked for the Nationalists as well as the Communist government or armies during the war. Communist Party cadres working with them during the war became key players dealing with Japan affairs for the People's Republic of China. And the large number of Japanese who had China experience and felt guilt or affection for China formed the social basis for "friendship" with China in later years.[25] In contrast, the far more "good Chinese" for imperial Japan,[26] as collaborators with a defeated country, played no visible role in postwar "friendship."

At least four arguments have been raised to showcase the powerful legacy of historical memories left for China as it reasserted itself under Communist leadership and Japan as it found a new direction through democracy dominated by one party. First, the long delay in normalization without Japan making genuine efforts toward reconciliation permitted the gap in national identities to harden. In modern times, failure to bridge differences from a war of such magnitude is a recipe for prolonged enmity, primarily from the victim's side. Second, a cause of this legacy can be traced to the abnormal national identity in postwar Japan, where refutations of the revisionist thinking of right-wing figures resonate weakly in a population distracted by other identity themes while the political system gives veto power to those with the strongest national identity consciousness. Illusions about China, such as that growing dependency on Japan would diminish historical resentments or that propaganda was solely responsible for enduring resentment, misled many Japanese. Third, exceptional features of Chinese national identity nurtured by Communist leaders also bear responsibility for this gap. If the Maoist approach to national identity spared the Japanese nation as a whole from blame, it also distorted history and international relations to such a degree that a balanced perspective on postwar Japan was unrealizable, even after the two countries normalized relations, leading to "friendship" ties. Starting in the mid-1980s, Chinese leaders had decided to oppose on moral grounds Japan's revival as both a political and military great power, and then, as revealed in the brief effort at "new thinking" in 2003, various one-sided interpretations of Japan were reinforced as part of China's identity. Fourth and finally, a failure to narrow the gap over pre-1945 history is rooted in competition for leadership in East Asia, in which China is driven to reassert its superiority and Japan is anxious to avoid any reinforcement of the opprobrium of its past immorality.

COLD WAR INTERACTIONS

China and Japan ended up in different places in postwar East Asian international relations defined by the Cold War. China was pulled toward world revolution, at first in the camp led by the Soviet Union, and Japan was directed toward pacifism and identity with the West rather than Asia. Thus the interactions between China and Japan in the years before their 1972 normalization were shaped in important ways by their evolving national identity complexes.

Japan could not establish diplomatic relations with China, even though many Japanese wanted to do so. The United States left some room for economic and cultural exchanges, being aware of China's prior economic importance for Japan and the consensus in Japan, not only for economic reasons, of the need to expand contacts with the Asian continent.[27] Japan's relationship with China was noticeably different from that between the United States and China.[28] Because of the Korean War, the United States had virtually no ties with China. By contrast, Japan's unofficial economic, cultural, and political contacts with China were upgraded over time to semiofficial status and increasingly served different national identity goals.

A combination of war guilt and revived appreciation of Chinese cultural influence on Japan helped the Japanese form a favorable view of China. Japan's progressive forces identified, to some extent, with a socialist China, while also finding it useful in their opposition to the U.S. alliance and American military bases in Japan. If conservatives stressed the value of the alliance and friendship toward Taiwan, many welcomed diversification through Asian networks in order to avoid subversion from a United States–centered national identity. However, they rejected the progressive tendency to use the China factor to bolster identity as a victimizer of Asia, fearing that Japanese youth would become masochistic in lieu of a positive understanding of Japanese history. On the basis of cultural affinities and experience in China, the Japanese tended to view the members of the Chinese Communist Party as nationalists who were bound to clash with the Soviet Union. Yoshida Shigeru predicted that China would eventually split from the Soviet Union, pointing to the "extremely proud" Chinese character.[29] The Japanese also felt that as fellow Asians, they understood China better than the Americans.

The Chinese government understood and took advantage of Japan's divisions over China and sense of war guilt and culture debt. Officials such as Zhou Enlai appealed to Japanese identity as a teacher and early modernizer and to a shared sense of Asian destiny.

From 1952 to 1972, China juggled several identities shaping its foreign policy: socialist identity, third world identity, victimization-based identity, and Asian identity. Due to its victimization identity, China criticized prime ministers Kishi Nobosuke and Sato Eisaku for reviving militarism, but Japan was a low priority compared with the Soviet Union and United States. Given frequent visits by Japan's progressive leaders, China had reason to emphasize Asian identity too.

Apart from its national interest in neutralizing Japan from a hostile encirclement of China in the 1950s and in seeking trade and technology in the 1960s, China's policy toward Japan was also shaped by its class-based ideology that the majority of Japanese people were victims of Japanese militarism and only a minority of Japanese militarists was responsible for a common disaster for the Chinese and Japanese peoples. Such an assessment played a central role in Mao Zedong's decision not to seek reparations from Japan out of concern that it would put too much of a burden on innocent Japanese. Given Mao's status and the authoritarian nature of Chinese politics, strong resentment against Japan among ordinary people was suppressed. China was preoccupied with frequent domestic strife, and thus it had plenty of "villains" at home for both its class struggle and demonization of first the United States as the capitalist/imperialist enemy and then the Soviet Union as the revisionist betrayer of socialist identity. This left Japan as mostly an afterthought.

Normalization of China-Japan relations led to the "1972 system," a carefully constructed framework for the bilateral relationship.[30] National interests were crucial, but national identities also played a role. In the 1970s, China tried to get Japan to play a more strategic role against the Soviet Union, but this did not have a visible effect on Japan's well-entrenched identity as a peaceful country not involved in international conflict, even though the country was allied with the United States and hosted American bases. Starting reform in 1978, China publicly sought out Japan's assistance, which reinforced Japan's identity as the most advanced country in Asia and alleviated its sense of guilt because it was helping the country it had victimized. In a dramatic shift, the Chinese government sought official development assistance, direct investment, and policy advice for economic activities.[31] This approach worked to a large extent because Japan's wartime generation largely felt guilty and expected resentment from the Chinese. The fact that the Chinese government seemed forward looking and sincere in forging a relationship fit with the Japanese desire to pay in some way for the past and then move on and be proud of themselves again. The Japanese were rightly proud of their postwar economic miracle, and by sharing their economic model with the Chinese, they expected to transform Chinese national identity away from socialism and victimization and toward shared modernization and Asian identity. Japan's large program of official development assistance was meant as compensation for past aggression, even if China barely publicized it.

In the 1980s, there were some incidents involving history textbooks and a prime ministerial visit to Yasukuni Shrine. China's pressure played into Japan's divided politics and achieved some results but could not solve the problem to its ultimate satisfaction because Japan had divided identities. This was still manageable because Japan could balance it psychologically as a teacher and by thinking that this phase would pass as China became more moderate as it developed. On the Chinese side, there was a division between the state and the society not far below the surface. The government handled Japan-related issues politically, often not to the satisfaction of much of the citizenry.

Postwar interaction between China and Japan was largely asymmetrical. Before 1972, the Japanese could deal with China only on a societal level, but Japanese officials and politicians also had ways to participate. On the Chinese side, it was a state-controlled process, consistent with overall foreign relations at the time. Private Chinese citizens could not take the initiative in engaging the Japanese. Such a pattern continued on the Chinese side in the 1970s. Japan's aggression was not studied, and scholars were urged to emphasize friendship, but history and victimization-based national identity loomed large in the background. On the Japanese side, the government took center stage after diplomatic relations were established, as the public gradually grew more enthusiastic.

With the economic reform in 1978, social restrictions in China began to relax, which led to greater direct interaction between Chinese and Japanese citizens. A new wave of Chinese students and trainees came to Japan, often funded by the Japanese government, foundations, companies, or universities. Japanese businessmen, scholars, and tourists became part of the Chinese scene. The drastic expansion of trade and investment during those years was also a powerful engine for the two countries. The two governments adopted policies to promote bilateral exchanges to lay a foundation for further friendship. As a dramatic example, Hu Yaobang, arguably the most pro-Japan Chinese politician since 1949, invited 3,000 Japanese youth to China in the mid-1980s. However, these intensified interactions did not prevent the relationship from deteriorating, and the interactions even had some negative short-term effects. With better access to China, the Japanese came to have a more realistic assessment of the situation in the country, adjusting overly rosy assessments of views of their country. On the Chinese side, those who came to Japan or interacted with Japanese tended to reject the excessively negative views of Japan ingrained in the Chinese public, but their new understanding was overwhelmed by the public's negativity.

If there had not been state-led bilateral interactions, the honeymoon would not have happened. Despite the sense of guilt, it would be hard to imagine that the Japanese elites would have felt as willing to cooperate if they had confronted the Chinese public's long-held anger at Japan. Indeed, as they acquired a better understanding, they could have responded with contempt for China. At the same time, it would have been better if the two countries had had more genuine interactions starting in 1972. Suppression of some emotions might have been expedient, but it pushed the problem toward the future. In fact, when the Chinese government's position changed and unleashed societal anger, the relationship was prone to suffer a greater shock. An accurate understanding of Chinese sentiment could have led the Japanese to view history differently and recognize the need for greater urgency. The older generations of elites arguably could have better handled a confrontation over the national identity gap. After all, they had seen the war, the worst kind of bilateral interactions, and had the credentials and experience to manage a public confrontation, which could have served as a kind of immunization for constructing a long-term, healthy relationship.

In the 1980s, conditions were more favorable for facing the emotions of clashing historical memories. Japan had an opportunity to proceed from confidence, while China was striving for inclusion in the regional and global community with no foundation for arrogance. Japan would have had to take the initiative to win the trust of the Chinese as well as convince the leadership, as Nakasone Yasuhiro tried to do with a flawed strategy in his dealings with Hu Yaobang. Not only did overconfidence expose Japan's lack of foresight, but the response in China as Hu was ousted revealed China's reluctance to narrow this identity gap. National interests were quite well aligned, but the national identity gap widened.

The Sino-Japanese relationship remained largely unchanged in its basic 1972 framework, which appeared special compared with their relationships with other countries, except for Japan's more special relationship with the United States. Ties were inconsistent with their national interests, and national identities were lurking in the background and even surfaced from time to time, because some Japanese leaders could not wait to press a revisionist agenda as they warned that China was intervening in Japan's internal affairs and hurting its prestige, while some Chinese leaders called the Chinese approach toward Japan too soft and insisted that Japan could not be trusted without confronting its history.

POST–COLD WAR INTERACTIONS

The end of the Cold War did not predetermine the nature of the Sino-Japanese bilateral relationship. Both sides had been struggling with their national identities as perceptions of how the other thinks fed into this process. In the first half of the 1990s, the focus in each state was on the United States. With the United States leading in isolating and sanctioning China, Beijing saw Japan as the weakest link, and thus made extra efforts to cultivate relations with Japanese visitors. The Japanese also had their own reasons to maintain good relations with China, sensing an opportunity to act as a bridge between China and the West, which could allow them to leverage better relations with both sides to their advantage. The Chinese felt Japan owed China a historical debt not to pressure it for human rights. The Japanese understood that in light of their troubled modern history in China and a stronger Asian identity after the Cold War, they had to keep a low profile. Many were concerned about China's collapse rather than its rise, renewing Japan's identity as a teacher that could lend a helping hand to a China in trouble. Soon, when Japan was challenging the Washington consensus, they also saw China's economic growth as confirming Japan's development model. If Japan had to do something in line with the West because it did not want to look too different, knowing well that much had been said about such differences in the heat of trade wars, China under-stood Japan's dilemma and wisely did not overreact.

New developments taking place at this time would have a greater impact in later years. The Japanese government openly talked about putting its relationship with China in a global context, which reflect-ed its desire to end the special relationship as its status in the world was rising rapidly. A globalized Japan-China relationship would work to its advantage by moving beyond the 1972 system in which Japan seemed to be bowing to its neighbors over history. The Japanese were also reacting to criticism of checkbook diplomacy during the Persian Gulf War. Many felt that Japan needed to make political and military contributions to acquire an international status consistent with its economic power. Given trade tension with the Bill Clinton admin-istration, the United States rather than China was at the center of Japanese identity consciousness.

In the early 1990s, a debate ensued about how to better assert Japan's identity, which had ramifications for the identity gap with China. One focus was internationalism and international contribu-tions. Ozawa Ichiro and Hashimoto Ryutaro stressed political and military contributions. Ozawa felt that Japan had to seek internation-al cooperation to ensure its security, which economic power alone could not do. Hashimoto talked more about Japan's unique traditions. In contrast, Takemura Masayoshi and Kaifu Toshiki focused on pacifist contributions, as the latter highlighted Japan's harmonious relations with the environment. All these politicians wanted Japan to emphasize greater contributions to the international community in exchange for higher standing,[32] presenting as a responsible member of the exist-ing legitimate international society. In the mid-1990s, Japan moved gradually toward greater security responsibilities, a shift mainly meant to shore up its alliance with the United States and help it to become a normal, great power respected in the world.

Japan tried to reconcile internationalism and Asianism at a time when there was much discussion of Japan "reentering Asia." This failed because of contradictions in the way Japan approached these identity issues and also because of China's new assertiveness rather than Japan's seizing the opportunity. To make Japan a normal state, some conser-vatives felt that they had to go back to the root of what they viewed as its abnormal status, which would reignite disputes with its Asian neighbors over history.[33] After the U.S. government adjusted its policy to strengthen the alliance, Japan continued to pursue Asianism in a cautious manner while testing China amid recurrent uncertainties in bilateral relations.

Japan's shift toward greater security cooperation in about 1994 was largely read as threatening in China, compounding the reaction to its growing revisionist views in Japan. The Chinese government turned to patriotic education as a way to shore up its legitimacy after the Tiananmen Square massacre in 1989, recalling its status as a great power for two millennia and as a victim in modern history.[34] This move was triggered mainly by China's negative reaction to the West; but once the patriotic campaign began, it could not help but focus on Japan, which did the most damage to China and gave the Chinese Communist Party legitimacy in the resistance struggle.[35] Japan remained the crucial "other" in China's victimization-based national identity.[36] One often hears people argue whether negative views of Japan come from the top or the bottom. Both are important. If resentment against the United States is often offset by admiration, the case of Japan aroused a more unambiguous reaction.

China took the first move, leading to a downward spiral. When Western pressure began to ease in 1994, the Chinese government became more critical of Japan, which in turn fueled Japanese resentment. The Taiwan Strait crisis began as a triangular dynamic involving Beijing, Taipei, and Washington but spilled over to Sino-Japanese relations when the issue arose of whether the United States–Japan alliance covers Taiwan, and Japanese saw it as added reason for strengthening the alliance. Feeling that only Chinese and Koreans were so critical when their country was respected in the rest of the world, the Japanese were alienated, and this was compounded by generational change. From 1981 to 2005, those who had experienced World War II had decreased from 46.2 to 16.0 percent, as a younger generation preferred to focus instead on Japan's positive contributions in the postwar era.[37] One senior Japanese diplomat explained to me that he felt that his grandfather's generation did bad things in Asia and was wrong, his father's generation tried very hard to be good, and now his generation is not denying history but does want to move forward.

Japan's identity as a democratic country also mattered. The difference in political regimes had become an important factor to explain why the two countries diverge, why the Chinese side behaves as it does, which should not be taken seriously, and why Japan cannot ultimately trust China. The Tiananmen Square massacre seriously damaged China's image, even though the Japanese government took a low posture, and its effect intensified with the widening identity gap in the second half of the 1990s. One way to reconcile internationalism and Asianism is to see Japan as a voice of human rights and democracy in the international community and in Asia. When Abe Shinzo and Aso Taro toned down their insistence on Japanese uniqueness in favor of claims to be pursuing value-based internationalism, they were in obvious tension with a nondemocratic China.[38] Although neither explicitly criticized China's nondemocratic values and systems while in office, both emphasized Japan's shared democratic values with the United States, India, and

Australia, and this explains a policy to improve strategic cooperation with major democracies as a check on China, which is increasingly viewed as a threat.

With Jiang Zemin's visit to the United States and Clinton's visit to China, the Chinese government grew more confident in dealing with Japan. Jiang's 1998 visit to Japan revealed his personal sentiments, but also his underestimation of Japan in contrast to the United States, which he saw as central to China's domestic reform and foreign relations. The ill will generated by this visit triggered popular reactions on both sides. With cybernationalism on the rise, Japan was a tempting target. In the years 2003–6, the absence of summits blamed on Koizumi Junichiro's Yasukuni Shrine visits further fueled these emotions.[39] A vicious cycle unfolded. The national identities of both sides clashed with each other. Both sought great power identities,[40] but they viewed each other as a main obstacle to that ambition. The compromise reached in October 2006 involved virtually no change of mind on either side. The Chinese and Japanese think less and less of each other because they think the other thinks less and less of them. In a speech on October 24, 2008, before Hu Jintao, Aso explained low mutually positive views despite strong economic interdependence by saying, "In both Japan and China, the percentage of people holding at least some degree of positive feelings towards the other country does not even reach 30." He then noted that "even if we hold different views, at a minimum, we should always have a correct understanding of what the other is thinking." He advocated youth exchanges as a way to show that what they have heard is not true. A Chinese youth may find out that Japan is not becoming militaristic and a Japanese youth may realize that "I had heard that in China there is strong anti-Japan sentiment, but in fact everyone I met was very kind."[41]

One important issue is where the Japanese or Chinese consider their country to be relative to each other. China has been gaining rapidly on Japan, which is affecting its identity. The Ministry of Economy, Trade, and Industry issued a report in the summer of 2009 that China would surpass Japan in gross domestic product by the end of year. Most elites with whom I talked in Tokyo at the time expressed sadness as Japanese.

As one put it, "Number 3 is not Number 2. Who cares about Number 3?" The fact that there was much discussion of the "Group of Two" between the United States and China for dealing with the 2008 global financial crisis adds to this anxiety about Japan's place in the world. The fact that the crisis started in the United States while China continues to grow is a serious worry for many Japanese commentators.[42] But more serious scholars and officials also see a sea change in world politics, in which China is rising, to which Japan has to adapt.[43] There is a broad concern over China's military modernization,[44] which is accompanied by reluctant acceptance of Japan's declining power position in the world.

To be sure, the Japanese are aware of the severe challenges that China is facing. A quick glance at the Yaesu Book Center near Tokyo Station will give one a strong impression of "negative" stories about income disparities, corruption, crimes, and so on, with new titles added frequently. However, such negative stories, which are often accurate portrayals of the situation in China, are nothing new. The dominant view among Japanese policy elites has recently tilted to the China rising theme rather than the China collapsing theme.[45] As a senior official of the Ministry of Economy, Trade, and Industry explained to me in July 2009, whereas he told people not to worry about China a number of years ago, now he wonders how much longer Beijing will maintain such a rapid pace of growth. He judges the Chinese government "wise enough" to continue China's economic success. Although he continues to view China as an opportunity for Japanese companies, he is not alone in being clearly concerned.

Partly because of a stronger yen, Japan barely maintained its position in 2009. But in mid-August 2010, news broke that China had surpassed Japan as the world's second-largest economy. The Japanese media did not play up the story. For example, *Yomiuri shimbun* reported on this on page 3 on August 17, 2010. The lead economic story on the front page was how to stimulate the economy. Even related to China, there was a much longer story on the front page about how China is expanding its English-language media presence in the United States. Given a lengthy heat wave in the hottest month since 1946, the strongest yen for the past fifteen years, a sharp decline in the stock market, and a high drama of political fights within the ruling Democratic Party of Japan, the Japanese public did not react to Japan's loss in status. Some commentators suggested that many Japanese had already been resigned to a declining Japan.[46]

Japanese resignation about their declining power does not mean that the Japanese are now ready to embrace China or that the government is no longer hedging against China's perceived expansion. According to a poll released by the *China Daily* of China and Genron NPO of Japan on August 14, 2010, 72.0 percent of Japanese said in interviews done in June and July that they had an unfavorable impression of China, citing poisoned food and China's pursuit of energy and natural resources. This was only slightly better than the 73.2 percent reported in 2009. By contrast, the Chinese view of Japan had improved more, with negative feelings declining from 65.2 percent in 2009 to 55.9 percent in 2010. The Japanese media believed that that was mainly due to the more positive media coverage of Japan in China. The Japanese fear of China is based on current events, whereas the Chinese think mainly about the past.[47] The Japanese government is becoming more concerned about China's military modernization and its intentions in the world. The Council on Security and Defense Capabilities in the New Era, a private advisory board, submitted its final report to Prime Minister Kan Naoto on August 27, 2010, prepared for a planned revision of the defense program outline for the country. The council study reportedly called for a more proactive defense and cited China's military buildup and naval activities.[48] The Democratic Party of Japan government's view was reflected in the Defense Ministry's annual defense white paper issued on September 10, 2010. This white paper used more space to express concern about China's rapidly increasing defense budgets and lack of transparency in its intention, detailing the Chinese navy's activities close to Japan.[49] The Democratic Party of Japan did not differ that much from the Liberal Democratic Party in this regard.[50]

There is virtually no Japanese acceptance of a scenario in which China would dominate in Asia, given Japanese identity. As one China school diplomat who favors good relations with China explained to me, Japanese are OK if the United States or France does better than

Japan, but not China. Yet there is a sense of resignation to the fact that Japan may not be able to compete with China over gross domestic product, given the country's demographic decline and unstable politics. There is a shifting focus on Japan's comparative advantage and options in a world of a relatively declining America and a rising China. Opinions vary, but a common theme is to subtly downplay hard material power resources and to favor Japan's soft power or unique contributions, such as "Cool Japan," which attracts the youth of the world. An illustration of this is Nakanishi Terumasa's view that Japan's real strength lies in its "solid" nature and that it is more important to be solid than strong. Japan also draws strength from its traditional values and the emperor system, its autonomy, its people, and its entrepreneurship.[51] This quest for pride in a unique identity is unlikely to produce any consensus, given the vagueness of any comparative advantage with China, whose national identity looms in the shadows of such claims.

The Taiwan issue was part of a broader Japanese tendency to view China as an empire with distinct ethnic groups. Such a tendency was used before the war to carve out the Japanese sphere of influence from China by defining certain regions as distinct from "China proper." A good example is an artificial Japanese definition of "Manchurians" as different from Han Chinese. In postwar periods, the Japanese continue to view China as a conglomeration of different nationalities, albeit not from an imperialist intent to divide and conquer. In recent years, there has been much interest in Tibetans and Uighurs and other minority issues. The current Japanese way of thinking is actually consistent with much of Western scholarship on China, but it nevertheless conflicts with Beijing's views. Japan's official position has been cautious, but underlying views of China guide some policy choices that have an impact on the bilateral relationship.

The United States continues to heavily factor in Chinese and Japanese thinking. On some level, a rising China means that the Chinese have gained more confidence and worry less whether the United States will lean toward Japan. As a matter of fact, from the Chinese perspective, the United States has always leaned toward Japan on issues that truly matter in the postwar decades. The Japanese have been more sensitive about the United States, treating China as more important while relegating Japan to a position of irrelevance. As a recent example, the Japanese media's initial reaction to Barack Obama's victory in the 2008 U.S. presidential election was that he would stress China's importance at Japan's expense.[52] This, of course, shows that the U.S. factor makes Japan view China as a competitor for America's attention, whether or not the Chinese are actually trying to be so.

Both Japan and China have been eager for some sort of Asianism to take root that would limit U.S. dominance in the region. Both have questioned U.S. values and looked for partners in Asia to gain leverage in asserting their own approach to values. After the Cold War, there was an upsurge in Japanese interest in Asianism.[53] Indeed, in the 1990s one may argue that China's economic success contributed to this rediscovered regional identity.[54] However, the window of opportunity for China and Japan to narrow their identity gap following this pathway, after fluctuating for more than a decade, has been closing. By the time China became serious about pursuing regionalism, Japan had grown more suspicious of China's intention to marginalize it. Starting in the early 2000s, it grew nervous about China's ambitions to gain dominance over Asia. In 2010, this turned into alarm. A decidedly more confident China was no longer reassuring Japan, as it had once done. With growing doubts about China's intentions vis-à-vis the East China Sea, the South China Sea, Taiwan, and the Korean Peninsula, the Japanese are in the midst of redefining China more negatively and reconstructing their own national identity in opposition to China's.

The Chinese and Japanese have studied each other extensively in recent years. The Japanese scholars have had the advantage of being in a more open society and freer academic environment. But studies of Japan in China have also improved. Some Japan-trained Chinese scholars are actively teaching and writing about Japan. A large number of Chinese citizens or China-born naturalized Japanese citizens teach and do research in Japan, and they have published a large number of books on various aspects of China and Japan, past and present, in Japan and China.[55] In recent years, Japanese students have also been studying for degrees in Chinese universities, and it is just a matter of time before some will publish books in Chinese.[56]

There is a positive trend of joint research projects that attempt to go beyond national borders.[57] The process of these projects and outputs can only deepen mutual understanding, if not friendship, in all cases. Even if scholars do not physically participate in collaborations, they are increasingly aware of academic writings from the other country, as shown in the reference lists in their works. Put simply, the Chinese and Japanese now have to imagine their national identities partly defined in relation to each other under the gaze of the other. But despite a better mutual understanding among some scholars, the identity gap between the two countries has not narrowed, as shown in opinion polls and in comments by observers on both sides.

For decades, it was assumed that the Sino-Japanese identity gap was largely about history—since the end of the Cold War, issues linked to history have been conspicuous in arousing national identity consciousness toward the other country—and that it would gradually diminish as the two countries interacted more closely and became more interdependent. The two countries have become highly interdependent economically, and person-to-person interaction has also expanded dramatically with an ever-increasing number of Chinese tourists going to Japan due to rising Chinese incomes and a corresponding relaxation of visa requirements by the Japanese government and a greater number of Japanese nationals studying and working in China.[58] Then why has the national identity gap not narrowed?

One immediate reason is that much of this interaction is driven by pragmatic economic motives. The Japanese welcome Chinese tourists as a source of income, which has been the case for China's view of Japanese tourists for a much longer period, and the increasing number of Japanese learn Chinese and go to China in order to advance their careers, similar to their Chinese counterparts in an earlier period. In fact, a persistently negative Japanese view of China results from a new source: ordinary Japanese being more exposed to Chinese nationals in Japan, who are often portrayed as not that well mannered.

A more fundamental reason for the persistent gap is divergence in recent aspects of worldview. For instance, despite Prime Minister Hatoyama Yukio's enthusiasm for cooperating with China in forging an East Asian community, there was no progress in narrowing differences in visions of what such a community signifies. The two states disagree on how to manage climate change, how to advance toward denuclearization, and how to combine market forces with state guidance of the economy—to mention three recent themes highlighted at global summits. Japan has drifted closer to the United States in advocacy of universal values at the very time China has become more assertive in challenging some of these values and pressing for a different regional and global order. Although clashing national interests are evident, the growing hiatus in foreign policy choices is couched in national identity thinking.

As a case in point, it is recognized by some of the most experienced observers of Sino–Japanese relations that the single most important bilateral issue now is the territorial dispute in the East China Sea, which starts with and feeds back into the identity gap. This was confirmed when a Chinese boat and two Japanese Coast Guard ships had a collision incident near the Diaoyu/Senkaku Islands on September 7, 2010, an accident waiting to happen. The Japanese government decided to try the Chinese captain in the Japanese court according to Japanese law while calling on the Chinese side to be calm. Predictably, however, the Chinese government took a strong stance, calling for the immediate release of the captain and then suspending the scheduled talks on the East China Sea and canceling a senior Chinese legislator's planned visit to Japan. The Chinese government was responding to public pressure for tough actions against Japan and was also clearly angered by Tokyo's initial downplaying of the seriousness of the incident, which fits their perception of an arrogant country wantonly disregarding the sentiment of its neighbors.[59] On the Japanese side, a question was raised in the media of why China was acting so tough, with one reason cited as China's stronger big power mentality.[60] The national identity gap thus contributed to the escalation of the incident.

The fishing boat collision incident also further enlarged the identity gap between China and Japan. Similar to the Americans and some of China's Asian neighbors, the Japanese view China as too aggressive since about early 2009. With China's protection of North Korea despite the sinking of the South Korean warship *Cheonan* in March 2010 and the North Korean shelling of Yeonpyeong Island in October 2010, along with Chinese tension with Vietnam and the Philippines in the South China Sea, the Japanese policy elites now feel strongly that China is an outlier in Asia and that Japan needs to cooperate more actively with the United States and other countries to force China to play by the international rules. Beijing's support for Kim Jong-un after his father Kim Jong-Il died in December 2011 further damaged its reputation in the eyes of the Japanese, even though Tokyo wants to utilize Beijing's perceived leverage over Pyongyang to advance its own policy objectives.[61] Conversely, for many Chinese, Japan's tougher stance proves their suspicion that Japan always wants to keep China divided and weak.

CONCLUSION

Looking back, the relationship between China and Japan seems to have a clear trajectory with good reasons why it makes a turn here or there. However, this relationship has never been predetermined, similar to all other bilateral relationships. Different historical outcomes could have been imagined and were imagined at different times. Specific to the focus of this book, national identities have been important but have had a complex causal impact on the bilateral relationship and have in turn been informed by it. There are layers of national identities, and how important they are is partially contingent upon the distribution of national interests at a given time and the internal dynamic of national identities enhanced by generational changes.

The national identity gap between China and Japan is now deeply ingrained, centered initially on an inability to achieve reconciliation over Japan's aggressive conduct up to 1945. Various attempts to narrow this divide over history have not succeeded.[62] The friendship mode of relations offered only a superficial approach to reducing tensions over history. Efforts to draw attention to other periods of history and patterns of mutual benefit failed to elicit public support, remaining peripheral to national identity. When circumstances were most favorable for reducing differences over history, the visit by Nakasone to the Yasukuni Shrine and the purge of Hu Yaobang with criticisms of his overfriendliness to Japan were symptomatic of the lack of receptivity in both countries. After nearly forty years of normalized relations, there is no sign that the tremendous benefits both sides have gained are being appreciated at the level of national identity. Instead, the divide over Japanese aggression is being compounded by a widening divergence in outlooks vital to national identity.

Looking into the future, there are strong uncertainties about how the Sino-Japanese relationship and the national identity gap will evolve. In the end, the Sino-Japanese relationship will largely be what the two countries will make of it. The national identities that may be positive or negative for the bilateral relationship are both present. Despite real underlying challenges to the relationship, what identities the Chinese and Japanese will seize upon will have a large impact on their future relations, which will in turn help shape their identities.

As for the identity gap, experience shows that the official relationship does affect the underlying perception and identity, but not in an immediate or one-to-one fashion. On the Chinese side, the positive tone set by the government may mean that there is room for a more complex discourse about Japan or past interactions with the Japanese, which may contribute to a narrower identity gap between the two nations. But the uncertainty lies in whether the periodic official warmth will last pending domestic and international developments.

Will greater economic and cultural interaction improve the two countries' mutual images? Such interaction has so far failed to close the identity gap, and some of the harshest critics of China studied in China. At the same time, it is likely that the interaction in recent years will come to play a bigger, positive role in the next round. After all, the promoters of Sino-Japanese interaction are mostly driven by a desire for the Chinese and Japanese to know each other more realistically with their own eyes, rather than viewing each other based on mere imagination or fed information. Logically, close interaction should help narrow the identity gap in the long run because much of the gap has been based on wild imagination, such as "Japan wants to revive militarism," even though one should not anticipate quick results.

NOTES

1   Ming Wan, *Sino-Japanese Relations: Interaction, Logic, and Transformation* (Stanford, Calif.: Stanford University Press, 2006), 158–65.

2   On the complexity of identities in China, see *China's Quest for National Identity*, edited by Lowell Dittmer and Samuel S. Kim (Ithaca, N.Y.: Cornell University Press, 1993).

3   Harumi Befu, ed., *Cultural Nationalism in East Asia: Representation and Identity* (Berkeley: Institute of East Asian Studies, University of California, 1993).

4   Samuel P. Huntington, *Who Are We? The Challenges to America's National Identity* (New York: Simon & Schuster, 2004), 23.

5   Atsuko Sakaki, *Obsessions with the Sino-Japanese Polarity in Japanese Literature* (Honolulu: University of Hawaii Press, 2006).

6   Shogo Suzuki, *Civilization and Empire: China and Japan's Encounter with European International Society* (London: Routledge, 2009), 46–55.

7   Joshua A. Fogel, *Articulating the Sinosphere: Sino-Japanese Relations in Space and Time* (Cambridge, Mass.: Harvard University Press, 2009), 7–13.

8   Yu Tatsun (Xiong Dayun), *Kindai Chugoku kanmin no Nippon shisatsu* (Tokyo: Seibundo, 1998).

9   Sakaki, *Obsessions with the Sino-Japanese Polarity in Japanese Literature*, 21.

10 Peter C. Perdue, *China Marches West: The Qing Conquest of Central Eurasia* (Cambridge, Mass.: Harvard University Press, 2005).

11 S. C. M. Paine, *The Sino-Japanese War of 1894–1895: Perceptions, Power, and Primacy* (New York: Cambridge University Press, 2003), 136–38.

12 John W. Dower, *War without Mercy: Race and Power in the Pacific War* (New York: Pantheon Books, 1986).

13 Fogel, *Articulating the Sinosphere*, 19.

14 Testuo Najita, *Japan: The Intellectual Foundations of Modern Japanese Politics* (Chicago: University of Chicago Press, 1974), 86–101.

15 Suzuki, *Civilization and Empire*.

16 Stefan Tanaka, *Japan's Orient: Rendering Pasts into History* (Berkeley: University of California Press, 1993).

17 Urs Matthias Zachmann, "Blowing Up a Double Portrait in Black and White:

The Concept of Asia in the Writings of Fukuzawa Yukichi and Okakura Tenshin," *East Asia Cultures Critique* 15, no. 2 (Fall 2007): 345–68.

18 Eri Hotta, *Pan-Asianism and Japan's War, 1931–1945* (New York: Palgrave Macmillan, 2007).

19 Mutsu Munemitsu, *Kenkenroku* (A diplomatic record of the Sino-Japanese War, 1894–1895), edited and translated by Gordon Mark Berger (Princeton, N.J.: Princeton University Press, 1982).

20 Paine, *Sino-Japanese War.*

21 Heng Teow, *Japan's Cultural Policy toward China, 1918–1931* (Cambridge, Mass.: Harvard University Asia Center and Harvard University Press, 1999).

22 Mark R. Peattie, *Ishiwara Kanji and Japan's Confrontation with the West* (Princeton, N.J.: Princeton University Press, 1975).

23 Fogel, *Articulating the Sinosphere*, 3–4.

24 Peattie, *Ishiwara Kanji*, 286–89.

25 Mizutani Naoko, *Hannichi izen Chugoku tainichi kosakusha tachi no kaiso* (Tokyo: Bungei shunju, 2006).

26 We are beginning to see in-depth studies of Chinese collaborators based on archives in China. See Pan Min, *1937–1945 Jiangsu riwei jiceng zhengquan yanjiu* (Shanghai: Shanghai renmin chubanshe, 2006); and Wang Shihua, *Riwei tongzhi shiqi de Huabei nongcun* (Beijing: Shehui kexue wenxian chubanshe, 2008).

27 Michael Schaller, *Altered States: The United States and Japan since the Occupation* (New York: Oxford University Press, 1997), 77–95.

28 Sadako Ogata, *Normalization with China: A Comparative Study of U.S. and Japanese Processes* (Berkeley: Institute of East Asian Studies, University of California, 1988).

29 Chin Chōhin (Chen Zhaobin), *Sengo Nihon no Chugoku seisaku: 1950-nendai Higashi Ajia kokusai seiji no bunmyaku* (Tokyo: Tokyo Daigaku shuppankai, 2000), 9–18.

30 Kokubun Ryosei, "Reisen shuketsugo no Nitchu kankei 72 taisei no tankan," *Kokusai mondai*, January 2001, 42–56.

31 Chae-Jin Lee, *China and Japan: New Economic Diplomacy* (Stanford, Calif.: Hoover Institution Press, 1984).

32 Koichi Nakano, "Nationalism and Localism in Japan's Political Debate of the 1990s," *Pacific Review* 11, no. 4 (1998): 505–24.

33 Tsuyoshi Hasegawa and Kazuhiko Togo, eds., *East Asia's Haunted Present: Historical Memories and the Resurgence of Nationalism* (Westport, Conn.: Praeger, 2008).

34 Michael D. Swaine, *China: Domestic Change and Foreign Policy* (Santa Monica, Calif.: RAND Corporation, 1995), 83–84; William C. Kirby, "Traditions of Centrality, Authority, and Management in Modern China's Foreign Relations," in *Chinese Foreign Policy: Theory and Practice*, edited by Thomas W. Robinson and David Shambaugh (Oxford: Clarendon Press, 1994), 13–29.

35 Christopher R. Hughes, "Japan in the Politics of Chinese Leadership Legitimacy: Recent Developments in Historical Perspective," *Japan Forum* 20, no. 2 (July 2008): 245–66.

36   Shogo Suzuki, "The Importance of 'Othering' in China's National Identity: Sino-Japanese Relations as a Stage of Identity Conflicts," *Pacific Review* 20, no. 1 (March 2007): 23–47.

37   *Yomiuri shimbun* War Responsibilities Examining Committee, *Kensho senso sekinin*, vol. 1 (Tokyo: Chuokoronsha, 2009), 222–24.

38   Abe Shinzo, *Utsukushii kuni e* (Tokyo: Bungei shunju, 2006); Aso Taro, *Jiyu to hanei no ko* (Tokyo: Gentosha, 2007); Aso Taro, *Totetsumonai Nihon* (Tokyo: Shinchosha, 2007).

39   Xu Wu, *Chinese Cyber Nationalism: Evolution, Characteristics, and Implication* (Lanham, Md.: Lexington Books, 2007).

40   Gilbert Rozman, "China's Quest for Great Power Identity," *Orbis* 43, no. 3 (Summer 1999): 383–402; Gilbert Rozman, "Japan's Quest for Great Power Identity," *Orbis* 46, no. 1 (Winter 2002): 73–91.

41   Aso Taro, "My Personal Conviction Regarding Japan-China Relations," talk given at the Reception to Commemorate the Thirtieth Anniversary of the Conclusion of the Treaty of Peace and Friendship between Japan and China, October 24, 2008, Great Hall of the People, Beijing; Press Release, Embassy of Japan, Washington, October 24, 2008.

42   See Moriki Akira, *Nichibei doji hasan Chugoku haken ni yoru otsuroshii jidaiga yatteguru* (Tokyo: Daiyamondo, 2009).

43   See, e.g., Sakakibara Eisuke, *Keizai no sekai seiriyokuzu* (Tokyo: Bungei shunju, 2007).

44   Kayahara Ikeo, ed., *Chugoku no gunjiryoku nisenniji yunen no shorai yotsuku* (Tokyo: Tsutsusha, 2008).

45   There are, of course, views by some leading thinkers that China's rise is not as impressive as it appears. E.g., Watanabe Toshio and Miwara Shumon view China's growth as merely based on processing. Watanabe Toshio and Miwara Shumon, *Nippon no katsuro* (Tokyo: Karyusha, 2009).

46   According to an earlier poll, the Japanese public was divided over whether it would be a problem to lose the number two position to China. And more than half those polled did not want Japan to be a great power. *Japan Times*, August 17, 2010.

47   *Japan Times*, August 16, 2010.

48   *Japan Times*, September 6, 2010.

49   *Asahi shimbun Evening*, September 10, 2010.

50   *Asahi shimbun*, September 11, 2010.

51   Nakanishi Terumasa, *Nippon no jiryoku* (Tokyo: Kairyusha, 2009). He also doubts the reliability of the United States, which necessarily pursues its own national interests.

52   Ayako Doi, "In Japan, the Picture Isn't Quite So Bright," *Washington Post*, November 16, 2008. My reading of selected Japanese newspapers confirmed her observation.

53 Gilbert Rozman, "Internationalism and Asianism in Japanese Strategic Thought from Meiji to Heisei," *Japanese Journal of Political Science* 9, no. 2 (August 2008): 209–32.

54 Yuichi Nakano, "Nationalism and Localism," 506.

55 For examples of these publications in Chinese in China, see Zhu Jianrong, ed., *Riben biantian minzhudang zhengquan dansheng jinjuli guancha* (Beijing: Xinshijie chubanshe, 2009); Li Xiushi, *Riben xinbaoshouzhuyi zhanlue yanjiu* (Beijing: Shishi chubanshe, 2010); and Wu Guanghui, *Riben de zhongguo xingxiang* (Beijing: Renmin chubanshe, 2010).

56 Even for those without Chinese degrees, we begin to see publications or blogging in Chinese. E.g., Fujiwara Daisuke, who was a correspondent for Japan's TBS, wrote in Chinese for a limited Chinese audience about some very sensitive topics voicing a Japanese perspective. Fujiwara Daisuke, *Chugoku shinshiko genekitokuhain ga mitaminjitsu no Chugoku senhappyaknichi* (Tokyo: Nippon kyohosha, 2008).

57 See, e.g., Ryu Ketsu (Liu Jie) and Kawashima Shin, eds., *Senkyuhyakuyonjugonen no rekishi ninshiki shusen o meguru Nitchu taiwa no kokoromi* (Tokyo: Tokyo daigaku shuppankai, 2009); Kishi Toshihiko, ed., *Mosakusuru kindai nicchu kankai taiwa to kyozun no jidai* (Tokyo: Tokyo daigaku shuppankai, 2009); Mitani Hiromi and Kimu Teichan, eds., *Higashi Ajia rekishi taiwa kokkyo to sedai o koete* (Tokyo: Tokyo daigaku shuppankai, 2007); and Ryu Ketsu, Mitani Hiromi, and Daqing Yang, eds., *Kokkyo to sedai o koeru rekishi ninshiki Nitchu taiwa no kokoromi* (Tokyo: Tokyo daigaku shuppankai, 2006).

58 Although Japan was viewed as a land of opportunity for young Chinese for a long time, China, particularly Shanghai, has become attractive in recent years for some young Japanese, particularly women, who find work more challenging and promotion more likely working in Japanese or foreign firms or starting their own business. For recent Japanese media coverage, see *Asahi shimbun*, September 6, 2010.

59 Chinese state councillor Dai Bingguo called in the Japanese ambassador at midnight, urging the Japanese government not to "misjudge the situation" and to make "a wise political decision." China News Agency, September 12, 2010, http://www.chinanews.com.cn/gn/2010/09-12/2527185.shtml.

60 *Asahi shimbun*, September 14, 2010.

61 This paragraph is based on my observations and conversations in Japan since August 2010.

62 He Yinan, *The Search for Reconciliation: Sino-Japanese and German-Polish Relations since World War II* (New York: Cambridge University Press, 2009).

CHAPTER 4

NATIONAL IDENTITIES AND SINO–SOUTH KOREAN RELATIONS

Scott Snyder and See-Won Byun

This chapter considers the influence of national identity on the management of the China–South Korea relationship based on the concept of national identity gaps. The China–South Korea relationship is the "newest" bilateral relationship in Northeast Asia and the only purely post–Cold War state-to-state relationship under study in this volume. Despite its relative newness, the historical Sino-Korean relationship stretches back centuries. However, differences in interpreting this history within the broader context of the national identity gap are a major issue influencing Sino–South Korean relations today.

A primary factor that pushes national identity issues to the forefront of the China–South Korea relationship is the presence of North Korea as a direct challenger to South Korea in an ongoing competition to shape the national identity of a reunified Korea. The North Korea factor influences the Sino–South Korean relationship in two respects. First, the existence of two Koreas underscores the fact that fundamental identity issues on the peninsula remain unresolved because both Koreas have historically aspired to achieve unification under their own rule. The identity debate divides the two Koreas and is also an underlying dividing line in South Korean domestic politics, with conservatives in favor of a strong alliance with the United States and progressives in support of reconciliation with North Korea. The Sino–South Korean relationship exists in parallel to the relationship between China and North Korea, and South Korea's management of it cannot help but be influenced by a sense of competition with the Sino–North Korean relationship.

Second, China's own policy toward the Korean Peninsula involves responding to two diametrically opposed "others," North Korea and South Korea. China's national identity formation, including the ideological dimension, is closely tied to that of North Korea, but China's economic reforms and international political interests have increasingly provided a basis for an expanded relationship with South Korea. Perceptions regarding the peninsula arguably have skewed Chinese foreign policy in such a way that China's handling of North Korea remains a special case, raising contradictions with the main strategic trends shaping its overall foreign policy and complicating Sino–South Korean relations.

The gap between China and South Korea has grown in the aftermath of the March 2010 sinking of the South Korean warship *Cheonan* and the November 2010 artillery attack on Yeonpyeong Island, which appeared to mark a shift in South Korean attitudes toward not only the North but also China. South Korean perceptions that China "protected" North Korea in response to these incidents have affected relations, arousing a domestic debate on the relative value of South Korea's security alliance with the United States versus its economic partnership with China, driving concerns about China's apparent prioritization of its "traditional friendship" with the North over its "strategic cooperative partnership" with the South, and revealing conflicting visions of Korean reunification.

Apart from North Korea, another factor that exacerbates tensions over national identity is the asymmetric nature of the Sino–South Korean relationship,[1] which is reinforced by the traditional concept of a hierarchical order in Asian relations that defined the nature of Korean interaction with China as the "Middle Kingdom."[2] South Korea's economic and cultural strength and emerging global leadership are countervailing forces to China's size, and until now have provided South

Korea with a sense of security and opportunity in the relationship. But as China becomes sufficiently competitive to challenge and surpass South Korea in many sectors, the asymmetry in relations is growing, creating a sense of vulnerability in South Korea that intensifies identity-related tensions with China.

The existence of the asymmetry in which China was at the center and Korea was subordinate provides a complex historical backdrop for the development of a "new" relationship between the People's Republic of China (PRC) and the Republic of Korea (ROK; South Korea) as equal nation-states. The efforts of both states to develop compelling national identity narratives as part of their respective efforts to mobilize public support have led to conflicting rhetoric, especially as it relates to the history of the ancient Koguryo Kingdom, which both states claim as their own. This conflict over history clearly reveals the gap in national identities between the two. The asymmetrical nature of the historical Sino-Korean relationship, as played out in respective interpretations of a historical era that could be interpreted to have marked a turning point in the historical power relationship between the two, also has resonance for the future as China develops instruments of national power and reasserts itself in ways that may revive some asymmetrical characteristics of the relationship.

Following a review of the historical antecedents of the modern Sino–South Korean relationship in the context of both dynastic and Cold War relations, this chapter considers contestations over national identity as manifested in three areas: first, the debate over the historical status of the Koguryo Kingdom, which stems from China's Northeast history project; second, the direction of North Korea's future, particularly in light of North Korea's own apparent weakness, which has deepened with North Korean provocations and the uncertainties of domestic political transition since 2009; and third, the transformation of the Sino–South Korean economic and cultural relationship in the international context. Tensions between China and South Korea in these areas are analyzed with reference to the six dimensions of identity discussed in this book as a way to deepen understanding of the role of the national identity gap and its effect on relations.

HISTORICAL CHARACTERISTICS OF SINO-KOREAN RELATIONS

The dominant characteristic of the Sino-Korean relationship, particularly from the fourteenth through the nineteenth centuries, was its tributary nature. Korea recognized China's cultural centrality, political influence, and suzerainty over Korea in return for ritual benefits, peaceful relations with a dominant neighbor, and semiautonomy to manage local affairs as it saw fit.[3] The Sino-Korean tributary relationship was part of a broader strategy whereby a Sinocentric hierarchical order provided security. Korea's cultural identity remained distinct, but its political leadership was dependent on adherence to China's centrality and respect for Chinese cultural and bureaucratic accomplishments. The Korean system of governance and social order modeled itself after China, implicitly affirming a hierarchical order in which Korea's elite not only accepted a subordinate role to that of China but also emulated China in many facets of intellectual and social life. The Yi (Chosun) Dynasty (1392–1910) adhered to orthodox principles within Confucianism more strictly than was the case in China. Korean intellectuals studied classical Chinese, bureaucratic governance involved an examination system modeled on China's system, and adherence to neo-Confucian thought elevated patrilineal family ties as the central feature of the social order. The Korean term to describe the Sino-Korean relationship, *sadae*, or "serving a superior," reflects the hierarchical nature of the relationship.[4]

Korean kings in the Yi Dynasty ritualistically received their governance rights from the Chinese authorities in exchange for an understanding that China would come to the defense of Korea from hostile attacks by "barbarians" outside the Chinese cultural sphere. Such a strategy of dependence on China as guarantor of Korean autonomy and stability minimized the costs of self-defense against hostility from both China and other neighbors. This system remained in place through the end of the nineteenth century, at which time cracks in the traditional order began to seep through with the influx of Western influence and the transition to the modern nation-state system. The transition worked to China's disadvantage versus Japan as Asia's early modernizer, with Korea as the primary victim.

China's loss of influence on the Korean Peninsula and Japan's rise as an imperialist colonizer had tragic effects for a Korean leadership that was unable to defend itself against Japanese imperial ambitions and came late to an understanding of the implications of replacing a Sinocentric world order with the Western nation-state system for conducting international affairs.[5] Korea's transition from China's sphere of influence to Japanese tutelage was made complete by Japan's extension of its own suzerainty over Korea and eventual formal annexation of the peninsula in 1910. During the decades following the Sino-Japanese war, and particularly after the annexation, China's influence on Korea was minimal, mostly in the context of Japanese efforts to extend its empire or Korean guerilla efforts to make common cause with the Chinese to fight Japanese imperialism—the origin of ties between the Chinese Communist movement and the Korean guerilla movement of which Kim Il-sung was a part.[6] Divided by ideology, South Korean political leaders had virtually no ties with the leadership of the PRC that emerged in 1949.

Mao Zedong's decision to enter the Korean War of 1950–53 under the name of the Chinese People's Volunteers remains in the memories of the South Korean conservative leadership, which until now has led South Korea's development for all but one decade (1998–2008). Following the negotiation of the armistice, in which Chinese advisers played a prominent part in talks with the United States–led United Nations command, there was virtually no contact between the governments of South Korea and the PRC.[7] Nixon's visit to China in 1972 came as a shock to the leaders of both Koreas, so much so that they initiated their own channels of contact in response to the shift in Asia's geostrategic landscape.[8] Opportunities to establish relations with PRC counterparts were slow in coming and were confined primarily to quiet South Korean trade through other Asian countries, sports diplomacy, and specific political incidents, such as the 1983 hijacking of a Chinese plane that landed in South Korea.[9] Throughout the 1980s, ideology was clearly incorporated into the Korean language through common usage of "Communist China" or "Red China" to refer to the PRC. It was not until economic and political opportunities requiring the opening of new ties began to develop that ideologically driven obstacles began to recede.

This brief historical review shows that the South Korean relationship with China is divided into two dramatically different forms of interaction. The traditional dynastic form was one in which Korea had a close relationship premised on subordination to China as the civilizational, political, and economic center of its universe. Korea was seen as a loyal subordinate in the overall tributary hierarchy and as a model for how the Middle Kingdom preferred to order relations with its neighbors. The beginning of the modern era in Asia's international relations marked a dramatic shift in this relationship to one in which South Korea moved into the U.S. orbit and was drawn to a maritime-based order versus the previous continentally focused order. Under Japanese colonial rule, Korea had no basis upon which to pursue relations with China, and during the Korean War, China became an enemy to South Korea. Conversely, China and North Korea have close fraternal bonds based on their shared revolutionary experience. China's ideological opposition to South Korea created a distance, whereas South Korea's close alliance with the United States engendered a certain wariness on the part of Chinese leaders inhibited by their own loyalties to North Korean cadres. The historical backdrop of the Sino–South Korean identity gap provides a mixed picture from which strands can be drawn to justify commonality or opposition, with the dividing line between the two shaped primarily by ideology.

THE KOGURYO DISPUTE AND THE NATIONAL IDENTITY GAP

Competing interpretations of history and related territorial claims have long characterized relations in Northeast Asia, where unresolved issues among China, South Korea, and Japan are recognized as fundamental constraints to political cooperation that reflect efforts to protect national identity as rooted in distinct historical experiences. Between China and South Korea, these tensions have been most apparent in their "history war" over Koguryo. To understand how identity politics have driven this dispute, we examine its respective Chinese and South Korean interpretations; strategies of national consolidation, including China's ethnic minority policy and the South's reconciliation with the North; and the role of this controversy in current bilateral interactions.

On July 1, 2004, the United Nations Educational, Scientific, and Cultural Organization (UNESCO) designated the remains of Koguryo in China and North Korea as part of the UNESCO World Heritage List, identifying it as "the dynasty that ruled over parts of northern China and the northern half of the Korean Peninsula from 277 BC to AD 668."[10] These remains included three sites in Northeast China that China was seeking to include on the World Heritage List in the preparation for the Twenty-Eighth Session of the UNESCO World Heritage Committee in Suzhou from June 28 to July 7, 2004.[11] China had blocked North Korea's efforts to list its sites since 2002, and China's active competition with North Korea to register their respective properties resulted in the listing of both Chinese and North Korean sites. After UNESCO's listing of the Koguryo sites, Chinese Cultural Minister Sun Jiazheng urged "domestic archeologists and scholars to undertake all possible cooperation with their peers in the DPRK [Democratic People's Republic of Korea, i.e., North Korea]."[12]

Beijing's drive to promote its Koguryo relics was part of its Northeast Project, a five-year campaign launched in 2002 to advance research on China's Northeast region with the objective of integrating the history of the region more closely into the PRC's national historical narrative. This project stirred heated debate in South Korea over perceived Chinese efforts to distort history,[13] starting in 2003, when the Chinese media began to recognize Koguryo as an ethnic Chinese administrative unit rather than an independent Korean dynasty, and in April 2004, when the Chinese Foreign Ministry deleted references to Koguryo from its official Web site. In response to Chinese state media claims in July 2004 about the significance of Koguryo to Chinese history, Park Heung-shin, director of culture and foreign affairs at the Foreign Ministry of the ROK, affirmed that "our basic stance is that Koguryo is part of Korean history."[14] The Koguryo debate flared up as a political concern when the Chinese Foreign Ministry in August 2004 dismissed

Seoul's demands to restore the Koguryo section of its Web site and instead removed all references to Korean history before the founding of the ROK in 1948.[15] In response, the South Korean Foreign Ministry spokesman reiterated Seoul's position that "Koguryo history is an indivisible part of our people's history," urging China to "stop distortions of Koguryo history, …as Koguryo history is the root of our people and a grave matter connected to our identity."[16] Although the two governments reached a five-point verbal agreement on making joint efforts to prevent the history dispute from developing into a political issue, the agreement was seen by Koreans as a "temporary compromise."[17]

Reporting on the UNESCO decision, the PRC's *People's Daily* on July 2, 2004, announced that "the capital city and tombs of the ancient Koguryo Kingdom of China" had been added to the World Heritage List.[18] Xinhua asserted that "Koguryo was a local government of China;…its politics and culture were heavily affected by those of the central government" and that the kingdom's remains "are a key part of Chinese history."[19] The *China Daily* added that "the Koguryo Kingdom once expanded to the Korean Peninsula."[20] The Koguryo controversy has drawn far less concern among the Chinese public than in South Korea, and scholarly views are divided.[21] A conference hosted by the Chinese Academy of Social Sciences' Center of China's Borderland History and Geography Research and Yanbian University in August 2004 produced "The Question of Koguryo: A Collection of Historical Papers," which reflects three schools of thought: (1) Koguryo belongs exclusively to Chinese history; (2) Koguryo constitutes a shared past between China and Korea; and (3) a more neutral stance dealing with historical perception and comparative historical studies. Han Chinese historians constitute the first group, whereas the second group comprises ethnic Korean scholars, suggesting that perceptions of identity strongly dictate assessments of Koguryo's historical significance.

China's handling of Koguryo's history is partly driven by an effort to reconcile understandings of ethnic and national identity among Northeast China's Korean minority population, who are recognized as both ethnic Koreans and Chinese nationals and have faced "identity confusion" over the course of China's reform and opening.[22] According to Yanbian University professor Xu Mingzhe, as ethnic Koreans in China seek to assimilate into Chinese society, "national identity is becoming a source of conflict over whether we can enter Chinese culture and whether the Chinese can accept us."[23] Identification with Korea among China's ethnic Koreans raises broad concerns about rising ethnonationalism and potential internal repercussions in China's other fifty-four minority communities, as was seen in 2001 when Beijing was reluctant to approve visas for South Korean legislators seeking to visit for research on revisions to the Overseas Ethnic Koreans Law.[24] Many ethnic Koreans in the Yanbian Korean Autonomous Prefecture in Jilin Province have moved to seek economic opportunities in South Korea, where thousands staged a hunger strike in November 2003 demanding that Seoul grant them South Korean nationality.

Chinese media reports have emphasized the significance of Koguryo to both ethnic and Chinese national identity, noting that "as one of the several influential regimes established by ethnic groups in northeastern China at the time, the Koguryo regime played a very important role in the development history of the northeastern Asian region."[25] The Northeast Project and the UNESCO World Heritage listing of the Koguryo ruins served to intensify provincial efforts to reinforce understandings of local Chinese history and culture. Jilin University professor Wei Cuncheng indicated that "Koguryo was a regime established by ethnic groups in northern China some 2,000 years ago, representing an important part of Chinese culture," and the deputy director of the Jilin Province Culture Department pledged that "we shall strive to better take care of the heritage so that more people can have a chance to enjoy the ancient Koguryo culture."[26] In its description of Koguryo relics in Jilin, the *People's Daily* highlighted their "unique ethnic features" as "a good example in China's architectural history" and "the impact of Chinese culture on the Koguryo, who did not develop their own writing."[27]

In South Korea, the escalation of the Koguryo dispute in the summer of 2004 was considered the lowest point in diplomatic relations with China since normalization in 1992, and it precipitated a decline in South Korean public opinion toward China.[28] As Peter Hays Gries indicates, Koguryo induces strong responses toward China, the primary "other" against which Koreans define themselves, and a symbol of heroic resistance against foreign invaders.[29] South Korean interpretations of China's Northeast Project fall into two main schools of thought: First, the defensive view is that the project is primarily reactive and domestic, driven by Chinese concerns that a unified Korea might make territorial claims to parts of southern Manchuria, efforts to maintain stability in Northeast China's ethnic Korean communities, and fears about the impact of potential North Korean collapse. Second, the offensive view is that the Northeast Project demonstrates China's goal of reasserting its influence over countries within its traditional sphere of influence to restore a Sinocentric structure of relations in East Asia.[30]

South Korean officials and scholars heavily criticized China's Northeast Project following the UNESCO World Heritage listing as challenges to Korean national identity. Foreign Minister Ban Ki-moon warned that "the issue of distorting Koguryo's history is a matter that shakes our national identity and people down to their roots."[31] Seo Young-soo of the Institute of Koguryo Studies asserted that "Koguryo is more than just an ancient kingdom for both Korea and China. It is a very significant part of history, being associated with their national identity."[32] And Yoon Deok-min of the Institute of Foreign Affairs and National Security argued that "this is a matter about our national identity. We should never make a compromise on this."[33] Chinese actions were attacked by both ruling and opposition party members at the Korean National Assembly in August 2004: A Grand National Party lawmaker, Lee Jae-oh, claimed that "China is trying to sway the identity and pride of our country from its roots by claiming sovereignty over Koguryo," and a Uri Party lawmaker, Lee Kyung-sook, criticized Beijing for attempting to "steal the Korean people's national spirit," noting that China's distortion of history is "led by its government."[34]

The Koguryo controversy reveals sensitivities in South Korea over the question of Chinese cultural superiority linked to historical experience. Many believe that Koguryo as a Korean dynasty has a negative legacy in China, whose Sui and Tang dynasties made several failed attempts to conquer the kingdom, driving current efforts to incorporate Koguryo into Chinese history. Referring to Koguryo as "a symbol of the unified power of the two Koreas," Seo Young-soo claimed that "China had tradition-ally downplayed the historical value of Koguryo out of an apparent fear of Korea's firmer historic and cultural identity."[35] The Koguryo dispute reflects sensitivities about not only historical relations with China but also China's strategic interests in Korea's future, indicating that it seeks to sys-tematically distort Korean history to maintain political influence on the peninsula in the event of territorial disputes following North Korean col-lapse or unification.[36] As the South Korean scholar Kim Woo-jun argued in 2004, "This is not a purely historical issue…. If Koguryo is incorrectly interpreted by China as China's old kingdom, the North Korean region becomes China's historical territory. And this can serve as justification for future Chinese intervention."[37]

China's competition with North Korea over the Koguryo sites led South Korean officials to present the issue as a cause for inter-Korean cooperation against Chinese claims.[38] North Korea began raising its voice on Koguryo by claiming in a September 2004 Korean Central News Agency article that "Koguryo was the most powerful state in the Korean history" and that the World Heritage status of Koguryo relics "is giv-ing great prides [sic] to the entire Korean people in the north, south and overseas."[39] South Korean Vice Unification Minister Rhee Bong-jo pledged to "explore diverse countermeasures" to jointly address the issue during proposed inter-Korean talks, and lawmakers called for establishing inter-Korean parliamentary exchanges to deal with "China's attempt to claim sovereignty over Koguryo."[40] Park Jin of the Grand National Party argued that "beyond the ideological differences, the two sides can use the Koguryo issue to solidify our national identity."[41]

South Korea's civil society groups and its media have perpetu-ated tensions by pressuring the South Korean government not to compromise and by keeping "Koguryo-consciousness" alive through broadcasting Koguryo-based historical dramas during 2006 and 2007.[42] These dramas had the explicit objective of raising national awareness of Koguryo identity as a "Korean" kingdom. Lee Hwan-gyeong, the writer of "Yongae Somun" asserted that "I felt frustrated by the Korean government's inactive response toward the Chinese distorted historical viewpoint over Koguryo. Through this drama, I hope to change people's mind [sic] and tackle China's unreasonable claims over Koguryo."[43]

The dispute over historical aspects of China's ties with the Korean Peninsula plays on concerns that modern Chinese behavior may seek to replicate a historical hierarchical relationship in which Korea was at a distinct disadvantage. South Korea's sensitive reaction betrays doubts about its own identity and power vis-à-vis China in the context of China's rise. China's handling of the issue also betrays its own potential vulnerabilities regarding national minority issues and potential separatist challenges to internal political control. The dispute also touches on Chinese concerns about whether a future unified Korea might be a source of renewed nationalism that could incite Korean minorities in ways that threaten Chinese internal stability and raise tensions between China and a unified Korea. Seeing developments in Korea through the lens of its own efforts to promote historical research in the service of nation building, China has had difficulty accepting that Korean efforts to promote greater consciousness about Koguryo are driven by pressures from civil society. Even Korean government-led initiatives have represented efforts to channel public frustrations constructively, such as the Northeast Asian History Foundation, which was established in 2006 and has focused on academic projects to promote a deeper knowledge base regarding historical issues that have become sources of political controversy.

The two governments have been relatively successful at preventing the political controversy surrounding Koguryo from affecting other aspects of the relationship. However, China took actions to prevent the airing of Koguryo dramas in China despite the overall popularity of Korean products there as part of the "Korean Wave." The strong South Korean public response to the Koguryo issue has also partly led to the decline of the Korean Wave as a cultural phenomenon in China. (The Korean Wave is discussed below.) Finally, this issue drives the two Koreas together in opposition against perceived Chinese efforts to develop a basis for claiming Koguryo as part of Chinese history and territory.

NORTH KOREA AND THE SINO–SOUTH KOREAN NATIONAL IDENTITY GAP

The most serious Sino–South Korean national identity–related conflicts have arisen over the future of North Korea. The trigger for these tensions lies in a perceived increase in North Korea's reliance on China as a result of its growing marginalization in the international community and increasing prospects for sudden internal instability or leadership succession problems. North Korea's provocations and domestic developments since 2009 have raised potentially serious questions in South Korea regarding North Korea's future and have revived long-standing debates over national identity. The relative disparity in power between North Korea and South Korea and growing perceptions that China holds the key, if not to North Korea's survival then at least to the outcome of diplomatic efforts to blunt the North Korean nuclear challenge, are factors that influence the two Koreas' quest for a unified national identity. To the extent that China utilizes economic tools to expand its political influence in North Korea or to shore up the North's stability, such actions are perceived as an attempt to deny a unified Korean national identity, with negative ramifications for Sino–South Korean relations. Competition for long-term influence in North Korea has emerged as a bilateral issue, revealing tensions over national identity in three major areas: the debate on Korean unification; Chinese diplomatic efforts to reconsolidate its "traditional friendship" with North Korea; and China's economic engagement with the North.

China and South Korea appear to have fundamentally different preferences regarding the desired end state on the Korean Peninsula. From a South Korean perspective, reunification is essential to the full recovery of Korea's historical identity, and the perception of great power opposition arouses suspicion. Although China rhetorically supports the objective of reunification, it appears comfortable with the status quo of a divided peninsula, whereas the official goal reflected in the Korean Constitution is a unified Korean Peninsula.

The importance of reunification as a fundamental issue of identity drives a willingness to make significant economic sacrifices toward this goal, causing the Chinese to use economic or political instruments to influence North Korea in ways that appear to defer reunification and thus create a source of distrust. Although a lack of contacts with North Korea has resulted in relative emotional detachment among younger South Koreans, one analysis asserts that "for those who do desire uni- fication, the motivation is often derived from South Korea–centered goals: unification for the benefit of South Korea or to prevent China's spreading influence over the North."[44] In contrast, Chinese concern has increased about individual irredentist Korean claims in support of a "greater Korea" extending to parts of Chinese territory.[45] Chinese analysts view the issue through the lens of their own challenges in man- aging a policy toward minorities and have aroused resentment among Netizens, which has seeped into the consciousness of security analysts focused on the peninsula.[46] China's expectations on the peninsula, Shi Yinhong indicates, are confined to a few "nonnegotiables": "The pen- insula must not threaten China's security through internal disruption or chaos; it must not function as a strategic fortress for U.S. "containment" against China; and it must not damage China's territorial and national integration by any irredentist and "pan-Korean" aspirations driven by extreme nationalism."[47]

Chinese debates about the implications of Korean unification for China intensified with the onset of South Korea's Sunshine Policy toward the North. And China's interest in playing a central role in reunification surfaced with reactions to the inter-Korean joint dec- laration of October 2007, which stated that the two Koreas would work together to advance cooperation on building a permanent peace regime on the peninsula among "the three or four parties directly con- cerned," a statement that appeared to exclude China from the process.[48] A Chinese Foreign Ministry spokesman on October 9 affirmed that "China, as an important nation in Northeast Asia and also a contracting party to an armistice agreement of the Korean War, will go on playing an active role in the process."[49] Quoting the inter-Korean statement, *People's Daily* editorialized that "China's role in Korean issue cannot be neglected."[50] A Chinese expert added that in the creation of a per- manent Korean peace regime, "if the United States is an indispensable power, China is an equally important player that can by no means be bypassed.… It is neither possible nor desirable to exclude China."[51]

South Korea's goal for the end state of the peninsula is embodied in its July 2009 Joint Vision Statement with the United States, which pledges that "through our Alliance we aim to build a better future for all people on the Korean Peninsula, establishing a durable peace on the Peninsula and leading to peaceful reunification on the principles of free democracy and a market economy."[52] This objective reflects both South Korea's growing confidence as an internationally responsible player and ally of the Obama administration, and increasing pessimism about whether the DPRK regime is sustainable in its current form. It also highlights differences with China on the values and worldview that constitute national identity. One Korean analyst argues that "we should accommodate the increasing economic relationship with China, but … China is not a democracy and is very different from the South Korean identity as a democracy and market economy—it is very different from us."[53] Although the Joint Vision Statement reassures South Koreans that the allies are aligned on unification, it raises questions about Chinese willingness to cooperate, given divergent views on the desired end state. After the Workers' Party of Korea (WPK) conference in September 2010, which marked the consolidation of the Kim regime, China's heir apparent, Vice President Xi Jinping, stated that "under the new leadership of the WPK, the DPRK people will see greater progress in developing its economy, improving living standards, achieving peaceful national unification and expanding foreign relations."[54]

Looking primarily through the lens of United States–China strategic relations, Chinese authors acknowledge that Beijing prefers a "strategically neutralized Korean Peninsula,"[55] rather than "a hastily unified Korea following the collapse of the North Korean regime" that would result in "loss of a strategic buffer."[56] A unified Korea under U.S. leadership would be unacceptable. "Beijing's long-term strategic concern is not whether there will be two Koreas or one reunified Korea, but how to reduce U.S. influence there."[57] Such sensitivity over United States–led unification has been most apparent during periods of perceived DPRK instability, such as during North Korea's famine in the mid–1990s in the aftermath of Kim Il-sung's death in 1994, and United States–led sanctions in response to DPRK military provocations have raised Chinese suspicions about attempts to drive early reunification under U.S. and South Korean terms. As one expert argued regarding the second nuclear crisis, "Obviously, the essence of the Bush administration's DPRK policy at the time was to force it to change its policy or bring about regime change by economically strangling, politically isolating, and militarily threatening it."[58] Although the domestic debate on North Korea's strategic value widened after the North's May 2009 nuclear test, there is an aversion to regime change or collapse, even among advocates of a tougher response.

The unification debate has significant national identity implications for South Koreans because it is shaping perceptions of the long-term U.S. presence on the peninsula, the core rationale for which is directly tied to deterrence against North Korea.[59] South Koreans view the security alliance with the United States as aimed primarily against the North Korea threat rather than China's rise or military intervention, but this perception inevitably influences South Korea's identification with China, given the tendency to view alignment with the United States versus China in zero-sum terms. Although the inter-Korean summit in 2000 marked a turning point in attitudes toward North Korea, exposing a division between conservatives who demand reciprocity from the North and progressives who seek a single Korean nationalism defined by reunification, the conservative Lee Myung-bak's foreign policy has resulted in greater tensions with China—despite upgrading the "strategic partnership" in 2008, partly due to perceived efforts to use the alliance as a tool to manage Chinese interests and influence on the peninsula. Chinese officials have expressed dissatisfaction with South Korea's apparent tilt toward the United States and "Cold War mentality" since Lee's first summit with Hu Jintao in May 2008.[60] South Korean public opinion trends in 2010 indicated an increase in both North Korea threat perceptions and support for continuation of the alliance, breeding further competition with China regarding Korea's future orientation.[61]

Both China and South Korea view North Korea as a "younger brother" based on their respective historical relationships. China's close identification with North Korea, based on a shared Communist ideology and a fifty-year alliance relationship, conflicts with South Korea's vision of a unified Korean Peninsula (with Seoul in the lead). In his message to Kim Jong-il on the sixty-fifth anniversary of the founding of the WPK, Hu Jintao praised "achievements in the DPRK-style socialist construction";[62] and during military talks with his DPRK counterparts, Defense Minister Liang Guanglie claimed that "the Sino-Korea friendship sealed in blood will last forever," pointing to "the Korean people's deep emotional attachment of friendship toward the Chinese people."[63] The proliferation in diplomatic exchanges since 2009 reflects joint symbolic efforts to reinforce the historical relationship and China's renewed commitment to advance future intergovernmental ties under a revamped DPRK leadership. That these interactions intensified despite the unprecedented level of DPRK provocations and fallout in inter-Korean relations heightened political tensions between China and South Korea, significantly souring South Korean public perceptions of China.

Differences over dealing with a belligerent North Korea—and the question of how to effectively influence Pyongyang's behavior—heightened with the reconsolidation of the China-DPRK "traditional friendship" in the aftermath of North Korea's May 2009 nuclear test. China's policy shift suggests an attempt to recover an apparent loss of strategic influence over Pyongyang following the first nuclear test in 2006, but this insistence on a special relationship challenges both the inter-Korean relationship and management of North Korean provocations. In 2010, the number of China's high-level exchanges with the North increased fourteenfold since the stagnation in contacts in 2007 and exceeded that with South Korea for the first time since normalization in 1992.[64] The leadership exchanges were widely perceived in South Korea as an affirmation of Chinese economic and political support amid leadership transition in Pyongyang, raising suspicions about China's long-term intentions. South Koreans reacted most negatively to China's protection of North Korea over the *Cheonan* incident, which marked a second downturn in ties after the 2004 Koguryo dispute. China's failure to back efforts to condemn Pyongyang at the UN Security Council was also a setback for South Korea's efforts to project its influence.

Commemorations of the sixtieth anniversary of China's entry into the Korean War revealed stark differences with South Korea. Xi Jinping referred to the war as "a great and just war for safeguarding peace and resisting aggression.... It was also a great victory gained by the united combat forces of China's and the DPRK's civilians and soldiers, and a great victory in the pursuit of world peace and human progress."[65] The ROK Foreign Ministry's immediate response defended South Korea's position and warned against the negative implications for China's global image: "That the Korean War broke out as a result of the North's southward invasion is an indisputable and historical fact that has been internationally recognized. China is a permanent member of the UN Security Council and a responsible member of the international community."[66] These competing efforts to shape respective understandings of national identity underscore not only conflicting interpretations of national history but also differences in worldview linked to clashing visions of the future of the peninsula.[67]

China's historical identification with the Korean Peninsula has also drawn criticism inside China. China's role in the Korean War was briefly a topic of public debate following North Korea's 2009 nuclear test, driving a growing interest in Korean War–related literature and heated Internet forum discussions on Cold War relations with the North. Negative Chinese views of the North as "unreliable" are based on the understanding that many pro-China members of the WPK were purged at the end of the 1950s and that a pro-Soviet Kim Il-sung intended to marginalize Chinese influence. Supporters of such views also point out that North Korean history textbooks downplay the role of Chinese volunteer troops during the Korean War, showing a characteristic tendency of not reciprocating Chinese trust and support.[68] Chu Shulong of Tsinghua University argues that "for many years, North Korea has ignored China's assistance during the Korean War, even denies China's qualifications to participate in the negotiation of a Peace Agreement to end the Korean War. How can China have any trust of and expectations for North Korea?"[69]

South Korean anxieties over the national identity implications of China's role on the peninsula are reflected in an acute awareness of the challenge that China's economic influence in the North poses for South Korean interests. Kim Dae-jung publicly stated his concern about North Korea's economic dependence on China as one of the main motives of continued inter-Korean reconciliation efforts. During the Roh Moo-hyun period, *Chosun ilbo* featured a series of articles assessing Chinese investments in North Korea as an attempt to transform it into "China's fourth northeastern province."[70] South Koreans perceive Chinese activities as driven by strategic interests of propping up the regime, thwarting unification, and maintaining long-term influence on the peninsula. Chinese food and material support for North Korea in the mid-1990s arguably played a major role in forestalling North Korean instability when famine and a deteriorating economy raised prospects of North Korea's collapse and the realization of Korean reunification.[71] The difficulty of distinguishing between state- and market-led trade and investment between China and North Korea exacerbates South Korean concerns.

The pattern of North Korea's trade with China and South Korea during the past decade suggests that there is Sino–South Korean competition for a dominant position in North Korea's external trade. During progressive South Korean administrations, inter-Korean trade accelerated, in 2004–7 approaching the level of China-DPRK trade. South Korea's share of North Korea's external trade dropped to 30 percent in 2009 under Lee, while China's share increased to more than 50 percent, fueling concerns about the displacement of South Korean economic influence. Although the decline in inter-Korean trade corresponds to a shift toward sanctions and a desire to use trade as a lever to drive North Korea back to dialogue, this effort has resulted in a widening gap with China-DPRK trade, which increased by 75 percent from 2007 to 2010, compared with 6 percent for inter-Korean trade.[72]

South Koreans are particularly sensitive to Chinese trade and investment in North Korea's key strategic sectors, including natural resources and infrastructure development. One highly touted outcome of the 2007 inter-Korean summit was an agreement to allow South Koreans to enter North Korea's natural resources sector, but China-DPRK investment deals secured during Hu Jintao's summits with Kim Jong-il in

2005 and 2006 raised alarms in South Korea concerning China's preferential access, as did those pledged by Premier Wen Jiabao in October 2009. Heightening this concern is a sense of entitlement over the North that stems from the commitment to reconciliation and reunification and a continuing desire to recover the identity of a reunified Korea.

The Sino–South Korean relationship faces significant identity-related challenges in its handling of North Korea issues. China's prioritization of its special relationship with North Korea is based on shared history and ideology. South Korea's own domestic political polarization on North Korea has shaped China's views and approach on the peninsula. Despite a period of intensified Sino–South Korean dialogue on the North Korean nuclear crisis in 2009, Chinese analysts remain uncomfortable with the direction of South Korean policy under Lee, expressing concern with the downturn in inter-Korean relations, the emphasis on the United States–ROK alliance, and South Korean public expressions of "extreme nationalism" over historical and territorial disputes with China.[73]

Whereas the normalization and development of Sino–South Korean relations was driven primarily by China's need to prioritize economic interests over national identity issues, its tendency to treat North Korea as an exceptional case has brought China and South Korea into conflict on identity-related issues. In addition, both countries appear to be in an economic competition as a way to secure a strategic advantage in shaping the situation on the peninsula. Differences over South Korea's independent and unruly civil society activism have spilled over into China and exceeded the strict limits that China is willing to allow. For example, although China showed some tolerance for the responses of South Korean civil society to the DPRK refugee crisis in the mid-1990s, the politicization of the issue in the early 2000s introduced a more adversarial component to aspects of bilateral relations that stem directly from differences in the two countries' social systems.

Finally, China has prioritized its own domestic needs and interests over international demands in dealing with North Korea. Its response to provocations has undermined regional perceptions of China's role as mediator of the Six-Party Talks and member of the UN Security

Council. Its tendency to see North Korean issues through the lens of the United States–China relationship suggests that China's main strategic priority on the peninsula is to protect its sphere of influence and limit U.S. influence and that of other outside powers.

SINO–SOUTH KOREAN ECONOMIC AND CULTURAL RELATIONS: COMPETITION ON THE GLOBAL STAGE

The global marketplace provides a venue for regulated competition among states and companies. Different capabilities and comparative advantages contribute to national identity by providing identifying characteristics that influence both international perceptions of a particular country and the self-image of that country compared with others. Questions of national identity can thus be associated with marketing and branding.[74] Because the Sino-South Korean economic relationship has been the primary catalyst for the development of a closer political relationship, it is worth examining bilateral economic trends to gain an understanding of the potential for national identity conflict that could escalate into a political dispute. In 2010, China accounted for 21 percent of South Korea's foreign trade, a proportion greater than that of South Korea's combined trade with the United States and Japan. China's entry into the World Trade Organization in 2001 accelerated economic relations, leaving a deeper impression in the minds of the respective publics regarding each other's place in national identity and creating the need for new political mechanisms both to manage bilateral problems as they arise and to provide support for enhanced trade opportunities.[75] To evaluate the effect of economic and cultural interdependence on national identity perceptions, two issues are paramount: (1) the impact on public perceptions of each other; and (2) the impact on national identity of China's growing competitiveness in third-country markets and traditional sectors of South Korean economic strength. Economic and cultural exchange can be seen as dynamic processes influencing identity perceptions.

Surveys by the Korea Trade-Investment Promotion Agency (KOTRA) show that Chinese consumers are drawn to South Korean goods by their design, price, reliability, and quality.[76] The South Korean government and businesses took active steps to promote Korean products and culture at the Shanghai Expo in May–October 2010, during which KOTRA reported an improvement in the Chinese public image of Korean corporations, with the strongest brand awareness in home appliances, cellular phones, computers, and fashion products. The popularity of Korean cultural products has contributed to a positive image of Korea during the past decade through the "Korean Wave" ("Hanliu"), a term coined by the Chinese media in the late 1990s amid the rising popularity of Korean television dramas in China. However, the appeal of Korean music, movies, and TV entertainment appeared to wane following the public clashes over Koguryo in 2004.[77] Surveys in 2009 indicated that 50 percent of Chinese respondents had a good image of Korean products, whereas 20 percent had a bad image, but the finding that older and more educated Chinese dominated the former group also suggested an increasingly negative image of Korea among the younger generation.[78] The success of Korean products and services has led to emulation by Chinese companies, posing competitive challenges across broad sectors.

Negative perceptions of South Korea emerged in the Chinese popular media, most notably during the 2008 Beijing Olympics. The Chinese were offended that the South Korean media released secretly recorded segments of the rehearsals of the opening ceremony, which highlighted Chinese national identity and accomplishments. Although the broadcaster, Seoul Broadcasting System, apologized for the incident, it unleashed a flood of angry debate on Chinese radio shows, newspaper commentaries, and Internet blogs.[79] The violent scuffles during the Olympic torch relay in Seoul between Chinese students and Korean demonstrators protesting against China's human rights violations led to an outpouring of confrontation in Internet forums on a host of identity issues, including traditional philosophy, art, and culture. One student at China Foreign Affairs University recognized that, "as people have come to have a strong national identity, some of the historical heritage that both China and South Korea had shared together before, have [sic] become a source of dispute." [80]

In recent years, Korean views of Chinese products have been colored by problems with quality control for food imports, the threat posed to Korean producers by low-cost Chinese goods entering the Korean market, and skepticism regarding the motives behind the investment by the Shanghai Automotive International Company in SsangYong Motor Company.[81] The threat of cheap Chinese products hit South Korea the hardest during the garlic and kimchi trade disputes in 2000 and 2005, respectively, which incited the public and also left a negative impression among South Korean officials regarding China's retaliatory trade tactics. South Korean concerns over Chinese product safety escalated with the scandal over melamine-tainted food in 2008, which soured public perceptions to the extent that survey findings in October 2008 showed that 69 percent of respondents were more worried about tainted food than North Korean nuclear weapons.[82] But as the potential for disputes has intensified, both governments have been relatively adroit at creating new mechanisms for handling such disputes at both bilateral and regional levels—for instance, in response to food and product safety concerns since 2005.

Although Chinese cultural products have not yet made big inroads into South Korea, there is no denying the increase in popularity of Chinese language study. Twenty-five percent of South Korean students studying abroad are in China, where South Koreans represent the greatest number of foreign students, more than doubling from 29,102 to 68,806 between 2006 and 2009.[83] The number of Chinese students in South Korea increased almost tenfold between 2004 and 2010, to 53,461, or 70 percent of the total foreign student body in South Korea,[84] although most South Koreans were not aware of the trend in South Korea until the clashes during the Olympic torch relay in 2008.[85]

With changes in the bilateral trade structure, Sino–South Korean competition in key export markets has shifted from labor-intensive to higher-end sectors, producing new trade frictions since the 2005 kimchi dispute and new political challenges that have an impact on national identity.[86] The Federation of Korean Industries in 2010 projected that South Korea may lose its technological advantages over China in fewer than four years in eight key export items such as semiconductors, automobiles, and steel, which in total represented 64 percent of all South Korean exports in 2009. Chinese competitiveness in global markets made itself felt in 2010, when China surpassed South Korea as the top shipbuilding country and as the biggest market for its own Hyundai Motors. The global trend is a major concern for South Koreans: Despite a much shorter record of internationalization, the accumulated outward foreign direct investment stock of Chinese companies reached $37 billion by the end of 2003, exceeding South Korea's $34.5 billion; and in 2005, 15 Chinese companies entered the "*Fortune* Global 500" list, surpassing South Korea's 11.[87]

One problem shaping Korean images is the preferential treatment of Chinese companies over foreign investors. Korean manufacturers have faced pressure to move plants to China in order to remain competitive in the international market, but China has demanded technology transfers and has adjusted its investment laws to provide incentives to companies that give higher-end production experience to Chinese workers. Once in China, operations may be subject to espionage or the theft of core technologies along with local competition from firms established to compete head to head with foreign counterparts. Although such obstacles of doing business in China are not unique, they may have a greater impact on the national identity gap given a deep Korean sense of vulnerability. Identity-related conflicts might become more prominent if China becomes the economically more advanced partner, eliminating the trade surplus that South Korea currently enjoys. Under these circumstances, the political and economic advantages would seem to lie with China, raising South Korea's sense of economic dependency on China and constraining South Korean options and competitiveness in global markets.

In general, the growing intensity of Sino–South Korean interactions represented by transborder economic and cultural trends has provided positive reinforcement to the relationship, with initial positive effects in closing the identity gap between the two. But the decline of the "Korean Wave" in recent years and a loss of South Korean cultural appeal in China pose a long-term challenge.[88] This trend appears to reflect growing grassroots resentment among Chinese of Korean cultural influence and increasingly negative associations with the Korea brand. Periodic trade and Chinese product safety disputes within the last decade have also contributed to a nationalist backlash from both sides compounding other issues of identity, including historical and territorial disputes. The Olympic confrontations in 2008 sparked a brief firestorm of exchange on such issues and most strongly illustrated how national identity frictions at the grassroots level could escalate into larger tensions requiring special handling by governments.

CONCLUSION: ASYMMETRY AND IDENTITY

We have found manifestations of a national identity gap between China and South Korea in confrontations over their shared history and the future of North Korea, and in the two countries' economic and cultural interactions in the context of globalization. The emergence of the Koguryo dispute in 2004 revealed the significance of national identity as a source of tension in the bilateral relationship. South Korea's own national identity debates on North Korea's future have exacerbated the potential for Sino–South Korean tensions over dealing with the North, raising doubts about China's willingness to accept reunification. Although complex economic interdependence has promoted cooperation, there is growing concern that a rising China will squeeze out South Korean comparative advantages on the international stage and challenge South Korea's global role and prestige.

The polarization of views toward China in South Korea appears to be an indirect result of the clear divisions regarding South Korea's relations with the United States and North Korea. Lee Myung-bak's emphasis on the alliance relationship with the United States and tougher policy toward the North compared with his predecessors highlighted aspects of South Korean identity as a U.S. ally that are perceived by some Chinese as incompatible with Chinese interests. Although progressive governments downplayed the alliance while promoting inter-Korean reconciliation, this was also a period of emerging competition with China for economic influence over North Korea and outbursts of Sino–South Korean historical, territorial, and trade disputes that required careful political management and revealed significant gaps in national identity perceptions. South Korea's foreign policy orientation under Lee has been the subject of intense criticism regarding the implications for Chinese regional interests.

South Koreans perceive China's historical and territorial claims as interference in their national identity, which surfaced most dramatically with the Koguryo dispute. China's commemoration with North Korea of the Korean War as a joint "victory" also pointed to an identity gap far greater than had been anticipated. The regional impact of North Korean provocations in 2010 represented what many perceived as a reversion to Cold War thinking in the region and exposed the limits of China's shift to a two Koreas policy.

In April 2009, the ROK Ministry of Strategy and Finance warned against a likely intensification of Sino–South Korean competition in trade and energy diplomacy, a sharp departure from previous favorable references to China's growth as an opportunity for South Korean exports since China's integration into the global economy in 2001.[89] The major trade disputes between China and South Korea raised concerns about China using economic tools of retaliation to meet political objectives, concerns that reemerged with China's handling of its territorial disputes with Japan in 2010. However, South Korean analysts remain aware of the need to maintain a favorable partnership with China. Although political tensions have not significantly undermined perceptions of each other's economic significance, a key challenge lies in building sufficient trust in Sino–South Korean relations to secure more active cooperation on sensitive political issues.

South Korean assessments of the relative importance of relationships with China and the United States emerged for the first time in a report by the Korean Institute for Defense Analysis in December 2008—titled *China or the United States?*—a debate that intensified in the aftermath of North Korean military provocations in 2010. Differences arise fundamentally from differing perceptions of strategic competition on the Korean Peninsula and the long-term role of the United States–ROK alliance, especially in scenarios of DPRK instability and Korean unification. South Koreans' preference for a continuation of the alliance risks misperception from the Chinese, who may see the alliance as targeted toward managing Chinese influence rather than deterring North Korea as the primary source of threat. At the same time, although Beijing has indicated that the United States–ROK alliance "would not be valid in viewing, measuring and handling the current global or regional security issues,"[90] South Korean views of the alliance as the primary source of security also reflect a reluctance to accept a Sinocentric regional structure.

The national identity gap is widened as a result of the asymmetrical nature of the relationship. This has the effect of amplifying bilateral differences or the likelihood of misunderstanding on sensitive issues related to national identity. The intensity dimension of national identity is especially pronounced in the context of regional perceptions of China's rise and the United States' decline. United States–China tensions on Korean Peninsula issues may reinforce South Korean self-perceptions as a "shrimp among whales." According to one Chinese assessment of the long-term geostrategic environment on the peninsula following North Korea's 2009 nuclear test, "The most decisive international development in recent years is China's rapid rise…. As Washington's requirement for (and even dependence upon) selective security cooperation with China continues to increase, China will sooner or later become the most influential major power on the Korean Peninsula."[91] A *Global Times* editorial similarly argued in October 2010 that "China should firmly insist on the protection of peninsular stability and oppose any country that seeks to undermine such a standpoint. As China's national strength rises, such a bottom line will be insisted on with greater seriousness."[92] These attitudes contrast sharply with past Chinese calls for strengthened cooperation with regional partners, including U.S. allies, as a "responsible stakeholder" in 2006.[93] Such assertions of power challenge South Korea's efforts to manage relations in the context of its growing international interests and efforts to carve out a leadership role on the global stage. The return to an asymmetric relationship may reveal historical parallels that make the identity gap a central diplomatic challenge.

NOTES

1   Brantly Womack, *China and Vietnam: The Politics of Asymmetry* (New York: Cambridge University Press, 2006); Brantly Womack, *China among Unequals:*

Asymmetric Foreign Relationships in Asia (Hackensack, N.J.: World Scientific, 2010).

2   David C. Kang, *China Rising: Peace, Power, and Order in East Asia* (New York: Columbia University Press, 2007).

3   Key-hiuk Kim, *The Last Phase of the East Asian World Order: Korea, Japan, and the Chinese Empire, 1860–1882* (Berkeley: University of California Press, 1980), 5–15.

4   Martina Deuchler, *Confucian Gentlemen and Barbarian Envoys: The Opening of Korea, 1875–1885* (Seattle: University of Washington Press, 1997), 1–10.

5   For a detailed account of how Korea's leadership rejected the Meiji Restoration based on a Chinese civilizational norm, see Hahm Chai-bong, "Civilization, Race, or Nation? Korean Visions of Regional Order in the Late Nineteenth Century," in *Korea at the Center: Dynamics of Regionalism in Northeast Asia*, edited by Charles K. Armstrong, Gilbert Rozman, Samuel S. Kim, and Stephen Kotkin (Armonk, N.Y.: M. E. Sharpe, 2006), 35–50.

6   Suh Dae Sook, *The Korean Communist Movement, 1918–1948* (Princeton, N.J.: Princeton University Press, 1967).

7   Chen Jian, *China's Road to the Korean War: The Making of Sino-American Confrontation* (New York: Columbia University Press, 1994).

8   Don Oberdorfer, *The Two Koreas: A Contemporary History* (Reading, Mass.: Addison-Wesley, 1997), 1–26.

9   Chung Jae Ho, *Between Ally and Partner: Korea-China Relations and the United States* (New York: Columbia University Press, 2007).

10   UNESCO, "Capital Cities and Tombs of the Ancient Koguryo Kingdom," http://whc.unesco.org/en/list/1135. South Korea recognizes a longer Koguryo history, beginning in 37 BC.

11   "China to Put Forward Three Historical Sites for UNESCO Heritage List," Xinhua, May 12, 2004.

12   Xin Dingding, "Koguryo Sites Put on Heritage List," *China Daily*, July 2, 2004, http://www.chinadaily.com.cn/english/doc/2004-07/02/content_344757.htm.

13   Lee Chi-dong, "Beijing History Distortion Mirrors Concern over Future: Scholar," Yonhap, August 9, 2004.

14   Lee Chi-dong, "China's Claim on Koguryo Kingdom Goes Too Far, Scholars, Lawmakers Say," Yonhap, July 5, 2004.

15   The Chinese Foreign Ministry also deleted all accounts of pre–World War II Japanese history from its Web site.

16   "China Erases All Pre-1948 Korean History from Ministry Website," *Chosun ilbo*, Aug. 5, 2004, http://english.chosun.com/w21data/html/news/200408/200408050035.html.

17   Seo Hyun-jin, "China-Korea Truce in Ancient-Kingdom Feud," *Asia Times*, Aug. 25, 2004.

18   "China's Ancient Koguryo Kingdom Site Added to World Heritage List," *People's Daily*, July 2, 2004, http://english.peopledaily.com.cn/200407/01/eng20040701_148209.html.

19 Lee Chi-dong, "China's Claim on Koguryo Kingdom Goes Too Far."

20 Xin Dingding, "Koguryo Sites Put on Heritage List."

21 Li Sheng, Piao Wenyi, et al., "*Gaogouli lishi wenti yanjiu lunwenji* (The Question of Koguryo: A Collection of Historical Papers), Koguryo Research Foundation, Yanbian University, 2005, http://english.historyfoundation.or.kr/Data/Jnah/J3_1_B1.pdf.

22 Kang Jin Woong, "The Dual National Identity of the Korean Minority in China: The Politics of Nation and Race and the Imagination of Ethnicity," *Studies in Ethnicity and Nationalism* 8, no. 1 (April 2008).

23 "Xu Urges Korean-Chinese to Balance Both Cultures," *Korea Times*, November 16, 2004.

24 Frank Ching, "Unruly Minority," *South China Morning Post*, Nov. 28, 2003.

25 "China Attaches Great Importance to Protecting Koguryo Heritage," Xinhua, July 2, 2004,

26 "China's Ancient Koguryo Kingdom Site Added to World Heritage List."

27 Ibid.

28 Chang Jae-hoon, "S. Korea, China Facing Hardest Test of 12-Year Relationship," Yonhap, August 23, 2004.

29 Peter Hays Gries, "The Koguryo Controversy, National Identity, and Sino-Korean Relations Today," *East Asia* 22, no. 4 (Winter 2005): 3–17.

30 Jae Ho Chung, "China's "Soft" Clash with South Korea: The History War and Beyond," *Asian Survey* 49, no. 3 (May–June 2009).

31 "Ban Pledges 'Stern Countermeasures' against History Distortion," Yonhap, August 11, 2004.

32 Lee Chi-dong, "Beijing History Distortion Mirrors Concern over Future Scholar," Yonhap, August 9, 2004.

33 Chang Jae-hoon, "S. Korea, China Facing Hardest Test."

34 "Lawmakers Slam China for History Distortions," *Korea Times*, August 12, 2004.

35 Lee Chi-dong, "China's Claim on Koguryo Kingdom Goes Too Far."

36 "S. Korea Closely Monitoring China's History Research Projects," Yonhap, September 8, 2006.

37 Seo Hyun-jin, "China-Korea Truce in Ancient Kingdom Feud," *Asia Times*, August 25, 2004.

38 Donald Kirk, "Chinese History: A Cause That Unites the Two Koreas," *South China Morning Post*, February 28, 2004; Khang Hyun-sung, "China's Historical Bid Unites Koreans," *South China Morning Post*, March 2, 2004; Lee Chi-dong, "China's Claim on Koguryo Kingdom Goes Too Far."

39 "Koguryo, Pride of Korean Nation," Korean Central News Agency, September 27, 2004.

40 Kim Hyung, "Seoul-Beijing Dispute over Ancient Kingdom Enters Critical Moment," Yonhap, August 6, 2004.

41 "Lawmaker Proposes Inter-Korean Parliamentary Meeting on Koguryo," *Korea Times*,

August 11, 2004.

42 Scott Snyder, "New Grounds for Contestation: South Korea's Koguryo-Era Historical Dramas and Sino-Korean Relations," in *U.S. Leadership, History, and Bilateral Relations in Northeast Asia*, edited by Gilbert Rozman (Cambridge: Cambridge University Press, 2011).

43 "Historical Dramas Strain Sino-Korean Relations," *Korea Times*, June 29, 2006.

44 Emma Campbell, "South Korea's G-Generation: A Nation within a Nation, Detached from Unification," *East Asia Forum*, April 13, 2010. Public opinion following North Korean military provocations in 2010 indicates that the younger generation increasingly identify themselves as South Korean rather than Korean and view dealing with North Korea as a security rather than a familial imperative. Brad Glosserman and Scott Snyder, "Confidence and Confusion: National Identity and Security Alliances in Northeast Asia," unpublished manuscript, March 2011.

45 Andrei Lankov, "The Gentle Decline of the 'Third Korea,'" *Asia Times*, August 16, 2007.

46 Scott Snyder, "Post-Olympic Hangover: New Backdrop for Relations," *Comparative Connections* (Center for Strategic and International Studies) 10, no. 3 (October 2008).

47 Shi Yinhong, "China and the North Korean Nuclear Issue: Competing Interests and Persistent Policy Dilemmas," *Korean Journal of Defense Analyses*, no. 45 (2009).

48 "Declaration on the Advancement of South-North Relations, Peace and Prosperity," October 4, 2007, http://www.korea.net/news/news/newsView.asp?serial_no=20071004023.

49 Foreign Ministry spokesperson Liu Jianchao's regular press conference, October 9, 2007.

50 Wen Xian, "China's Role in Korean Issue Cannot Be Neglected," *People's Daily*, October 10, 2007, http://english.peopledaily.com.cn/90001/90780/91343/6280449.html.

51 Ren Xiao, "Korea's New Administration and Challenges for China's Relations with the Korean Peninsula," *Asian Perspective* 32, no. 2 (2008), http://www.asianperspective.org/articles/v32n2-h.pdf.

52 "Joint Vision for the Alliance of the United States of America and the Republic of Korea," June 16, 2009.

53 Author's interview in Seoul, October 2008.

54 "China Vows to Work with DPRK's New Leadership to Boost Ties," *Xinhua*, October 8, 2010, http://news.xinhuanet.com/english2010/china/2010-10/08/c_13547869.htm.

55 Xiaoxiong Yi, "A Neutralized Korea: The North-South Rapprochement and China's Korean Policy," *Korean Journal of Defense Analysis* 12, no. 2 (2000): 71–118.

56 Jing-dong Yuan, "China and the North Korean Nuclear Crisis," Monterey Institute of International Studies, January 2003.

57 Xiaoxiong Yi, "Neutralized Korea."

58 Wang Lianhe, "Chaoxian wenti jiejue lujingde sange cengci xuanze," *Xiandai guoji*

guanxi, January 20, 2009.

59   Hahm Chaibong, Kim Jiyoon, et al., *AIPS Opinion Survey 2010: Report on Korean Attitudes toward the U.S.* (Seoul: Asian Institute for Policy Studies, 2010); Victor Cha and Katrin Katz, *Report on U.S. Attitudes toward the Republic of Korea* (Chicago: Chicago Council on Global Affairs, 2010).

60   Foreign Ministry spokesperson Qin Gang's regular press conference, May 27, 2008.

61   Hahm Chaibong et al. *AIPS Opinion Survey 2010*; Nae-young Lee and Han-wool Jeong, "The Impact of North Korea's Artillery Strike on Public Opinion in South Korea," East Asia Institute Issue Briefing 91, December 2010.

62   "Full Text of Hu Jintao's Congratulatory Message to DPRK's Kim for 65th Anniversary of Ruling Party," Xinhua, October 9, 2010.

63   Kim Hyun, "China Seeks to Strengthen Military Bond with N. Korea: Reports," Yonhap, Nov. 25, 2010.

64   Scott Snyder and See-Won Byun, "DPRK Provocations Test China's Regional Role," *Comparative Connections* 12, no. 4 (January 2011), http://csis.org/files/publication/1004qchina_korea.pdf.

65   "China Commemorates 60th Anniversary of Participation in Korean War," Xinhua, October 26, 2010.

66   "Korea, U.S. Rebut Chinese Vice President's Rhetoric," *Chosun Ilbo*, October 28, 2010.

67   Xi's statement contrasted sharply with Obama's Veteran's Day remarks at South Korea's Yongsan base: "Sixty years have come and gone since the Communist armies first crossed the 38th Parallel. . . . As we look around in this thriving democracy and its grateful, hopeful citizens, one thing is clear: This was no tie. This was victory." Remarks by the President Honoring Veterans Day in Seoul, U.S. Army Garrison Yongsan, Seoul, South Korea, November 10, 2010, http://www.whitehouse.gov/the-press-office/2010/11/10/remarks-president-honoring-veterans-day-seoul-south-korea.

68   Zhu Feng, "North Korea Issue Divides China," Asia Security Initiative, June 17, 2009, http://asiasecurity.macfound.org/blog/entry/north_korea_issue_divides_china/.

69   Chu Shulong, "The North Korea Nuclear Issue Calls for New Thinking and New Policy," Asia Security Initiative, September 3, 2009.

70   Ji Hae Beom, "Buk, Joonggukeui Dongbuk je 4 sung dwena," *Chosun ilbo*, July 14, 2005.

71   Nicholas Eberstadt, *The North Korean Economy: Between Crisis and Catastrophe* (New Brunswick, N.J.: Transaction, 2007), 99–126.

72   "Pyongyang's Reliance on China Grows," Yonhap, March 24, 2011.

73   Scott Snyder and See-Won Byun, "Sweet and Sour Aftertaste," *Comparative Connections* 10, no. 4 (January 2009), http://csis.org/files/media/csis/pubs/0804qchina_korea.pdf.

74   Keith Dinnie, "Repositioning the Korea Brand to a Global Audience: Challenges, Pitfalls, and Current Strategy," *KEI Academic Paper Series* 4, no. 9 (December 2009).

75 See-Won Byun and Scott Snyder, "China-ROK Trade Disputes and Implications for Managing Security Relations," *On Korea: Korea Economic Institute Academic Paper Series* 4 (2011): 29–52.

76 See the Korea Trade-Investment Promotion Agency Web site, www.kotra.or.kr/wps/portal/dk.

77 Korean TV drama exports to China and Japan more than halved between 2006 and 2007 and declined by a further 35 percent in 2008. See http://english.yonhapnews.co.kr/news/2009/01/09/0200000000AEN20090108006900315.html.

78 "Samsung Most Famous Korean Brand in China," *Chosun ilbo*, September 21, 2009, http://english.chosun.com/site/data/html_dir/2009/09/21/2009092100261.html.

79 Sunny Lee, "Internet Rumors Roil China-Korea Ties," *Asia Times*, August 9, 2008, http://www.atimes.com/atimes/China/JH09Ad02.html.

80 Kurt Achin, "Massive Chinese Crowds Overwhelm Olympic Torch Protests in South Korea," Voice of America, April 27, 2008.

81 The Shanghai Automotive International Company took a 51 percent stake in SsangYong in 2004, and following deep financial troubles from 2008, SsangYong was acquired by an Indian firm in February 2011. During the Shanghai Automotive International Company's ownership, South Korean counterparts accused the Chinese company of technology theft and failure to meet investment commitments.

82 Bae Ji-sook, "Tainted Food Concern Parents More Than Nuclear Threat," *Korea Times*, October 17, 2008, http://www.koreatimes.co.kr/www/news/nation/2008/10/117_32879.html.

83 Ministry of Education, Science, and Technology of the Republic of Korea. In contrast, the number of South Korean students in the United States increased by 19 percent, from 57,940 to 69,124, during the same period.

84 Sohn Woo-hyun, "Chinese Students Ride Korean Wave to South Korea," Yonhap, September 20, 2010.

85 Achin, "Massive Chinese Crowds Overwhelm Olympic Torch Protests."

86 Zhou Shengqi, "Sino-South Korean Trade Relations: From Boom to Recession," East Asia Institute Background Brief 508, March 3, 2010.

87 Friedrich Wu, "The Globalization of Corporate China," *NBR Analysis* 16, no. 3 (December 2005), http://www.nbr.org/publications/analysis/pdf/vol16no3.pdf.

88 Scott Snyder and See-Won Byun, "Year of China-DPRK Friendship: North's Rocket Fizzles," *Comparative Connections* 11, no. 1 (April 2009), http://csis.org/files/media/csis/pubs/0901qchina_korea.pdf.

89 "S. Korea Wary as China Rises to Economic Power," *Shenzhen Daily*, April 14, 2009, http://paper.sznews.com/szdaily/20090414/ca2911920.htm.

90 Foreign Ministry spokesperson Qin Gang's regular press conference, May 27, 2008.

91 Shi Yinhong, "China and the North Korean Nuclear Issue."

92 "Stable Sino–N. Korea Ties Benefit Region," *Global Times*, October 11, 2010,

93 Jing Huang and Xiaoting Li, "Pyongyang's Nuclear Ambitions: China Must Act as a 'Responsible Stakeholder,'" Brookings Institution, October 12, 2006.

CHAPTER 5

THE REDISCOVERY OF THE TIANXIA WORLD ORDER

Yongnian Zheng

One of the important elements of national identity is an idealized statement of a country's international position. It depicts the positive influence the country is supposed to exert, avoiding any negative overtones of its ability to project power. As China's precipitous rise as a global power continues, the search is proceeding for a worldview that presents its role in the surrounding region and beyond in the most favorable light. After the reform and opening policy, China started to search for a new identity on the world stage, a sense of a distinctive international mission.[1] With China's continuous rise, the Chinese have become increasingly confident about their tradition, looking to it for guidance. One intriguing part of this search is the revival of a historical worldview known as Tianxia (All-under-Heaven). After all, throughout its imperial history China was obsessed with casting its state conduct, especially for the well-being of its people but also in dealing with its periphery and the outside, as a test of virtuous rule. The revival of Tianxia thinking is not the only force in the recent quest for the clarification of national identity related to international relations, but more than any other force it captures the renewed spirit of self-justification and uniqueness in China's identity.

China's rise is occurring in the context of an international system that is dominated by the United States and a regional environment where many states are wary of a rising power, which carries the weight of millennia of Sinocentrism linked to a hierarchical and unequal order. If revived Tianxia discussions do not directly address the contradictions with these ways of thinking, they implicitly rebuke them. There is a dyadic undertone of contrast with the U.S. worldview, presenting a Chinese national identity at odds with how many in the West perceive China and critiquing the U.S. national identity used to justify a different approach to international relations. Although this chapter does not focus on the Sino-U.S. dyad, it depicts emerging strands of the Chinese national identity that loom in the background as the struggle intensifies to reconcile divergent approaches.

This search is associated with China's changing role in the world. Since the early 1990s, with its rapid economic development, China has begun to take a more active role in world politics. It has played by the rules of multilateral institutions at the global level, and thus has actively sought membership in the World Trade Organization and other established international organizations.[2] Meanwhile, China has turned to the Asian region that it had previously ignored, even playing a leading role in establishing new institutions, including the Shanghai Cooperation Organization and the Association of Southeast Asian Nations (ASEAN)–China Free Trade Area.[3] Whereas Communist China once vehemently condemned "illegitimate" international institutions, which served the interests of the West, China is now an important player in the existing international system and has finally gained the power to reshape these institutions. Therefore, it seems inevitable that China will bring changes to the regional as well as international order.[4] Whereas some project a benign China, others see its rise as a threat to the established order.[5] At the root of these conflicting predictions are contrasting assumptions about its evolving national identity. People outside China are uncertain about its future. The recent debate about the meaning for China's leaders of the concept of Tianxia is a reflection of this divergence.

China is believed to have achieved a central status in regional affairs, positioning itself at the center of the division of labor in East Asia and becoming a locomotive of intraregional trade.[6] Its actions may be driven largely by strategic considerations, rather than economic benefits, as argued in the article "How China Is Building an Empire," by Michael Vatikiotis and Murray Hiebert. They suggest that while in the short term China sought little more than closer trade and economic ties, "longer term, with China's sustained economic growth, it could see the recreation of the kind of strategic centrality that China enjoyed at the height of imperial rule, when Asian states paid tribute to Beijing and recognized its preeminence in return for favorable terms of trade."[7] Many ask whether China is going back to the days of the Middle Kingdom.[8] They want to know if revived interest in the core of China's past worldview is but a prelude to a Sinocentric identity at odds with recent principles of global relations.

In the West, how the rise of China is perceived depends on which theoretical framework is employed. Such frameworks have often defined international relations debates. In North America and some parts of Europe, realism and liberalism have dominated the field for decades, imposing the Western scientific tradition on East Asia. Neoliberalism and neorealism do not differ much from the older versions, and both emphasize power relations, the former viewing China's rise as an opportunity and the latter seeing it as a threat. China does not fit well into these two major frameworks. If the influence of a state is proportional to its power, then China has long seemed to be far less influential than its rising power permits. (This situation is reflected in the fact that the post–Deng Xiaoping regime did not assert Chinese power in the region or the world in proportion to its potential and instead harped on its peaceful rise.) Distinctly nonrealist, it has apparently idealistically promoted the ASEAN–China Free Trade Area and ASEAN's role in the driver's seat for regional integration. It also does not fit into the concept of liberalism, given its readiness to strike back when its perceived core national interests are threatened (e.g., in the war against Vietnam in 1979, assertiveness over Mischief Reef in 1995, and missile firings across the Taiwan Strait in the mid-1990s) and when it suspects the West of attempting to promote democratization in China.

Some writers in the West have also employed constructivism to depict China's past interstate experience and explain its international behavior, but they have faced many doubts.[9] Writers in China are often suspicious of explanations or predictions about China by Westerners; however, they have been slow to provide an alternative approach to China's international behavior. Observers in the West have searched for an answer to the question: What is China's new identity in international relations? Chinese experts themselves have also tried to answer this question. As in the West, their perceptions of China in the world depend on what approach they apply. Within China, the discipline of international relations first emerged as an autonomous academic discipline in the early 1980s, when the post–Mao Zedong reform and open door policy began. During the past three decades, the discipline has grown in spite of severe political inhibitions and ideological constraints into a vigorous field. China can now boast of one of the largest epistemic communities in the world in numbers of students, faculties, research centers, policy analysts, and practitioners. This expansion has been accompanied by outward signs of Americanization, as specialists have borrowed concepts and theories developed out of Western experiences to advance studies. However, many have determined that a mechanical application of the existing concepts and theories does not suffice in researching a proper understanding of China's international behavior.[10] They also have been prompted to put a different face on China's trajectory by situating it in a distinct theoretical orbit.

One option that is of considerable appeal inside China but is also gaining popularity abroad is to go back to Chinese traditional philosophy, interpreting it in today's context to explain the country's international behavior.[11] Many have endeavored to uncover deeply rooted cultural elements in China's contemporary behavior, shaping the way its national identity is framed as the blueprint for what the emerging world order should look like and how it should be achieved. In 2005, the philosopher Zhao Tingyang published the book *Tianxia tixi* (The All-under-Heaven system).[12] In 2009, he followed with the book *Investigations of the Bad World: Political Philosophy as First Philosophy*. Taking a philosophical perspective, Zhao's concept of the Tianxia system aroused persistent discussion among Chinese specialists. Many greeted this system as the Chinese ideal of international relations. During its long history, China had endeavored to establish such an order, and today building it looms as a civilizational mission if China does not want to repeat what the West has done to the world.

Outside China, in 2006, Wang Gungwu chose "Tianxia and Empire: External Chinese Perspectives" as the topic for his inaugural Tsai Lecture at Harvard University and thus introduced the Tianxia system to those in the English-speaking world who do not follow Chinese history. In the same year, a conference was held at the University of Nottingham to examine the contemporary relevance of John Fairbank's treatment of Tianxia as the "Chinese world order."[13] In 2009, another conference in Singapore in honor of Wang drew further attention to Tianxia.[14] Scholars have striven to rediscover the traditional Chinese world order and to assess the chances of its rebirth in the contemporary era.

Drawing on the growing body of literature on rediscovering the Chinese Tianxia world order, this chapter addresses three key questions: (1) What was the Tianxia system as seen through the lens of national identity? (2) How did the tributary system, a practice linked to this concept, serve to reinforce national identity? (3) To what degree can the Tianxia concept represent China's contemporary international identity?

THE TIANXIA SYSTEM AS CIVILIZATIONAL IMAGINATION

The Tianxia concept differs from Western international relations theories in its assumptions and conceptual framework, and in its understanding of power. According to this concept, the state is not viewed as the core or as an independent actor. In contrast, even a state that dominates the world order is depicted as so enmeshed by world institutions that world politics has become the prerequisite for domestic politics. To maintain domestic order, states must establish an orderly international environment. Although the world order is hierarchical and states are not endowed with equal sovereignty, this does not mean that the dominant state has despotic power. It cannot afford to confront the alliances formed by other, weaker states. The Tianxia concept highlights the close relations between power and legitimacy. For the ruler, hard power is not the only source of power. Instead, the virtue of the ruler and his ability to establish commonly accepted world institutions matter. The ruler should seek to realize worldwide harmony and benefit all actors that join the system. The world order should be reciprocal, though hierarchical.

According to Zhao Tingyang, Tianxia is a concept with a trinity of meanings: the geographical world (the Earth), the psychological world (the hearts of all people), and the political world (world institutions).[15] This implies that an emperor (*tianzi*, the son of the Heaven) does not really rule his empire of All-under-Heaven, even if he conquers an extraordinary vastness of land, unless he receives the sincere and true support from the people. Zhao cites the Chinese philosopher Xunzi (313–238 BC):

> Enjoying All-under-Heaven does not mean to receive the lands from people who are forced to give, but to satisfy all people with a good way of governance.

Moreover, a commonly accepted institution is necessary. Zhao argues that the empire of Tianxia does not mean a country but instead signifies an institutional world.[16] World politics is the prerequisite for the politics of an individual state; and an orderly world is one necessary condition for an orderly state. As a consequence, world governance becomes necessary for governance over the individual state.[17] The relationship between world and domestic politics could be better understood if we examine the origin of the Tianxia system. Zhao traces it to the Zhou Dynasty (1045–256 BC), contending that compared with the Shang, the previous dominant state, the Zhou was weak in military power. The emperor of the Zhou, however, was skillful in practicing virtue-centered diplomacy. As a consequence, the Zhou won support from other states and successfully toppled the Shang. In the aftermath, one major challenge the emperor faced was how to govern so many states. Because the Zhou was weak in military power, it could only rely on commonly accepted or new institutions that were able to reduce conflict or increase cooperation among states. Establishing a world institution with universal legitimacy became the prime political issue it faced.[18]

According to Zhao, to ensure the success of the Tianxia system, two political strategies are crucial: virtue and harmony. The former deals with how interests and power are allocated, emphasizing the principles of justice and kindness while highlighting that ordinary people should be endowed with interests and meritocrats should obtain power.[19] In other words, the ruler has the responsibility to take care of his subjects. If the ruler is immoral, people have the right to rebel. If we apply the strategy of virtue to international relations, it means that hierarchy is not a bad thing as long as the dominant state exercises self-restraint and behaves altruistically. It is also the responsibility of the dominant state to take care of weak states and to ensure that they can benefit from international institutions.

In sum, the Tianxia system is based on reciprocal relations among states. Every state can obtain certain interests, and the advantages of joining the system are obviously greater than those of remaining outside the system. Cooperation therefore becomes the best choice. States are willing to acknowledge the leadership of the dominant state and join the system. This may appear utopian, as Zhao acknowledges. Many Chinese emperors attempted to establish it but never succeeded satisfactorily, as in the case of the tributary system. Yet, for Zhao, globalization has intensified interdependence among states and made the Tianxia system more relevant to reality.

Tianxia also highlights the oneness of the world, or the "all-inclusive" principle (wuwai), which implies that no one should be excluded from the world system. In the context of Chinese philosophy, there is no incompatible otherness. The pattern of relations can only be characterized as close or estranged, rather than confrontational or incompatible. There is no element of cultural fundamentalism and no basis for a clash of civilizations.[20] This system ideally appreciates the differences among various cultures. The rights of governing the world are "open" (available) to any nation.[21]

The world order imagined by Tianxia is an extension of the domestic political and social order. Traditionally, Chinese emperors ruled the country by creating a "natural" hierarchical and, thus, antiegalitarian political order. Tianxia, presided over by the son of Heaven, embraced the whole world and claimed to be a natural order because it was based on the relationships that existed between family members in the private sphere, such as father and son, and husband and wife. These were simply extended to the relationship between emperor and minister in the public sphere and then to China's external relations with the non-Chinese. In the West, the domestic political order and the international order are constructed in accordance with abstract concepts, such as "nature" and "God." In contrast, it seems that the Chinese intellectual imagination did not go beyond this world, making the individual within a family the natural starting point for both the internal and external order. This natural order proceeded from individual to family, from family to state, and from state to other states under Heaven. Because this was a natural order, it was also universal.

THE TRIBUTARY SYSTEM AND CHINA'S HISTORICAL MEMORY

The tributary system is a practical application of the Tianxia concept. Throughout China's long history, almost all external relations were conducted through this tributary system. Joseph Whitney offers a geographical presentation of it, dividing the world known to China into three zones: the ecumenical and extra-ecumenical zones, and the contact zone between the two.[22] Within the ecumenical zone, there were three areas. The first was the core area: the apex of the hierarchy of national space where the water economy was most intensively developed. The second was the intensive ecumenical area. The third was the extensive ecumenical area: the minimally effective areas within the ecumene characterized by poor resources, low population densities, and a minimal degree of spatial interaction. This was the area with the greatest concentrations of non-Han people, who either had actively resisted assimilation or were not considered by the Chinese to be sufficiently civilized to become subjects of the empire.

Between the ecumenical and extra-ecumenical areas was the contact zone, which consisted of transitional areas where assimilation into and spatial interaction with the ecumene took place to varying degrees. The contact zone is where non-Han people with extensive land usage interacted with the intensively organized ecumene. Next to the contact zone was the outer zone (which includes Tibet, parts of Xinjiang, and Outer Mongolia), whose extreme cultural and political distance from the ecumene reinforced centrifugal tendencies. Beyond the outer zone were territories within the peripheral zone that fit the Chinese model of the world as "colonial," including dependencies like Korea, Annam, and Burma, or those that had a more tenuous relationship, notably tribute-bearing states such as Afghanistan and Ladakh.

Throughout most of Chinese history, these territories of the inner and outer zones posed complex problems for Han administrators; however, with the coming of other imperial powers in the nineteenth century, the nature of the problem changed. Earlier, there had been no other known power that could challenge the cultural and technological supremacy of the Tianxia empire. Barbarians in the peripheral areas might rise from time to time and conquer China and impose alien rule on it, but such non-Han usurpers quickly adopted the look and lifestyles of traditional Chinese emperors, and did everything they could to uphold the legitimacy and supremacy of imperialism.

A key feature of this system was that it was formed by the "natural" expansion of the Middle Kingdom, not by conquest. Other historical empires were formed by conquest over long distances and even across oceans, and their life span depended on whether their military forces were victorious. This was not the case with China for most of its two thousand years of imperial history. With the exception of the short Mongol period of ninety years, when China was part of the world empire of the Mongols, no armies marched out of the traditional Middle Kingdom lands. The Mongol expeditions that burst far into Eurasia, and across the sea to Japan and Java, were strictly non-Chinese. The successor dynasty of the Ming, which was led by Han Chinese, strongly resisted the Mongol worldview. After three decades of exceptional voyages by Admiral Zheng He early in the fifteenth century to the South China Sea and across the Indian Ocean to the shores of East Africa, the Ming emperors insisted on returning to the control of traditional lands and forbade foreign adventures.[23]

Given these facts, it is worth asking how the Middle Kingdom projected its power and maintained the tributary system. Although force was
occasionally used, hard power is not the only way the Middle Kingdom
exerted its influence on vassal countries. At the normative level, it was
believed that the virtue of the emperor legitimized China's rule. Chinese
philosophy attaches great importance to ethical governance. To maintain power, rulers have to win the "hearts of all peoples." This kind of
philosophical thinking was also reflected in China's relations with vassal
countries, as emperors placed great emphasis on the power of virtue and
often took a high moral tone. Because the emperor asserted himself to
be the son of the Heaven, who ruled all mankind, including Chinese and
barbarians, the emperor was expected to treat vassal countries and their
people justly and benevolently. For instance, Hongwu, the first emperor
of the Ming, used to assure his tributaries that "every land on which
the sun and moon shine I look on with the same benevolence."[24] In
the tributary system, the Middle Kingdom was the creator of the world
order and the major provider of public goods. Though this world order
was hierarchical, it was widely accepted by other countries. By receiv-
ing the symbolic submission of vassal countries, the Middle Kingdom
further enhanced its centrality and superiority. Most emperors knew that
they should avoid overstretching the Middle Kingdom's power. Khubilai's
failed military actions against the Southeast Asian countries demonstrated
that it might be easy to achieve victory at the beginning, but it would
be difficult to rule neighboring countries in the long run. Therefore, it
was more sensible to take a defensive stance and maintain the nominal
dominant-submissive relationship.

Vassal countries embraced this hierarchical system for different reasons. It cannot be denied that the Middle Kingdom was a military
threat to them in some historical periods. Although Khubilai's invasion
was finally frustrated, ruling elites in Southeast Asia probably drew the
conclusion that they could defeat Chinese armies, but only after suffering terrible devastation, and that a successful defense of territory
was no guarantee that another invasion would not follow.[25] Therefore,
they chose to recognize China's status of suzerain. Meanwhile, China
also provided protection to vassal countries and acted as an arbitra-

tor. A vassal country often chose to use the Middle Kingdom to balance other powers in the subregion. Another important motive was
trade, which was the lifeline of some vassal countries. According to John
Fairbank, the tributary system was a political framework for trading
states. Countries looking to trade with China were expected to do so
as tributaries. Thus, their trade must be regarded as a boon granted to
their ruler by the emperor and must be accompanied by the formalities
of presenting tribute through missions to China.[26] Usually, the principal
economic problem was the conflict of interest over trade, but the rulers
of China declared themselves ready to sacrifice economic substance to
preserve political form.[27] Martin Stuart-Fox asserts:

> Small kingdoms like Melaka and Brunei, that feared being
> absorbed by powerful neighbouring mandalas, eagerly sought
> protection. Medium polities such as Champa and Cambodia,
> worried about pressures from neighbors, looked to China to
> maintain the status quo. Larger kingdoms such as Vietnam or
> Ayutthaya, expansionist themselves, resisted intervention, while
> promoting trade with China.[28]

Another important source of the Middle Kingdom's power was its
cultural superiority. Fairbank and S.Y. Têng argue that the tributary system was a natural outgrowth of the cultural preeminence of the early
Chinese.[29] This helps to explain the longevity of the tributary system
despite the waxing and waning of dynastic power. Shogo Suzuki notes
that in some cases member states even remained loyal to a deposed
Chinese dynasty, citing Korea's Yi Dynasty of the seventeenth century.
In spite of increasing coercion by the newly established Qing Dynasty,
the Koreans remained loyal to the Ming, which cannot be explained
by power-based international theories. Suzuki argues that if the tributary system was sustained only by military threats and material benefits,
we should expect constant cost and benefit recalculations whenever
China's power and concomitant ability to provide material carrots
and sticks declined. There is no evidence that China's neighbors had
sought to overthrow the tributary system until Japan did so in the late

nineteenth century.[30] One possible explanation is cultural affinity. Some have argued that in the early fifteenth century, the Japanese shogun Ashikaga Yoshimitsu sought Chinese investiture simply because of "the factor of Chinese prestige in Japan."[31]

THE TRIBUTARY SYSTEM IN CONTRAST TO IMPERIALISM

The tributary system has several characteristics that differentiate it from imperialism. First of all, it was not established to transfer economic resources to the suzerain. As a matter of fact, the Chinese emperor accepted tributes from vassal countries and gave more expensive presents in return. Tribute from foreign countries recognized the legitimacy of the emperor as the son of the Heaven and the cultural superiority of the Middle Kingdom, and this satisfied the court. Because the emperor claimed the mandate of the Heaven, it was important that the barbarians acknowledge his rule. If not, how could the emperor convince the Chinese that he was the son of the Heaven? As argued by Fairbank, "the important thing to the rulers of China was the moral value of tribute. The important thing to the barbarians was the material value of trade."[32] The Middle Kingdom gave up some economic interests in exchange for recognition, whereas foreign countries joined the system voluntarily for the material incentives. As a consequence, a balance of interests formed and the system continued.

The submission of the barbarians and their acknowledgment of the emperors' virtue were ritualistic. In a certain sense, the tributary system was more closely related to paying respect to the court than to real strategic interests. Chinese bureaucrats even redrafted correspondence from foreign rulers to make it more submissive. Some scholars think that the Chinese Court required foreign envoys to kowtow to the emperor to humiliate barbarians. As a matter of fact, the kowtow was the necessary ritual for all meeting the son of the Heaven, including Chinese officials.

Sometimes the tributary relationship was sustained nominally to save the face of the court. For instance, after the Ming were defeated in Vietnam in 1428, the tributary relationship was restored. Vietnam was no longer a province of China, but a nominal vassal. In the early nineteenth century, despite the decline of China's power, there was a decided increase in tribute missions, which were motivated by material incentives. Fairbank insightfully argued that "possibly this prostitution of the tributary system for commercial ends served to confirm the Chinese idea of superiority just when it was most urgently necessary to get rid of it."[33] In this sense, the tributary system was defensive in nature.[34] The royal court was unwilling to intervene in regional affairs, as long as vassal countries demonstrated their respect for the Middle Kingdom. It waited for foreign countries to approach voluntarily. Whoever wanted to develop a relationship with the Middle Kingdom had to accept the supremacy of the Chinese emperor. As argued by T. F. Tsiang:

> Out of this period of intense struggle and bitter humiliation [the eleventh and twelfth centuries], the neo-Confucian philosophy, which began then to dominate China, worked out a dogma in regard to international relations, to hold sway in China right to the middle of the nineteenth century.... That dogma asserts that national security could only be found in isolation and stipulates that whoever wished to enter into relations with China must do so as China's vassal.... It must not be construed to be a dogma of conquest or universal dominion, for it imposed nothing on foreign peoples who chose to remain outside the Chinese world.[35]

The tributary system was also an open system. Its openness was embodied in many aspects, including culture diversity. The *Interpretations of Rites* (500 BC) said:

> It is proper to learn values from others whereas unjust to impose one's values onto the others. Or to say, the values are to be learnt by rather than to be taught to the others.[36]

In practice, though the Middle Kingdom claimed cultural superiority, Chinese culture was constantly influenced by foreign cultures. Consider, for instance, the spread of Buddhism in China. According to Chinese

philosophy, there are fundamental differences between harmony and similarity. Similarity is viewed as a bad thing, because it destroys the variety of
the world and the creativity of life. In contrast, harmonious coexistence
and cooperation—of different things, for instance—bring about better
results. Politically, the Chinese Court neither acted actively to prevent
other major powers from exerting influence nor forced vassal countries
to choose their side. Many vassal countries did not place only China
at the apex of the international hierarchy. In the seventeenth century,
Siam accorded similar recognition to ambassadors from Mughal India
and Persia as they did to envoys from China. Stuart-Fox argued that India
was always an alternative pole of attraction for Buddhist kingdoms for the
same reason that Mecca was for Muslim politics:[37]

> For all their acceptance of the Chinese world order, Southeast
> Asian kingdoms never saw themselves as committed to that order
> alone. Their foreign relations cultures, while hierarchical, recog-
> nized several potentially competing centers of power, and made
> allowance for shifting power relationships.[38]

TIANXIA AND CHINA'S IDENTITY IN THE CONTEMPORARY WORLD ORDER

Vassal countries stopped sending missions to the Qing Court in the late
nineteenth century, leading to the collapse of the tributary system. Since
that time, China has learned from the West how to become a great power
and behave like one. Understandably, China's conception of the "international order" also tends to be based on the Western model, jettisoning the feudal idea of the tributary system. As Wang Gungwu stressed,
despite the long history of the tributary system, China has accepted the
independence of both Korea and Vietnam. It has also acknowledged the
independence of the Mongolian Republic.[39] Thus, "the references to a
possible return to a threatening tributary system in the future not only
misrepresent the system to imply dominance and potential expansionism,

but are also anachronistic. Given the system of nation-states and the inter-dependent networks of a market economy, any return to a system largely based on feudalistic relations is unacceptable, even to the Chinese."[40]

Today, the Chinese no longer believe that China is the Middle Kingdom; nor do they believe that China's external relations can be established and maintained by a feudal system like the tributary system. However, the transformed mindset of Tianxia continues to be relevant, when China is fast rising as a great power. Since the beginning of modern times, China and other states in the region, many of which were within its tributary system, have struggled to achieve an independent sovereign status. A world of sovereign states does not contradict China's old idea of Tianxia, except that China can no longer regard itself as the center of the world. A Tianxia system without China as the center is completely new to the Chinese and to the rest of the world.

The effort to reconceptualize the Tianxia system and reinterpret the tributary system serves at least three purposes. First, it is expected that doing so will lead to the development of Chinese theories of international relations. The Chinese saw that the Western discourse on international relations, be it realism or liberalism, has dominated the interpretation of the international behavior of sovereign states, including China. This discourse has been very powerful in helping the West search for its identity and exercise soft power worldwide. Without its own theories of international relations, the Chinese doubt that their country will construct an identity capable of convincing the outside world. Second, it can help the Chinese understand the current America-dominated system, including identifying common characteristics between it and the Chinese-dominated tributary system. And third, such reflections will help guide China's international behavior, particularly its relations with the most powerful, namely, the United States. Should China behave like a "tributary state" toward the United States and wait for the latter's decline, or should it rise to challenge the United States? The Chinese believe that they can learn a great deal by considering their own past.

The Chinese are conscious that the norms of behavior and discourse of the existing order have been established by the West, and that these norms come from a distinct political culture that evolved from a particular state system in Europe. The Chinese accepted these norms for practical as well as cultural reasons. At the practical level, to accept them is to protect China's sovereignty and national integrity, given that this order recognizes each member's sovereignty. At the cultural level, the Chinese were confident that they could learn much from another culture. Alastair Iain Johnston convincingly shows how China was socialized by the West to be a more cooperative partner in international relations.[41]

However, there is also another, and probably far more important, reason for the Chinese to accept the existing international order: They have a deep cultural belief in "the prevalence and inevitability of change."[42] For the Chinese, the only proposition that does not change is that everything else is subject to change, a belief that stems from the *Book of Change*—"the nearest thing to a universal guide to Chinese thought and action ever since their civilization emerged some 5,000 years ago."[43] The state system of the great powers is not fixed, and it has itself been evolving. China's post-Mao leaders do not find it difficult to join the world. More important, they were willing to change China's existing laws and institutions— or, in Chinese conceptual terms, to gear itself (*jiegui*) to the international order. By accepting and joining this international order, their country is socialized by this order, but other countries can also be socialized by China. The existing international order can be interpreted in different ways. When the Chinese accept it, they have their own expectations. The central question is: What is the ideal international order? Chinese scholars find the answer in the traditional concept of Tianxia, which they had to forsake when their country was weak.

GLOBALIZATION AS A MECHANISM OF POWER RELATIONS

In the contemporary era, China considers that it appreciates globalization more than any other country. At the philosophical level, the Chinese find elements of convergence between globalization and their own tradition of Tianxia, a hierarchical but open interstate system. According to Zhao Tingyang:

All-under-Heaven appears much like globalization, but is essentially different as it contains no such sense of the "-isation." All-Under-Heaven indicates globalism instead.[44]

Moreover, the concept of Tianxia is as rich as that of globalism. Qin Yaqing, the president of China Foreign Affairs University, argues that Tianxia is not only a material concept but also a social, spiritual, and cultural one.[45] Globalization requires corresponding institutions through which global governance can be realized, as does the Tianxia ideal. Globalization intensifies interdependency among states and creates favorable conditions under which cooperation becomes the best choice of states and more states are attracted to join the system, rather than remain outside. A world order (not an international order) with Tianxia becomes more promising due to globalization.

In practice, the Chinese perceive globalization as a mechanism of power relations. Although China does not want to become a revolutionary force in the existing international order, it is a rapidly rising power and thus must find a way to solve the contradiction between maintaining the existing order and pursuing its own rise. It therefore perceives globalization as a mechanism for its peaceful rise. As pointed out by Zheng Bijian—then the executive vice president of the Central Party School, and who proposed the concept of peaceful rise—when China stresses its intended peaceful rise, it puts much emphasis on globalization as the mechanism.[46] The Chinese also see globalization, an important element embedded in the existing system, as a tool, acceptable to other powers, for helping China expand its influence as a great power. Viewing globalization as a dense network in which states influence each other, the Chinese believe that whereas the influence within this network is hierarchical, with great powers exercising more power than small states, the interactions will not be a zero-sum game; instead, it will be a win-win situation.

More important, the Chinese believe that globalization not only enables China to expand its external influence, at least in economic terms and in a peaceful manner, but also leads it to a new international order in a peaceful manner. Globalization has brought China and the international order together, and the two are now mutually transformative. Thus, while China tries to reshape the world, the world also tries to reshape China. In other words, a new international order will not be imposed by any great power or a group of powers but by the interaction among all powers.

After nearly three decades of reform and an open door policy, China is now an integral part of the world economy, an important link in the entire chain of global capitalism. China's expanding role in the world economy has been mainly driven by "invisible hands" (market forces) without a strategic plan on the part of the government. Of course, this does not mean that the "invisible hands" are not without problems in the world market. Sometimes political interference becomes necessary. This is reflected in the massive efforts made by the Chinese leadership in its pursuance of a policy of "going global" (*zou chuqu*) in recent years.[47] To become a global power, China certainly cannot rely on its economic power alone, given that many severe external constraints will need to be overcome by noneconomic factors. China's practice of "resource diplomacy" in recent years is a good example. The Chinese believe that if conflicts arise between China and other powers, it will be easier to solve them within this dense network than outside it.

Recently, China has used the concept "harmonious world" in foreign affairs. In comparison with the earlier concept "peaceful rise," this is more consistent with Tianxia. It is applied widely to relations with the "developing world," participation in international organizations, and the promotion of Chinese culture. The "harmonious world" concept was first introduced at the Afro-Asia summit in Jakarta in 2005 as justification for China's strong push to further diplomatic ties across Central Asia, Africa, and South America. If China's past goal had been to forge a united front for ideological struggle, its current objective is to amass primary resources to further its economic boom. The "harmonious world" theme signals China's intention to remain "nonintrusive" and "noninterventionist," treading carefully to avoid the image of a postmodern colonialist on the prowl.[48] Another logical choice is international organizations, given the overlap between the terminology of "harmonious world" and that of most multilateral organizations. Finally,

China's establishment of hundreds of Confucius Institutes serves to promote Chinese culture around the world, including language-training facilities. All these initiatives are depicted as indications of China's determination to support a "harmonious world."

INTERNATIONAL ORGANIZATIONS AND REGIONALISM

China today appears to be one of the strongest supporters of the world order established by the victors in World War II, treating the United Nations Security Council as the pillar of the existing world order. For the Chinese, although the UN's structure is unable to impose an ideal order on the world, it is the best form of organization that the world has and the only international organization that could constrain the great powers. The Chinese also believe that the UN structure is open to all sovereign states and protects their interests, especially those of small states. Calling for the UN to delegate more power to the developing world, China regards this as the only way to provide a workable model for a multipolar world. China has become proactive in taking part in all kinds of activity under the UN structure.[49] Despite dissatisfaction from time to time, China does not want any revolutionary changes to be introduced to the UN structure, especially its Security Council. It has been cautious about proposals to reform the UN, fearing that changes will undermine the current foundation.

To emphasize the UN structure does not mean that China neglects great power politics. China has actively interacted with the United States and other great powers, either within the UN structure or on a bilateral basis. Although accepting that every sovereign state is equal, China recognizes that an order based on great powers is hierarchical. Yet all powers must be restrained for this order to be sustainable. China is, therefore, trying to develop a balanced and multipolar world order capable of restraining the United States, whose power is often based on its superior military might.[50] The Chinese do not believe that a system devised to serve the interests of a single superpower can be stable for long. From their own past experience of dealing with neighboring states within the Chinese orbit, they understand that what is needed is a "competent hegemony," a strong but responsible power that could protect the world from anarchy.[51] At this stage, China is not capable of becoming such a competent hegemon. Only the United States can perform such a role. In this sense, China does not seek to challenge the United States itself; nor does it expect other countries to do so.[52] According to Wang Jisi, "in the long term, the decline of U.S. primacy and the subsequent transition to a multipolar world are inevitable; but in the short term, Washington's power is unlikely to decline, and its position in world affairs is unlikely to change."[53] What China can do is to work with the United States closely to push it toward that goal.

Furthermore, the Chinese are confident that they can work with the United States and other great powers, because, as Wang Gungwu argued, Chinese culture tends to stress a humanistic rationality that is compatible with the Enlightenment histories experienced by the other four permanent members of the United Nations Security Council— the United States, Russia, Britain, and France. The Chinese see their civilization as comparable to that of others, and they believe that there are no serious obstacles to absorbing modern values.[54] China wants to see a world that recognizes its own rightful place in world history, one in which it can make its own distinctive inputs. Toward this goal, China has accepted a rule-based global market system. More important, China has learned, by trial and error, how to make a contribution to the existing system, such as offering alternative routes to development that have worked better than those offered by the World Bank and International Monetary Fund models.

In Southeast Asia, a China-centered economic order has arisen as a natural outgrowth of China's economic expansion and as a harbinger of a "harmonious world," in the eyes of many Chinese. The end of the Cold War facilitated a readjustment in China's policies toward neighboring states. In 2004, Hu Jintao reportedly pointed this out in an internal speech, asserting that "China's opportunities and challenges—lie in (its relations with) peripheral countries; the latter provide China with hope, but also can be a source of instability."[55] As China rises and there is more conflict in Sino-U.S. relations, neighboring states will be crucial in bilateral relations as well as in China's rise. To enhance its status in the region and reassure its neighbors, one effective strategy is to enable them to benefit economically. In 2003, Wen Jiabao first put forward the policy of building "an amiable neighborhood, a tranquil neighborhood, and a prosperous neighborhood."[56] China offered a number of sweeteners to the ASEAN countries beyond what its economic interests would justify, and its trade deficit with ASEAN skyrocketed; at the same time, states in Southeast Asia have become more dependent on China. Although some warn that this will lead to Sinocentrism, the region remains open to outside powers. The "harmonious world" ideal, however vague it remains, has not been interpreted as Sinocentrism or even Tianxia.

CONCLUSION

Modern international relations concepts and theories are based on the historical experience of European countries. Chinese scholars once imported these concepts and theories and applied them to explain the world, including China itself, while Western scholars also interpreted China from the Eurocentric perspective. Westernization is largely confined to the economic realm. In the intellectual world, vestiges of Chinese tradition are still exerting influence on the mindset of the Chinese as well as on their behavior. It is reasonable to expect that with China's continuous rise, the influence of its traditions will become even greater. As China gains more economic power, the Chinese tend to become increasingly dissatisfied with importing values from the West and are eagerly seeking to revive their own philosophies and traditions. The international relations studies community has greatly facilitated the emergence of Tianxia identity. Many Chinese look back to traditional philosophical thinking, and their academic efforts further influence decisionmaking on the part of the state. Chinese leaders now tend to borrow more and more from their traditional philosophy to elaborate on China's foreign policy, concepts, and theories that were long badly under attack by the Chinese themselves when they lost confidence in their own traditions in modern times. Moreover, because of its newly gained economic power, China has more means to exert influence and shape the international order according to its civilizational imagination and historical memory. In the process, China is clarifying its national identity and is seeking to inform the world how it will behave when it becomes a dominant power.

In comparison with modern international relations concepts and theories in the West, the Tianxia system adopts fundamentally different assumptions and presents an alternative conceptual framework. It assumes that the international order is hierarchical but based on reciprocal relations. It also develops a different understanding of power. If the dominant state wants to maintain its status, it should not rely only on hard power; morality (virtue) and the capability to build a commonly accepted world order are just as important. The tributary system is different from imperialism in the West. Although the Middle Kingdom was on top of the regional hierarchy, the submission of vassal countries was symbolic and was driven by material and cultural incentives. The power of the Middle Kingdom came from its cultural superiority and the economic opportunities it provided to vassal countries.

Although the tributary system collapsed, the old idea of Tianxia is still relevant. For the Chinese, the world of sovereign states does not contradict it. In the real world, the hierarchy among states still exists, though nominal equality is recognized. The Chinese perceive convergence between the Tianxia system and modern phenomena and institutions such as globalization, the United Nations, and regional integration. The difference is that China can no longer regard itself as the center of the world. The Tianxia mentality continues to influence China's international behavior. Although China has begun to join and benefit from the international system, it also relies on its newly gained economic strength and establishes reciprocal relationships with its neighbors that give it a leading regional status. This contributes to the Tianxia mindset, yet it does not mean that China is trying to revive the feudal tributary system. China regards the principle of sovereignty as the most important mechanism to protect itself as well as other states from unjustified intervention by great powers. Chinese perceptions of the international order now are a mixture of Western and Chinese experiences. China can neither go back to its own traditional practice of foreign policy nor become another Western power. In this sense, China and the world are mutually transformative. The Chinese will confidently draw on their own tradition of external relations to guide their behavior in international affairs, while believing that China can make a civilized contribution to the future order.

NOTES

1   Lowell Dittmer and Samuel Kim, "Whither China's Quest for National Identity?" in *China's Quest for National Identity*, edited by Lowell Dittmer and Samuel Kim (Ithaca, N.Y.: Cornell University Press, 1993), 240.

2   Alastair Iain Johnston, *Social States: China in International Institutions, 1980–2000* (Princeton, N.J.: Princeton University Press, 2008).

3   See Lowell Dittmer, "China's New Internationalism," in *China Turns to Multilateralism: Foreign Policy and Regional Security*, edited by Guoguang Wu and Helen Lansdowne (London: Routledge, 2008), 21–34.

4   Denny Roy, "Consequences of China's Economic Growth for Asia-Pacific Security," *Security Dialogue* 24, no. 3 (June 1993): 182, 184; Denny Roy, "Hegemon on the Horizon? China's Threat to East Asian Security," *International Security* 19, no. 1 (Summer 1994): 156; Aaron Friedberg, "Ripe for Rivalry: Prospects for Peace in a Multipolar Asia," *International Security* 18, no. 3 (Winter 1993–94): 5–33; Gerald Segal, "East Asia and the Constrainment of China," *International Security* 20, no. 4 (Spring 1996): 107–35; Gideon Rachman, "Containing China," *Washington Quarterly* 19, no. 1 (Winter 1996): 131–33; Robert S. Ross, "The Geography of the Peace: East Asia in the Twenty-First Century," *International Security* 23, no. 4 (Spring 1999): 81–119.

5   For a summary of the cases for and against viewing China as a threat, see Denny Roy, "The 'China Threat' Issue: Major Arguments," *Asian Survey* 36, no. 8 (August 1996): 758–65. Also see Audrey Kurth Cronin and Patrick M. Cronin, "The Realistic Engagement of China," *Washington Quarterly* 19, no. 1 (Winter 1996): 144–46. For a depiction of China's nonimperialist tendencies, see Chen Jian, "Will China's Development Threaten Asia-Pacific Security?" *Security Dialogue* 24, no. 2 (June 1993): 193–94.

6   Deng Ziliang and Zheng Yongnian, "China Reshapes the World Economy," in *China and the New International Order*, edited by Wang Gungwu and Zheng Yongnian (London: Routledge, 2008), 127–48.

7   Michael Vatikiotis and Murray Hiebert, "How China Is Building an Empire," *Far Eastern Economic Review*, November 2003, 30.

8   See, e.g., David Shambaugh, "Return to the Middle Kingdom? China and
     Asia in the Early Twenty-First Century," in *Power Shift: China and Asia's New
     Dynamics*, edited by David Shambaugh (Berkeley: University of California Press,
     2006), 23–47.

9   Alastair Iain Johnston employed a constructivist approach to reinterpret
     China's international behavior in the Ming dynasty. His book *Cultural Realism*
     shows how Western scientific approaches could be used in constructing a
     theory of China's international behavior; see Alastair Iain Johnston, *Cultural
     Realism: Strategic Culture and Grand Strategy in Chinese History* (Princeton,
     N.J.: Princeton University Press, 1995). For a criticism, see Anthony A. Loh,
     "Deconstructing *Cultural Realism*," in *China and the New International Order*,
     ed. Wang and Zheng, 281–309. For David Kang, China's rise makes it possible
     for the country to become a source of stability in the region; see David
     Kang, *China Rising: Peace, Power, and Order in East Asia* (New York: Columbia
     University Press, 2007).

10   On the establishment of a Chinese school of international relations studies, see
     Ren Xiao, "Toward a Chinese School of International Relations?" in *China and
     the New International Order*, ed. Wang and Zheng, 293–309. The issue is more
     broadly framed by Wang Gungwu, "Nationalism and Its Historians," in *Bind Us
     in Time: Nation and Civilization in Asia*, by Wang Gungwu (Singapore: Eastern
     Universities Press, 2003), 12.

11   See, e.g., Xuetong Yan and Jin Xu, eds., *Pre-Qin Chinese Thoughts on Foreign
     Relations* (Shanghai: Fudan University Press, 2008).

12   Zhao Tingyang, *Tianxia: Shijie zhidu zhexue daolun* (Nanjing: Jiangsu jiaoyu
     chubanshe, 2005); Zhao Tingyang, *Huai shijie yanjiu, zuowei diyi zhexue de
     zhengzhi zhexu* (Beijing: People's University Press, 2009).

13   *China and the New International Order*, ed. Wang and Zheng, is a collection of
     papers presented during that conference.

14   The participants examined the continuities and discontinuities of Chinese
     traditional foreign behavior. See Yongnian Zheng, ed., *China and International
     Relations: The Chinese View and the Contribution of Wang Gungwu* (London:
     Routledge, 2010).

15   Zhao Tingyang, "Rethinking Empire from a Chinese Concept 'All-Under-
     Heaven' (Tian-xia)," *Social Identities* 12, no. 1 (January 2006): 39.

16   Ibid., 30.

17   Zhao Tingyang, *Huai shijie yanjiu*, 80.

18   Ibid., 78–79.

19   Ibid., 117–18.

20   Zhao argues that cultural discrimination against "periphery areas" or "barbarians"
     is an infringement of the All-Under-Heaven system, insisting that such prejudice
     by Confucians emerged under the threat of other nations or invasions.

21   Zhao Tingyang, *Huai shijie yanjiu*, 92–93.

22 Joseph B. R. Whitney, *China: Area, Administration, and Nation Building*, Research Paper 123 (Chicago: Department of Geography, University of Chicago, 1970), 26–45.

23 Gungwu Wang, *The Chinese Way: China's Position in International Relations* (Oslo: Scandinavian University Press, 1995), 54.

24 Martin Stuart-Fox, *A Short History of China and Southeast Asia: Tribute, Trade and Influence* (Sydney: Allen & Unwin, 2003), 74.

25 Ibid., 67.

26 John K. Fairbank, "A Preliminary Framework," in *The Chinese World Order: Traditional Chinese Foreign Relations*, edited by John K. Fairbank (Cambridge, Mass.: Harvard University Press, 1968), 4.

27 Ibid., 12.

28 Stuart-Fox, *Short History*, 92.

29 J. K. Fairbank and S. Y. Têng, "On the Ch'ing Tributary System," *Harvard Journal of Asiatic Studies* 6, no. 2 (June 1941): 137.

30 Shogo Suzuki, *Civilization and Empire, China and Japan's Encounter with European International Society* (London: Routledge, 2009), 41–51.

31 Wang Yi-T'ung, *Official Relations between China and Japan 1368–1594* (Cambridge, Mass.: Harvard University Press, 1953), 35.

32 J. K. Fairbank, "Tributary Trade and China's Relations with the West," *Far Eastern Quarterly* 1, no. 2 (February 1942): 139.

33 Ibid., 145.

34 Ibid.

35 T. F. Tsiang, "China and European Expansion," *Politica* 2, no. 5 (March 1936): 3–4, quoted by Fairbank and Têng, "On the Ch'ing Tributary System," 141.

36 *Interpretations of Rites* (500 BC), chapter on Qu-li, quoted by Zhao Tingyang, "Rethinking Empire," 36.

37 Stuart-Fox, *Short History*, 94.

38 Ibid.

39 Wang Gungwu, *China and Southeast Asia: Myths, Threats and Culture* (Singapore: World Scientific and Singapore University Press, 1999), 33.

40 Wang Gungwu, *China and Southeast Asia*, 34.

41 Alastair Iain Johnston, *Social States: China in International Institutions, 1980–2000* (Princeton, N.J.: Princeton University Press, 2008).

42 Wang Gungwu, "China and the International Order: Some Historical Perspectives," in *China and the New International Order*, ed. Wang and Zheng, 23.

43 Ibid.

44 Zhao Tingyang, "Rethinking Empire," 39.

45 Qin Yaqing, "Introduction II," in *World Politics, Views from China*, vol. 1, edited by Wang Jisi and Qin Yaqing (Beijing: Heping Press, 2007), xix.

46 Bijian Zheng, "China's 'Peaceful Rise' to Great Power Status," *Foreign Affairs* 84, no. 5 (2005): 18–24. Also see Zheng Bijian, *Lun Zhongguo heping jueqi fazhan xin daolu* (Beijing: Zhonggong zhongyang dangxiao chubanshe, 2005).

47 Yongjin Zhang, *China Goes Global* (London: Foreign Policy Center, 2005); Deng Ziliang and Yongnian Zheng, "China Reshapes the World Economy," in *China and the New International Order*, ed. Wang and Zheng, 127–48.

48 "Mbeki Warns on China-Africa Ties," BBC News, December 14, 2006.

49 Bates Gill and James Reilly, "Sovereignty, Intervention and Peacekeeping: The View from Beijing," *Survival* 42, no. 3 (2000): 41–59.

50 On multipolarity, see Yong Deng, "Hegemon on the Offensive: Chinese Perspectives of U. S. Global Strategy," *Political Science Quarterly* 116, no. 3 (2001): 343–65; Qin Yaqing, "A Response to Yong Deng: Power, Perception and the Cultural Lens," *Asian Affairs: An American Review* 28, no. 3 (2001): 155–59; and Yan Xuetong, "The New Trend in the Power Configuration of the International System," *Contemporary International Relations*, no. 10 (2005): 5–7.

51 Wang Gungwu, "China and the International Order," 28.

52 Jin Canrong, "The U.S. Global Strategy in the Post–Cold War Era and Its Implications for China–United States Relations: A Chinese Perspective," *Journal of Contemporary China* 10, no. 27 (2001); Jia Qingguo, "Learning to Live with the Hegemon: Evolution of China's Policy toward the U.S. since the End of the Cold War," *Journal of Contemporary China* 14, no. 44 (2005); Shen Dingli, "The Decline of the U.S. May Not Be a Good Thing," *Global Times*, December 19, 2005.

53 Jisi Wang, "China's Search for Stability with America," *Foreign Affairs* 84, no. 5 (2005): 39–48; the quotation is on p. 40.

54 Wang Gungwu, "China and the International Order," 29.

55 Quoted by Mingjiang Li, "Explaining China's Proactive Engagement in Asia," in *Living with China: Regional States and China through Crises and Turning Points*, edited by Shiping Tang, Mingjiang Li, and Amitav Achary (London: Palgrave Macmillan, 2009), 31.

56 "Wen Jiabao Highlighted China's Policy of 'Building an Amiable Neighborhood, a Tranquil Neighborhood, and a Prosperous Neighborhood,'" *China Youth Daily*, October 8, 2003.

PART II

NATIONAL IDENTITY GAPS AND THE UNITED STATES

INTRODUCTION:

THE U.S. FACTOR AND EAST ASIAN NATIONAL IDENTITY GAPS

Gilbert Rozman

National identities influence bilateral relations, but to explain systematically how this happens one needs a framework for moving beyond the identities of individual states to a dyadic approach. For this purpose, I introduce the concept of national identity gaps. These are measures of how substantial and sensitive differences in identities are. States with a narrower gap arguably have an easier time improving bilateral relations than those with a wider gap. Of course, serious bilateral clashes may occur between states in close proximity that share many civilizational attributes in common. The degree of gap is clearly not a function of how different their civilizational background is. Instead, I look to other attributes of national identity in order to specify how gaps can be calculated. This means recognizing that some states achieve special meaning in the way they are treated as part of the identity of other states. They are "significant others." Bilateral relations in East Asia involve states having this kind of significance and operating in ways that reveal the presence of a gap at an elevated level. For each of the major East Asian states, there is also considerable sensitivity about national identity issues centered on the United States.

The six-dimensional approach developed for the earlier study of national identities that was used to demonstrate the East Asian National Identity Syndrome can be extended to the study of gaps.[1] For the ideological dimension, I ask how much country B matters for the ideological identity of country A. Whether the ideology is Communist, progressive, or conservative, it can vary in the degree to which it depends on assertions about another country to justify its appeal, marginalizing a centrist worldview. In the temporal dimension, country B's meaning for A is separated for premodern / pre–Cold War history, for the Cold War era, and for the post–Cold War period. Obviously, if country A focuses on country B in all these periods, the meaning will be compounded. For the sectoral dimension, there is possible meaning in country B's presence for cultural, economic, and political identity. Claims that country A is unique and presumably superior in one or more of these aspects may come at the expense of positive views of country B and shared global practices. For the vertical dimension, the critical question is whether country B is perceived as interfering with country A's sovereignty. By influencing the intermediate level, such as nongovernmental organizations with the goal of promoting civil society, or the state level, is it regarded as an identity problem? Most clearly, the horizontal dimension refers to the relative significance of foreign states, especially the United States, but also neighbors as they figure in Asian regionalism. If the dimension of intensity drew separate attention in the syndrome, calculating the strength of the other five dimensions of gaps already offers a measure of it. Taking the dyad as the basic unit of international relations and assessing the intensity for each dimension on both sides, the approach here allows one to estimate a composite score for the five dimensions.

Countries that face each other with mainly national interests in mind are likely to take a pragmatic, problem-solving approach. Although their national identities may focus on different ideals, their gap is zero. In contrast, countries obsessed with each other for their significance in influencing national identity may score high on the gap index, even in the most extreme case reaching the maximum score of 5 on each dimension and a total score of 25. Estimating national identity gaps according to a scale of 1 to 5 allows comparison across time and space. If two countries demonize each other with little restraint, the score is 5. If they are prone to criticize each other harshly but in limited respects, then a middle range score of 3 applies. And if they are significant for each other but have largely kept national identity concerns to the side-lines, a score of 1 is appropriate. One does not need precise measures of each dimension of identity to approximate the score on the basis of the evidence given in a wide range of publications. The final tally is the sum for all five dimensions.

The gap may be driven largely by one country's obsession with the other. In that case, the combined score for each dimension would be less than 5 and the total tabulation would be well short of 25. With this approach, one can estimate the scale of a gap; its one-sidedness, which would be indicative of unrequited antipathy; and its composition across dimensions. This first stab at estimations is only intended to be sugges-tive of the relative size of identity gaps. They await refinement through methods such as content analysis applied with precision. The following sections cover the five dimensions separately and then tabulate the total for each of the three dyadic relationships. Taking late 2010 as the base-line, we will be in a position to keep track of subsequent transforma-tions in identity gaps as a factor in bilateral relations.

THE IDEOLOGICAL DIMENSION

Despite claims that East Asian states do not permit ideology to interfere with ties to other countries (e.g., the Yoshida Doctrine focusing on Japan as an "economic merchant," Deng Xiaoping's image of pure pragmatism with an "open door" to all, and South Korea in the post–Cold War era putting anticommunism behind it with "all-around diplomacy"), I find evidence that ideologies are a major source of identity gaps. Revisionists in Japan, progressives in South Korea, and China's fervent Communists each resisted advice from diplomats on how to manage bilateral rela-tions. They were driven by assumptions about national identity to deny a tone of compromise in favor of one of resistance. Such leaders as Prime Minister Li Peng, President Roh Moo-hyun, and Prime Minister Abe Shinzo were seen as holding strong ideological views, gathering around themselves others who were like-minded. An ideological leader could strategically seek to narrow an identity gap, but that does not mean that eventually ideological changes sought by the leader's supporting group would not exert a powerful impact on perceptions of bilateral relations.

None of these forces had an unrestrained voice in bilateral relations. In 2005, their impact seemed to peak, as Koizumi Junichiro persisted in visiting the Yasukuni Shrine each year, despite negative ramifications; Roh turned decisively against Japan over the Dokdo/Takeshima Island territorial issue, which was wrapped in history; Hu Jintao countenanced massive demonstrations against Japan, as it sought permanent membership in the United Nations Security Council, in spite of failing to address its historical transgressions appropriately; and Chinese leaders approved writings claiming that the ancient Koguryo state was really Chinese, reviving memories of Sinocentrism. As diplomats made progress in overcoming each of these problems, none was fully resolved. In 2008, Sino-Japanese diplomacy sustained a two-year record of keeping the lid on history issues, Japanese–South Korean relations kept putting out small ground fires over history under the stewardship of Lee Myung-bak, and even Sino–South Korean relations appeared to have moved beyond the Koguryo issue. We see a record of smoldering identity issues under control for a time, but they could be explosive if put in a revived ideological perspective. Although this did not happen in Japan or South Korea, it did in China, where ideological boosters not only had not relinquished power but also were waiting for growing confidence in national power to press their case.

In 2010, Japan's ideological forces had only a minor impact. South Korea's had also receded. China was the exception, because ideology was a rising force. If the revisionists in Japan had earlier raised the ideological gap toward South Korea and especially China to a level of 2 out of 5, after the election of the Democratic Party of Japan, the score fell toward South Korea to as low as 1 and, with Hatoyama's encouragement, did not at first rise toward China, despite new concerns. Only China's provocations reversed this trend, as revisionists jumped on the bandwagon of alarm by embracing ideological differences. Yet Japanese ideology was secondary, mostly a response to China's demonization of Japan. If one combines a 5 for China and a 3 for Japan, the score for this one-sided gap reaches 4. Ideological diatribes against Japan in late 2010 put this relationship at risk, intensifying the identity gap.

Despite growing concern over Sinocentrism and less deference by conservatives, the South Korean score toward China was just 2 out of 5, but it had risen from 1 a few years earlier. Anticommunism was now a minor force. After many years during which the ideology of Korean victimization had concentrated on Japan and downplayed China, it was now possible to envision China's score exceeding Japan's. On the Chinese side, the decisions to demonize South Korea with both an ideological and a historical emphasis, charging that it was under the sway of Cold War thinking, widened the gap sharply. If the prior gap with South Korea had risen to 2 as a mark of dissatisfaction with Lee Myung-bak, it jumped to 4 in 2010. The joint score was 3. As discussed below, China was demonizing South Korean national identity, although not as vehemently as it vilified Japanese national identity.

With progressives out of power and conservatives putting priority elsewhere, I estimate that South Korea scored 3 of 5 in dealing with Japan after reaching a figure of 4. In turn, the Japanese score toward South Korea had fallen to a 1, because the leadership of the Democratic Party of Japan, more than that of the Liberal Democratic Party, was intent on improving the atmosphere for relations. The joint score of 2 again reflects a one-sided gap, driven by ideological arguments on the Korean side.

Chinese ideological reinvigoration made its weight felt on identity gaps, although Japanese and South Korean restraint put a brake on them. Estimating the scale of the gaps being driven by ideologically charged leaders produces a scale with the Sino-Japanese at the top, the Sino–South Korean gap rising to the middle, and the Japanese–South Korean gap narrowing to the bottom rung on the scale by 2010. Each gap was one-sided in nature.

These estimates of 4 for Sino-Japanese relations, 3 for Sino–South Korean ties, and 2 for Japanese–South Korean ties in 2010 suggest the relative scale of identity gaps under the influence of ideology. All the gaps had been changing in recent years. Given the role of ideology in an emboldened China, these identity gaps have little likelihood of closing.

The ideological dimension is active in setting a negative tone in all three dyads when seen from both sides. In 2007 Abe Shinzo thought better about applying it to China, and in 2008 Lee Myung-bak tempered

sharp emotions toward Japan, while Hu Jintao did not allow the nationalist fervor during the Beijing Olympics to drive diplomacy toward Japan.
Yet in 2010 the ideological dimension further strained two East Asian
dyads, climbing to levels unseen since the normalization of bilateral relations. More strident ideology in China became the main factor heightening this dimension in the dyad, with a more conservative South Korea
and with a long-vilified Japan. If Chinese animosity is mostly unrequited,
a one-sided gap also has a tendency to arouse the other side. The de-ide-
ologization seen in Japanese–South Korean relations is also partly China's
doing, a sign that national identity gaps are interrelated and can be greatly
influenced by changes in the ideology of one state.

THE TEMPORAL DIMENSION

Although there was positive recall of shared premodern histories for more
than a thousand years, memories fixated on divisive forces in one era or
another were powerful enough to widen the national identity gap, with
spillover to other eras. The Chinese focus on how Japan joined the forces
of humiliation, causing the gravest damage to their nation and to their
political national identity. Allowing demonization of Japan for the period
from the 1890s to 1940s to fester contributed to criticism of Japan for all
periods. Koreans assail Japan, above all in the 1900s to 1940s, and they also
assail China in the premodern era for treading on their nation's political
national identity and suppressing its cultural national identity. Even the
Japanese have managed to assuage their postwar guilt with views of these
neighbors in the Cold War era and beyond denying Japan's positive history, intending to damage its political and cultural national identity. With
such fixations about the past, there is very little room to recover a shared
history. If the Sino-Japanese summits of the years 2007–8 produced gestures of respect for shared cultural history from the highest leaders, they
drew little notice against a setting where China was intent on showcasing
an extreme gap. Despite the fact that the premodern era held promise
as the best chance to narrow differences, in 2010 Chinese criticisms of
premodern Japan and Korea were exacerbating the gaps.

The specter of the 1930s and 1940s looms over national identities in these three states. And it is not receding. China decided to reemphasize it in the 1990s as part of a blueprint to give greater legitimacy to the Communist Party. A democratic South Korea faced increasing public pressure to retaliate against Japan's wavering on historical apologies. Moreover, a troubled post–bubble economy Japan offered more space for historical revisionism among its conservative leadership. Joint history projects have failed to narrow the gaps. In 2010, a more assertive China gave vent to wide-ranging historical criticisms of Japan, while the preference for North Korea as the heir to the anti-Japanese forces puts South Korea in a less favorable light, even for the wartime period and especially in the early postwar years.

Memories of the Cold War era are less intense. Japanese guilt toward China and a sense that it was on the periphery of the Cold War exploring a "friendship" policy, even when diplomatic relations were not possible, calm emotions. Successive improvements in ties in the 1970s and 1980s leave images of a sort of "golden age." Japanese–South Korean normalization was slowed up to 1965 and political ties only haltingly improved in the 1980s, so memories remain ambivalent without specific symbols of humiliation. Sino–South Korean memories could be most troubled because they were adversaries in the Korean War, but the South devoted so much effort to boosting ties in the years 1988–92 that the cloud over this era was partially lifted. Yet, China is reviving antagonistic memories with its reaffirmation in concert with North Korea of the glorious nature of the Korean War and with a reemphasis on the Cold War as a just struggle against anticommunism. The result is that the national identity gaps in looking back to the Cold War era are widening. Meanwhile, all three states center much of their attention for this period on the United States, leaving others as secondary concerns.

The post–Cold War era has redirected ambivalence about each other's significance for national identity. The Chinese and South Koreans have intermittently refocused on Japan, blaming rising rightist forces for offending their sense of national honor. The Japanese, in turn, blame these neighbors for repeatedly raising the history issue, defaming their honor, and giving no credit to current-day Japan for its positive contributions to peace and prosperity. China, above all, now minimizes the positive cooperation of this period in favor of an extension of the humiliation narrative. In the case of Sino–South Korean relations, the gap was quite narrow until recently, as neither focused on negative moves by the other in the post–Cold War environment. Yet in the years 2008–9, Lee Myung-bak aroused concern in China, and distrust over how the other is handling North Korea is affecting national identity on both sides. Downplaying joint internationalism in facing global problems and regionalism, China is the state making it difficult to narrow differences in line with rising economic integration.

Memory dwells on ideals of an earlier era with insufficient regard for today's realities. China refuses to consider how Japan and South Korea view the Sinocentrism of premodern times, as it anticipates recreating its essence in a new regional order. Being focused on humiliation and hegemonism as its replacement, the Chinese lose sight of critical factors in regionalism. Japan confuses some idealistic claims of the decades leading up to 1945 with the harsh realities of the times. When the Japanese insist that they do not need to issue more apologies, they often obscure the message that the real aim for many is to reclaim the past with arguments that idealism, more than imperialism, motivated their nation. South Korea in vain pursues Koreanness linked to taking charge of peninsular reunification in the face of grave doubts that great power maneuvering along with the North Korean leadership will allow this escape from dependency. These obsessions with divisive ambitions distort the practical possibilities of building mutual trust and stable international relations. Recently, China has reemphasized history in all these periods, widening two identity gaps.

In these circumstances, emotionally charged symbols replace pragmatic interests in debates about bilateral relations. Threats centered on values and perceived challenges to sovereignty take precedence over terrorism and the proliferation of weapons of mass destruction. They appear to be existential, rather than material, threats. Charges that another state is "bashing" one's state or even "passing" it are more matters of honor or face than of interests. Bilateral relations become ensnarled in small-scale obsessions—the Chinese focus on the Yasukuni Shrine, the South Korean focus on Dokdo/Takeshima Island and the Koguryo state, and the Japanese focus on pressure to apologize. Given the fact that the two other foreign relationships of greatest significance—with the United States and North Korea—are also tied to national symbols, it is hard to refocus. Another factor is the legacy of Confucian thinking vis-à-vis identities of all types as less about broad principles that can be uniformly applied than dyadic relations. What applies to the self also applies to the nation; bilateral ties to significant others acquire a distinct character that is not subject to universal values or principles. In this case, as on other dimensions, Japan and South Korea have advanced much further in accepting universal principles than has China.

In 2010, the Chinese approach to the temporal dimension with Japan was clearly a maximum score of 5, and the score with South Korea had risen to as high as 4. Given the rise of Japan's and also South Korea's score toward China, the composite temporal gap is estimated as 5 and 4, respectively. It rose with the specter of Sinocentrism. Confucianism changed from a shared legacy to a reason for civilizational arrogance and antagonism. The Koguryo controversy has boosted the Sino–South Korean gap abruptly, arousing Chinese opposition to negative Korean memories of *sadae*, or one-sided dependence on China, and South Korean views of China as standing in the way of full Korean identity coalescing in a manner that would have led to responding effectively to imperialism in the nineteenth century. With China's insensitivity to South Korean feelings and charges that the South Koreans are biased regarding history, China has made the premodern period a fundamental part of its own identity gap widening. It has also made the Cold War and post–Cold War eras additional sources of gap widening. As for the Japanese–South Korean gap, it remains under the shadow of Japan's period of colonialism. Although Japan's thinking is less intense, and the gap is narrowing for other periods, a score of 4 is still applicable.

THE SECTORAL DIMENSION

Bilateral relations figure in the sectoral dimension to the extent that symbols of cultural, economic, and political national identity focus on other states in East Asia. Culturally, China is increasingly laying claim to the region's past and to being the driving force as a new alternative to the Western influence that prevailed starting in the late nineteenth century. Japanese and South Korean claims to cultural identity in the Cold War era were directed against the West, represented by the United States, and this resistance still matters. Yet the rising role of China in the past two decades has transformed optimism about the beneficial, if decidedly modest, value in recalling joint cultural roots (e.g., the Kanji cultural sphere, Confucian capitalism, Asian values), to competition for the sake of cultural national identity. In the case of South Korea, such rivalry with Japan was most significant before Kim Dae-jung's 1998 agreement to open his country to Japanese movies, television shows, and the like. Some in Japan took the popularity of Korean TV dramas by 2003 as proof of shared values. Although that hope diminished for a time, it has grown again, with an emphasis on universal values.

As China's cultural offensive gathered steam, the gaps with Japan and South Korea widened in the years 2008–10. Neither Japan nor South Korea had experienced cultural alienation to this degree, because they generally refrained from blaming Chinese culture. Thus, an estimate of 4 on the Chinese side toward Japan and 3 toward South Korea is matched by a figure of 2 on the two other sides, again revealing a one-sided gap. The Japanese and South Koreans are inclined to blame Chinese culture in response, as they too are contributing to a widening gap. If the Chinese in 2010 showcased a cultural gap in the way they criticized the cultural history of Japan and South Korea and their approaches to universal values such as anticommunism, the Japanese and South Koreans had been inclined to see similarities in the Confucian cultures of East Asia, but their attitudes toward Chinese culture were hardening in the new, tenser atmosphere.

Economic national identity might be expected to have little meaning as the three states of East Asia become ever more closely integrated through massive levels of trade and investment. From the 1960s to the 1990s, Japan's economic national identity was boosted by its claims to be leading the modernization of the region, gaining new force after China made economic reform and openness its priority. In the 1990s,

South Korean economic national identity gained some traction in relation to its neighbors as that country became a model for China and saw
Japan's economy tottering. Of late, China's economic confidence has
surpassed the others' and has begun to influence bilateral relations. Its
assumption that it wields the levers because its neighbors are dependent
on it has led to arrogance in pressing its advantage and alarm in Japan
following the temporary suspension of China's exporting of critical
rare earth metals, along with apprehension in South Korea that its technological edge is declining amid the unscrupulous practices of China.
All three states have strong protectionist aspects to their thinking about
certain sectors deemed crucial. As they explore establishing a free trade
agreement with each other, this thinking matters. Given how far they
have come in economic integration, a shared score of 2 in the Chinese
dyads is a recent indicator of problems. China's sense of economic superiority is widening the gap. Not long ago, the Japanese–South Korea
dyad also had a score of 2, but it has fallen to 1.

As for political national identity, sensitivities toward neighbors are
highest here. South Koreans treat relations with Japan as a prime test
of their national identity. Despite Japan's focus elsewhere for political
breakthroughs since the diplomatic normalization with South Korea in
1965 and with China in the 1970s, the possibility of appearing weak
before either country has loomed in public discourse as a serious threat
to national identity. For China, too, the nation's pride is at stake in dealing with the past aggressor Japan from a position that has an appearance
of weakness or with the past vassal state Korea without the ritual signs
of China's superior status. Prior success in calming emotions on all sides
suggests that these potentially explosive matters were kept under control, but a shared score of 4 out of 5 shows the volatility of this factor.
China's claims to political superiority are rivaled by apprehension over
China's political danger. In the case of Japanese–South Korean relations,
the political gap has narrowed, roughly to 2.

The composite score for the sectoral dimension is 3 out of 5 for
China's gap with its neighbors, but only 2 and, perhaps, falling toward 1
for the Japan–South Korea dyad. As in the case of the ideological dimension, there was a shift after 2005 from Japan to China, stirring the most

emotions related to national identity. This is seen in a growing sensitivity toward China in Japan and South Korea and, no less, in the growing
impact of the sectoral dimension on Chinese national identity.

The shadow of the United States looms over the sectoral identity
gap. All three of these states have long been obsessed with differences
with the United States, striving to escape from its shadow in order
to construct a more robust national identity. Their economic ties with
each other were deemed helpful in this quest, even while political and
cultural ties won approval for their national identity consequences, apart
from South Koreans' fear of Japanese cultural dominance. Whereas the
temporal dimension has long complicated dyads in Northeast Asia, only
recently has the sectoral dimension posed serious obstacles.

THE VERTICAL DIMENSION

Differences in the vertical dimension affect how societies build networks
and trust to improve bilateral relations. Although all three East Asian core
states privilege the state in an unbalanced internal hierarchy, they differ
in the focus given to the intermediate level. Japanese and South Korean
societies are democracies in which political opposition forces forge ties
across national boundaries. Local governments enjoy a degree of autonomy in nurturing sister-city relations. Moreover, there is more room to
explore values as a factor that can draw the peoples of the two countries
closer. China's insistence on the monopoly nature of its national identity,
to the exclusion of other types of identity, sets it apart from Japan and
South Korea and handicaps each of its bilateral relationships.

The gap on the vertical dimension between Japan and China is growing. China is again claiming that its system is socialist and contrasting it
to those of capitalist states, which have fared poorly in the world financial crisis. This compounds the deepening criticism of the Japanese and
South Korean systems for bringing to the fore leaders who supposedly
play up the China threat. In turn, Japan and South Korea, which long
ago divorced their perceptions of China from the evils of Communism,
have reverted to accusations about the dangers of China's system.

I rate the gap between China and its two neighbors as 3 out of 5. The gap between Japan and South Korea from this perspective is a minimal 1 out of 5. They have much in common in their domestic structure and considerable potential to develop networks at both the elite and popular levels for better understanding, although this process has been slowed by distrust. The state's growing role in China's economy is another factor that concerns its two neighbors, which fear manipulation and distorting market forces. Chinese writers frequently refer to the negative effects of different social systems, and this has become a self-fulfilling prophecy.

China has long claimed that it is opposed to interference in the internal affairs of other states. It has no problems with diversity, but it charges that other states, in their obsession with human rights and democratization, are driven by small-mindedness. To the extent that an identity gap exists, it follows that other states are the cause. Yet the rhetoric in China has veered in the direction of criticizing Japan and South Korea for their political choices and the systems that have led to them. On this dimension, the gap is not one-sided. In the years 2011–12, China's growing repression further darkened its image in these neighboring states.

THE HORIZONTAL DIMENSION

Normalization of relations—by Japan with South Korea in 1965, Japan with China in 1972, and China with South Korea in 1992—came with caveats. In the case of Japanese–South Korean relations, formal diplomatic ties came without political reconciliation or a lowering of cultural barriers. A quarter century after the agreement, ties remained fragile, apart from economic ones, and even two decades later public trust was lacking between Japanese and South Koreans; but the gap has started to narrow. After all, their views of the U.S. alliance and China have led to triangulation, their views of regionalism and North Korea are drawing much closer, and their views of the international community now overlap. The gap on the dimension has closed to about 1 out of 5. The "friendship" mode for Sino-Japanese normalization brought superficial toasts without addressing serious problems, and as it faded after 1989, there was much talk of economics being hot but politics being cold, and even when the politics were better managed, they continued to be fragile, while cultural ties rooted in public opinion remained cold. The disparity in views of the United States, East Asian regionalism, and the international system has abruptly widened to 4 out of 5. In the case of Sino–South Korean ties, China's decision to rebalance its political ties with North Korea and South Korea and its difficulty in building trust with other states, including Japan, also left reconciliation incomplete. This gap grew to roughly 3 in 2010 and is likely to remain wide due to contrasting views of the U.S. role on the Korean Peninsula, North Korea, regionalism, and the international system. Bilateral relations not only have yet to be fully normalized between China and its neighbors, the gaps are now widening.

When symbols such as the Yasukuni Shrine, Dokdo/Takeshima Island, and the Koguryo state enter the picture, they conjure up historical memories linked to uncertain future intentions capable of triggering a national identity alert. The fact that the other state broached this sensitive subject in a manner deemed to have crossed a red line gave confirmation to fears that its intentions were hostile. At stake was not only the issue at hand but also respect for one's national dignity. A loss of face could follow without a vigorous response. Given authentic memories of historical transgressions, responses to Japan by China and South Korea and by South Korea to China need little explanation, but responses by China to South Korea and Japan to both its neighbors require some attention. Because these countries are dissatisfied with bilateral U.S. relations as an answer to their identity concerns, they put added pressure on their neighbors to give them status that would go a long way to answering their quest for Asianism or Sinocentrism.

In the Cold War era, China and Japan suffered from status denigration. The gap had widened between what China's leaders considered the rising status of their country after a century of humiliation and the way it was being treated by the United States and its neighbors. Normalization of relations with South Korea in 1992 did not resolve the matter, because the South maintained its alliance with the United States and deferred much more to its ally in strategic decisionmaking. Resentment toward South Korea persisted, as seen in the years

2008–9, when both public and high-level attitudes hardened in the face of perceived disrespect. In the case of Japan, there was also a large gap between status expectations by the 1980s and 1990s and in the way the country was treated, especially by neighbors but also by its ally. If Koreans viewed historical issues as a matter of justice along with an acknowledgment of a past infringement on status, the Japanese blamed the South Koreans' inward-looking emotionalism for the fact that they were not only ignoring legal justice but also denying Japan suitable status consideration. East Asians are conditioned to conduct interpersonal and interstate relations in accord with established rules of etiquette. Violating these rules makes rebuilding ties difficult. Given disagreement on the correct status hierarchy, the rules are easily breached.

China appeared to narrow the divide on the horizontal dimension with an agreement on the United States' role in the region, eagerness for multilateral partnerships in keeping with regionalism, and momentum toward improving ties with both Japan and South Korea as recently as 2007. Yet in changing direction on all these issues, China caused the identity gap in 2010 to grow to as much as 4 for Japan and 3 for South Korea, reflecting discourse on the full panoply of security issues and the values associated with them. More than the temporal divide, the horizontal dimension is foremost in discussions of the national identity gaps in East Asia, as highlighted in chapter 7.

COMPARISONS OF THE THREE DYADS

The Japanese–South Korean dyad appeared to be the most volatile identity gap. It was relatively immune to realist considerations, because both states were secure under the protection of the United States. The end of the Cold War saw both states maneuvering to gain leverage in Asia and diversifying beyond dependence on the United States, leading at times to efforts to narrow the identity gap and at other times to an explosive widening of the gap. The reconciliation of 1998 and a decade later, from 2008 to 2010, was proof that the overall trend was toward narrowing, which was made easier by rising concern in both states about North Korea and

China. Because the gap was sharply focused on the temporal dimension, it was easier to control. The horizontal and ideological dimensions increasingly faded as matters of conflict, especially after progressives lost power in South Korea. Moreover, the sectoral and vertical dimensions lost their poignancy. Just a few symbols associated with history, including the territorial dispute, kept the gap at a rather high intensity, even as leaders on both sides in 2010 were eager to narrow it in line with new conditions. Still, I estimate the composite gap as about 10 on the 25-point scale, a sharp drop from about 15. This drop did not guarantee a further narrowing of the gap, as was seen in new tensions over the territorial issue in 2011 and in Lee Myung-bak's decision in December 2011 to focus a bilateral summit on the issue, when polls showed the conservatives losing support and the progressives gaining before new elections.

The conservative/progressive divide in both countries was changing in its impact on their identity gap. As Japanese progressives lost ground in the 1990s and North Korea became a more obvious threat, the critique of South Korea subsided. Conservatives were now pursuing regionalism and looking afresh at Asianism, both of which were favorable to closer ties to South Korea. When the progressives were discredited in the South by 2008, this removed the biggest barrier to identity narrowing with Japan. As Chinese ties worsened, Japan was seen in a new light.. Yet South Korea's national identity remained more volatile, as did its relations with North Korea.

The Sino-Japanese and Sino–South Korean dyads varied somewhat in the themes raised and the timing of their transformation, but the trajectory was similar. Both Japan and South Korea preferred to narrow the identity gap with China and were hesitant to admit that the gap was widening sharply. In the mid-1990s when Sino-Japanese problems intensified, and a decade later when that happened again, Sino–South Korean ties seemed to be unrelated, bereft of the insidious wartime legacy. Yet by 2010 the parallels in the two identity gaps with China were striking (see table I.1). In the Chinese narrative, both allies of the United States were guilty of the same provocations, which justified a widening gap. The driving force in this process was not Japanese revisionism—after all, South Korea had no history of imperialism in China—but Chinese

Table I.1. Estimated National Identity Gaps in East Asia

Dimension of Gap	Sino-Japan Gap	Sino–South Korea Gap	Japan–South Korea Gap
Ideological	5	3	2
Temporal	5	4	3
Sectoral	3	3	2
Vertical	3	2	1
Horizontal	4	3	2
Total	20	15	10

Note: Gaps are measured on a 5-point scale, with a higher number signifying a greater gap. For the details of each of the five dimensions of the gaps, see the text.

antipathy to their association with Western civilization and their rejection of a Sinocentric approach to regionalism. All dimensions were in play in the intense identity divide that arose and seemed destined to endure. The estimate for the Sino-Japanese gap is about 20, whereas that for the Sino-Korean gap stands at about 15, up sharply from about 10. In the past decade, there has been a reversal in the Sino–South Korean and Japanese–South Korean gaps, whereas the Sino-Japanese gap is the widest and has grown appreciably wider along with the Sino–South Korean identity gap. Even so, the Japanese–South Korean temporal dimension gap centered on the first half of the twentieth century remains acute, keeping the prospect of volatility in relations high.

Estimates of national identity gaps, however preliminary, direct our attention to what drives strategic thinking and foreign policy decisions. They offer a mechanism for conceptualizing perceptions in bilateral relations and changes in multiple dimensions. At the core of such research is an awareness of national identities as a subject for systematic scholarship. Critical to any methodology for studying them as well as national identity gaps is the necessity to immerse the researcher in primary sources, many of which were written for a domestic audience. Indeed, the internationally minded, foreign-trained experts are least likely to accurately reflect the essence of national identity. Communications in English and contacts with those whose views overlap the most with one's own are a recipe for misjudging national identity gaps. Deductive theorizing also falls far short of these needs.

China seemed intent on reducing its national identity gaps with both Japan and South Korea as recently as 2007, when Fukuda Yasuo and Roh Moo-hyun were treated rather positively and talk concentrated on increasing regional cooperation and warming up cultural ties and trust to be more consistent with "hot" economic ties and thawing or already-warm political ties. Although Lee Myung-bak came to power with a more conservative agenda, he expressed no intention of widening the identity gap with China; nor did Japan's succession of prime ministers after Fukuda. Rather, it was Hu Jintao's China in the preparation for the selection of new leadership in 2012 that changed its thinking toward these two neighbors. In the three chapters of part II, these changes are clarified. Chapter 6 presents the context of international relations studies into which national identity gaps fit. Chapter 7 details for each of the dimensions the Chinese views of Japan and South Korea. Chapter 8 then extends the analysis to the United States, pointing to demonization of it at the same time China was widening the identity gaps with Japan and South Korea. By jointly considering gap widening with all three partners of China, we can see how shifts in national identity drive changes in identity gaps, not as isolated developments but together as an indispensable perspective on international relations.

NOTE

1   For more on this syndrome, see this book's companion volume: Gilbert Rozman, ed., *East Asian National Identities: Common Roots and Chinese Exceptionalism* (Washington, D.C., and Stanford, Calif.: Woodrow Wilson Center Press and Stanford University Press, 2011), esp. the introduction to part I.

CHAPTER 6

EAST ASIAN NATIONAL IDENTITIES AND INTERNATIONAL RELATIONS STUDIES

Gilbert Rozman

As China is leading East Asia onto center stage in new great power maneuvering, scholarship on how states manage relations with each other bears refocusing. In this work, I identify national identity studies as the framework of analysis, specify dyads as the unit for analyzing identities in international relations, and concentrate on China, Japan, and South Korea as three states whose foreign policy thinking exemplifies the framework's utility, including their ties to the United States. Any observer of post–Cold War relations in which these states were involved is aware of striking anomalies that raised the prospect of sharp shifts in bilateral relations and obliged analysts to scramble to find an explanation. Their experiences challenge us to consider the study of international relations anew.

The study of international relations keeps racing to catch up. It is burdened by the primacy of realism, when so many of the important developments do not conform to any predictions based on assumptions about a world where perceptions do not matter. Adding constructivism as a catchall label for interpretations of international relations inclusive of the perceptions of states and their representatives provided a necessary corrective, but its vagueness as a residual category offers scant guidance on how to proceed. The power of liberalism, whereby economic integration leads inexorably to trust and reconciliation, is increasingly in doubt as states that are joined by the World Trade Organization in ever-tighter webs of trade fail to overcome their mutual suspicions. China's break with the Soviet Union in the late 1950s and 1960s steered China's foreign policy into a dead end and occurred despite Nikita Khrushchev's attentiveness in boosting relations. Those who argue that Soviet assertive control offended the Chinese usually overstate what proved provocative. Likewise, those who emphasize China's determination to regain territory lost to Russia overlook the temporary, expedient nature of vast territorial claims, which were easily dropped as relations normalized. Often missing is an awareness of the feverish pitch of Chinese national identity, which leaders had aroused in a series of campaigns, with spillover effects in foreign policy. In particular, "big brother," which had become the dominant factor in the Chinese worldview, was vulnerable to China's identity upsurge.[1] A subsequent spike in national identity in 2010 and other lesser crests are further proof of this powerful force in China, which for more than half a century has had a far-reaching impact on foreign relations.

Other anomalies appear in the shift of South Korea away from the United States in the years 2000–5 and then the shift of Japan away from the United States in 2009, each following signs of new unease obscured by optimism about increasingly close relations under Kim Dae-jung in 1998–99 and Koizumi Junichiro in 2003–6. Given North Korea's nuclear threat and the rapid rise of Chinese power, it has proven difficult to explain the electoral victories of Roh Moo-hyun in South Korea, riding a wave of anti-Americanism, and the Democratic Party of Japan, led by Hatoyama Yukio, calling for Japan to take the lead in forging an East Asian community with a U.S. role in doubt. The centrality of the United States in each ally's identity fueled a spike in emotionalism, which reverberated in a shift in diplomacy that surprised observers, even if the underlying conditions limited how far the shift might proceed under current circumstances.[2] Although emotions were less intense than in China's identity outbursts, they too were unexpected. Established international relations theories stumble before these shifts of the two U.S. allies.

Ferment over Japan in South Korea, peaking in 2005, also reflected the arousal of national identity with the Asian financial crisis, the Sunshine Policy, and the instability of the North Korean nuclear crisis following George W. Bush's unilateral condemnation of the North as part of the "axis of evil." Despite a 1998 breakthrough in cultural exchanges with Japan and the salutatory impact of the South's cohosting the 2002 World Cup and the "Korean Wave" (see chapter 2) intensifying at the same time, Japan became targeted once again for its historical revisionism and aspirations to be a "normal power." Afterward, South Korean alarm turned to China, whose new claims to the historical Kingdom of Koguryo (see chapter 4) struck a blow against Korean national identity. China has begun to loom so large in the South Korean worldview that the emotions associated with national identity now gravitate toward it.[3] South Korea's identity gaps with its neighbors defy the expectations of conventional theory.

Any list of anomalies would be incomplete if one omitted China's response to the United States in the years 2009–11. Despite Barack Obama's strenuous efforts to engage China, avoiding the downturn in relations that had occurred at the beginning of every presidency from the time of Ronald Reagan, an emboldened China showed little inclination to find compromises as its tone grew more hostile. This was not a realist response to heightened threats, but it could be traced to a compounded national identity buildup, as the leadership used the Beijing Olympics to arouse emotions, insisted that interference in internal affairs linked to the Tibetans and Uighurs was a grievous affront, and demonized the United States over numerous matters rather than searching for common ground. Given the fact that a rising power was challenging the world's foremost power, many were content to dismiss national identity concerns, as if Deng Xiaoping's pragmatic legacy that had shed most of the ideological rhetoric of traditional Communism was proof that China was only focused on maximizing its comprehensive national power. However, the evidence from Chinese writings—gravitating from alarm over bourgeois peaceful evolution to condemnation of hegemonism to attacks on interference in internal affairs—suggests that the theme of national humiliation keeps reappearing, whether as

Western and Japanese imperialism, Soviet revisionism, or finally U.S. containment. More than other East Asian states, China is now driving the surge in national identity as a force reshaping international relations in the twenty-first century.[4] International relations theory continues to be caught flat-footed by China's adjustments.

China's national identity gaps with the United States, Japan, and South Korea pose a challenge to international relations scholarship. A static notion of China's national identity fails to address the ups and downs in foreign relations. But a fluid notion of it is prone to become of merely descriptive utility, accounting in retrospect for every twist and turn in foreign policy with no predictability. In developing a framework for studying gaps in national identities, I seek to avoid such extremes while differentiating this approach from what is habitually considered the mainstream in international relations studies.

What is distinctive about the approach used here? First, it treats the dyad as the basic unit of analysis. Instead of starting from a single country, usually the United States, and assessing its approach to foreign policy, it assumes that the foundation for analysis is the way two countries interact over time. Second, it covers the identities of both parties, introducing the concept of a national identity gap that can be measured and traced over time. Third, this approach concentrates on the state with limited regard for checks on a nation's identity from ethnic, religious, or groupings of nongovernmental organizations, recognizing that in East Asia the state's claim to represent the nation is little challenged, as indicated by the evidence assembled on the vertical dimension. Ethnic groups in outlying areas of China—such as Tibet, Xinjiang, and Inner Mongolia—at times make conflicting identity claims, but the mainstream dismisses them as inconsequential. Even when existing political leadership is authoritarian and defies what many regard to be the will of the nation it claims to fully represent, the gap between nation and state is tempered by the prevailing notion that the state embodies the nation and is its only legitimate expression. Fourth and finally, this approach is consistent with the tendency to view dyads not through the lens of general principles of conduct but through relational identities, in which a state's approach is conditioned more by past bilateral relations than by any application of universal standards. These regional characteristics give a distinct cast to international relations, not just with those states closely associated with one's own national identity through past experiences but also with the other great powers active in the region—Russia and, especially, the United States. National identity studies offer a prism for the study of international relations, demanding close attention to self-images while observing their impact over time on critical dyadic ties.

The study of dyadic national identity gaps puts a premium on understanding the domestic forces behind foreign policy decisions. One can visualize the research process as a series of steps. The starting point is appreciation for the core national identity and how symbolic issues related to identity have recently been debated. This combines historical background with media savvy. The next step is political insight into how various forces are struggling to shape identity debates combined with public opinion awareness to show how manipulation may be tried and effective. That leads to a focus on bilateral relations and how they are shaped by leaders alert to national identity gaps and to events that may narrow or widen them. Apart from the character of identities in East Asia that leave a legacy conducive to national identity spikes in dyadic relations, one can point to strong historical memories, accumulating driving forces, recurrent public anxieties, supportive national leaders, and occasional precipitating factors. This sequence characterizes many disputes centered on symbols of victimization and lack of respect. In East Asia, where history is deeply imprinted in claims of regime legitimacy, past bilateral ties retain their relevance. How they are invoked is subject to broader currents in bilateral relations, given that various types of problems can serve as driving forces shaping the national consciousness. When established red lines are crossed, an anxious public is prone to attribute greater significance to them than would otherwise be warranted. National leaders may pursue power or attempt to solidify it by capitalizing on these anxieties and arousing emotions. Finally, the flaunting of defiant behavior puts a clash of two identities in the forefront.

One regional legacy that shapes the horizontal dimension of national identities is the image of relations between states as inherently bilateral (without alliances to counter one strong state or to ensure stability) and hierarchical. There was no balance of power or incipient transnational community to mitigate this image before the twentieth century, and the arrival of the Western powers left states in the region with little trust in a different set of claims that modern relations are premised on equality among states. During the Cold War, China quickly rejected using the Soviet lens on countries such as Japan, North Korea and South Korea, and the United States to view bilateral relations. Similarly, Japan, despite its alliance ties to the United States, strove to frame bilateral relations with China, North Korea and South Korea, and the Soviet Union differently. South Korea had less leverage before the end of the Cold War, but it also departed from the U.S. approach in the 1990s. Each state saw itself as part of a complex of dyads, with none lacking contested hierarchical significance.

International relations studies long rested on assumptions that were grounded in thinking in Western nations about their civilizing or democratizing mission and also on polarization in the face of totalitarian opponents. The peak of the Cold War heightened these contrasts and left a legacy that would not be easy to change. In the process of adjustment, ideas about the ways civilizations change and interact were in the forefront of discussions on new ways of approaching interstate conflict. Although some international relations studies incorporated national identities, they did not point the way to joint study of East Asian identities or awareness of their important influence on dyadic and multilateral relations.

Building on constructivism, Anne Clunan developed a systematic approach to national identity and has applied it to Russia's resurgence since the 1990s. She calls her approach "aspirational constructivism." On the basis of elite debates, in which actors with their collective identities centered on the state seek self-esteem, she stresses the salience of common historical memories. Actors compete through support for national self-images—beliefs about a state's appropriate system of governance and mission and ideas about its international status—which are tested until convergence is reached when one view gains dominance even as it is further contested. Her approach emphasizes the aspirations of elites for national self-esteem, interprets them within the context of historical memories, links historical assessments to perceptions of current conditions as images compete for legitimacy, and engages with realism in ways often missing in other scholarship on national identity.[5] Compared with other analysts, Clunan makes clear the various sources of national identity, including the need for collective self-esteem through the national self, the role of historical memory in establishing the variance attached to identities, and the framework for understanding change in national identity. She extends her framework to the study of how national identities operate in shaping foreign policy orientations, introducing two case studies of Russia's security interests in Europe and in nuclear arms control. Though not stressing dyads, she distinguishes in-groups and out-groups and notes the importance of "others" as part of identity management strategies. Clunan's approach puts constructivist scholarship on a firmer footing, one that is consistent with the approach taken here to East Asian identities.

Clunan's framework clarifies the conceptual ground for national identity studies, but it is not a guide to comparative analysis or a blueprint for identifying the dimensions of national identity and how they interact with historical memory. She shows an example of an aggrieved nation aspiring to collective esteem choosing among national images to fill a vacuum left suddenly by the collapse of the previous established identity, while still influenced by elements of that identity. As a reconstructed identity takes hold, she finds that the frustrations associated with the collapse and the vacuum can boost its intensity.

Diverse circumstances lead to a surge in the intensity of national identity. The anguish of dashed expectations has that effect. After the collapse of the Soviet Union, Russia was ripe for a strong negative reaction to those associated with its decline, both at home and abroad. In the 1990s, Japan also suffered a letdown after high expectations during its period of a bubble economy, fueling an upsurge in revisionism. This occurred against the backdrop of the far-reaching collapse of national identity starting in 1945. China's isolation after the Tiananmen Square massacre on June 4, 1989, also lent support to a spike in resentment directed outward. Again, the scene was set by the abrupt shift away from the main pillars of national identity forged by Mao Zedong's leadership up to 1976. South Korea in the years 2001–3 also found itself unable to sustain the Sunshine Policy that had breathed life into its optimistic post–Cold War worldview, and a mood of frustration gave progressives a chance to press for policies that had once seemed radical but could be justified by national identity. This too can be set against the national identity vacuum during Japan's occupation and the sudden shifts in 1987 due to democratization and in 1997 due to the Asian financial struggle that left perceptions of identity unsettled. Finally, the backlash against Barack Obama's domestic and foreign policies in the years 2009–10 is further proof of how a country suffering from a letdown after the Bush agenda had failed falls prey to emotional attacks that are critical of pragmatic approaches. National identity lurks in the background and is invoked from time to time, until people lose hope or confidence, often following a spike in unrealistic expectations. It is mobilized by leaders or rivals to focus on symbols that serve as the standard for judging policies. The international relations field can benefit from a systematic outlook on spikes in national identity, including how they arise and how they are manifested in dyadic identity gaps.

Arrogance can also trigger national identity intensity to a degree comparable to the impact of anguish. Indeed, it is the double whammy of a bout of arrogance followed by a bout of anguish (or the other way around) that has special poignancy. The two sources of emotionalism feed off each other. Anguish mounting over a long time may turn into intense arrogance, as with China in the years 2009–10, when its rejection of globalization, apart from some economic aspects, exceeded that by Japan in its late 1980s' heyday when the Japanese felt superior and by the United States at the peak of Bush's unilateralism in the years 2002–6. When the various dimensions overlap in support of overconfidence about one's nation, there is less reason to listen to the voices of other nations. Yet this also results from perceptions that the national identity gap with particular nations has grown to an unacceptable level, allowing lower levels of intensity about overall identity to play a greater than normal role.

THE IMPACT OF EAST ASIAN NATIONAL IDENTITIES ON INTERNATIONAL RELATIONS

The three core states of East Asia have each experienced periods of low, moderate, and high intensity in national identity since the 1950s and a great flux since the 1990s. In the times of low intensity—Japan from the 1950s to the 1970s, South Korea in the 1960s and 1970s, and China in the 1980s—they appear to have been open to the ideas associated with modernization, along lines championed by the United States, and cooperation with the international community without challenging U.S. leadership. Yet there was unmistakable evidence that national identity was resistant to such convergence or dependency. International relations analysts were, on the whole, loath to recognize the deep-seated domestic thinking—not interest groups nor foreign policy alternatives—that drove their resistance. The Japanese debates on China in the 1970s and the Soviet Union in the 1980s, the South Korean debates on Japan in the 1970s and 1980s and on China in the 1990s, and China's debate on the Soviet Union in the 1980s and 1990s all signaled divergence from or disquietude with the pathway that many observers assumed would be followed. A search had begun for a new approach.

The first place to look for each country's search is the ideological dimension. As the heir to Communism, China has a deep-seated incentive to raise the heat of its identity search in opposition to the spread of a global civilization associated with U.S. leadership. In the 1990s and 2000s, the intensity of its identity quest grew in response to a sense of isolation and then of growing great power clout, and starting in 2008 one can detect high-intensity identity assertiveness as China anticipated superpower status. Given an ideological base of Communist messianism, such growing intensity should not be surprising. Yet this is not Communism alone, because the Confucian heritage of Sinocentrism provides an ideology that is also supportive of identity assertiveness. It is exclusive in its claim to be civilized, as the "great tradition" that coexists with multiple "little traditions," and it sets an example for all "barbarian" peoples. Japan's prewar claim to be a "divine nation" also has an ideological foundation, which despite official disavowals over sixty-five years that contrast with the continued Chinese state support for Communism, has enduring effects. Although the peak of its revival as right-wing revisionism appears to have been Abe Shinzo's tenure as prime minister in the years 2006–7, there is no reason to think that support has declined appreciably. Moreover, on the left and to the right of center, the old ideology may survive in a less obtrusive form. This was the case during the high intensity of national identity in the late 1980s, when the far right was less vocal, and at a time of overlap in leftist and rightist thinking on Asianism, as seen in Hatoyama's worldview in the years 2009–10.

South Korean progressives are less clear about their ideology in the shadow of North Korean "Juche Communism," which claims leftist national identity, whereas rightists never emerged from the United States' shadow after anticommunism lost its appeal. Yet the ideological appeal of "Asian values" and even the Sunshine Policy found support from both sides. The progressives increasingly have been the ones to sustain an ideological orientation.

International relations theory struggled against claims that Communist ideology is a driving force and then confronted Islamic fundamentalism in resistance to globalization. Yet the former produced the Sino-Soviet schism, and the latter remains centered more on nations than on a pan-Islamic ideal. Reinterpreting ideology as civilization filled a gap in the post–Cold War era but blurred the linkage between ideology and national identity. In East Asian states, once-popular Marxist-Leninist thought faded without stripping many boosters on the left of the core of their ideological beliefs. Progressivism did not depend on its tenets so much as on a worldview centered on critical symbols of national pride. In Japan, they combined pacifism with constitutionalism. In China, they focused on Mao's historical role and the legitimacy of the Chinese Communist Party. In South Korea, they rejected anticommunism for some optimistic assumptions about the path to reunification. Ideology survives after the veneer of traditional Marxist-Leninist thought is removed.

Images of the past are frequently being reconstructed, adding another dimension to national identity. In Japan in the 1950s and China in the 1980s, the recent past offered scant reassurance about the future. Eventually, however, the past acquired a much more positive gloss—even when negative impressions had scarcely been refuted. Such images have implications for policymaking. In South Korea, symbols of Japan's past aggression repeatedly complicated relations, as did reminders from 2004 of Sinocentric views of the past, with possible echoes in policies toward North Korea. Sino-Japanese relations were notably mired in historical imagery, complicating ties after the Cold War as identities grew more intensely historical in both states. As the Japanese grew more interested in *sensoron* (views of the war) and the Chinese took new interest in Tianxia, they revisited worldviews that had once been marginalized but now were becoming increasingly vital for grasping national identity in a changing international environment. Japanese sought national self-esteem at a time when it appeared to be slipping away—frustration over a loss of status and relevance, and criticism from some significant states whose major memories demonized their country. Anne Clunan refers to history testing during periods of fluidity, striving to avoid a past inferior status in order to gain esteem from another past status.[6] In recalling its grandeur as the "Middle Kingdom," China had available a source of considerable national esteem. If Japan had no similar option, it could at least find relief in an active effort to reduce worrisome views of its past.

International relations theory has lacked a systematic approach to the incorporation of historical memories. Despite their recurrent prominence in East Asia, many generalists do not dwell on these memories, often only mentioning them in passing as if they have no more than ad hoc significance or are merely rationalizations for policies. This is consistent with views that lack a long-term perspective on humiliation, victimization, and grievances. Among those steeped in East Asian thinking rooted in Confucianism, few would make this error.

The unusual overlap of cultural, economic, and political identity in East Asian states has not been captured by comparative social science studies or the international relations field. The intense sectoral identity that can result is subject to the vagaries of world affairs. In the 1950s, Japan clung to a disputed cultural identity, kept its political identity from collapsing by maintaining the imperial line and fully embracing democracy as the wave of the future, and held aloft a rosy economic future despite troubled times. In the 1980s, China also struggled with suspicions over its cultural identity, took desperate measures to maintain its political identity, and abruptly shifted claims about how it would achieve remarkable economic success. Similarly, in the period 1965–75 South Korea asserted strong cultural claims in the face of denials, struggled for political legitimacy in opposition to the North, and followed Japan's example in making the case for an economic miracle. An anticipated sharp rise in the hierarchical ranking of nations in each of these countries was predicated on state guidance, social harmony, and national will, grasping international opportunities but not succumbing to the forces of convergence. They were export driven but careful to avoid some common markers of dependence. Foreign ideas flooded into the country, but state controls limited their appeal. International relations theory had little to say about the way: Modernization through integration into the world economy does not lead to convergence, alliances do not forge a shared sense of international responsibility, and images of a distinct social order stand in the way of democratization or civil society. The fact that states that have been left far behind are able to catch up rapidly while clinging to claims of superiority and implementing policies to reinforce those claims is not well understood.

Countries whose sectoral identities are compounding at a high intensity succumb to arrogance, which influences foreign policy decisions. Japan's policies toward Moscow, Pyongyang, Seoul, and Beijing in the years 1988–92 reflect its national identity surge, as did its reduced deference to Washington. South Korea's policies in 1998–2007 carried the weight of its surge, even as the surge waxed and waned. In particular, China's policies in 2008–11 capped a precipitous upsurge in confidence from all sectors. States grow more assertive at times unanticipated by international relations experts, who pay little attention to the changes in national identities as states rise or fall in the global order.

In addition to the ideological, temporal, and sectoral dimensions of identity, there are vertical and horizontal dimensions that figure into our comparative analysis. As for the former, international relations theory has overlooked the sociological analysis of the relative importance of collective identities and how this affects national identity. Where religion, ethnicity, and civil society identities fail to put pressure on elites intent on state identity gaining overwhelming dominance as a collective identity, they can make a strong case for the legitimacy of their conception of a strong state urgently in pursuit of greater esteem. In Japan and South Korea, democratization has redressed some of the imbalance in the vertical dimension by highlighting competing national images and opening space for contesting elites. Chinese Communism since the demise of Maoist class struggle and continued censorship on many sensitive subjects linked to identity gives the state much more of a monopoly over national identity and the collective esteem of the populace.

The internal breakdown of collective identities was long obscured by a one-sided emphasis on social class, because Marxists insisted that class serves as the primary orientation. In recent times, race and gender have drawn more attention as sources of identity. Especially ethnicity has taken center stage in discussions of multiculturalism and clashes that extend to differences over national identity. In heterogeneous countries where ethnicity, religion, and national origin are associated with deep cultural divides, contested images of identity may matter greatly, although care should be taken to keep in sight the power of the state's identity. In East Asia, national identity is built on a foundation of homogeneity due to the marginalization and lack of alternate national identities of ethnic groups with notable differences. Gender identities have proven less significant as collective markers than in most developed states. Hierarchical principles of organization and conceptualization back the state's claims to identity. The prevalence of single-party rule also bolsters continuity. As a result, the vertical dimension in Japan, South Korea, and, above all in recent times, China puts a high premium on national esteem over all other collective identities.

The horizontal dimension refers to other states and the global community as out-groups in the construction of national identity. Such a group exists when there is a desire to compete with it in order to overturn the perceived negative status of the nation as an in-group or to express hostility owing to its perceived negative political purposes.[7] For all East Asian states, the United States is the most important out-group.

This applies to both historical memory and current policy calculations. In Japan and South Korea, too, national discourse centers on diversification, on finding an Asian referent for self-esteem to provide some balance with the preoccupation with the United States. Japan's quest for "reentry into Asia" and South Korea's Sunshine Policy were both linked to clear symbols of normalization as well as to a search for more wide-ranging images of the "other" that would be useful for national self-worth. Internationalization appeared to serve this objective as well, but there was never much success in differentiating that from the United States–led global community.

The horizontal dimension has somewhat different significance for China. Because it is not an ally of the United States and has long criticized the West, China finds promise of self-esteem in contrasting more than a century of humiliation by foreign powers with pride in three millennia of centrality without imperialism. China's significant other looms as a more unmitigated negative force, and its historical memory of how it contrasts with the United States provides grounds for greater glorification. The potential for self-esteem mixed with demonization is far stronger in China than in Japan or South Korea. If for a time it agreed to cooperation and obscured some of its identity claims, mounting calls for pressing the national identity agenda signaled what would follow in a manner that studies based on international relations theories were prone to overlook. Narrow thinking about relations with the United States does not do justice to the diversity of horizontal images.

On all the above dimensions, there is a difference in degree between China and its two neighbors. As its national identity climbed to a high intensity in 2010, the field of international relations studies had good reason to pay close attention. A continued rapid upsurge in China's comprehensive national power can be extrapolated to fuel even more aspirations for national esteem, which are associated with potent symbols such as reunification with Taiwan. However, the frustration that would be associated with a sudden dashing of expectations if China's bubble economy (in real estate and the stock market) were to collapse also could lead to an urgent search for symbols of self-esteem to cushion the blow. Japan's disappointments in the 1990s led to an upsurge of revisionism, albeit centered on symbols, but not an assertive foreign policy; and South Korea's dissatisfaction in the years 2001–5 led to provocative rhetoric toward some states, even if a middle-power status limited how far it would go. In contrast, in China expectations have been raised much higher and the intensity of national identity is, this book argues, much greater. Although Chinese leaders are alert to the need for efficacy tests for how they present the national identity and how it influences both the rhetoric and the policies selected in addressing international relations, they are steering their country closer to a possible international conflict than many have recognized. Rhetoric arousing the Chinese to perceive a wider national identity gap deserves theoretical consideration.

National identity gaps are pronounced in dyadic relations within East Asia and in the especially important relationship with the United States. Ideological differences have long focused on this country above others. Sectoral identities—cultural, economic, and political—treat the United States as the most significant "other." Historical memories are most poignant with the United States or Japan, making dyads with these states especially sensitive to spikes in national identity. Vertical identity centers on differentiating what is deemed specific to one's domestic order from the U.S. model. Looking closely at the horizontal dimension gives one insight into the struggle that combines a search for more self-esteem in dealings with the United States, aspirations for a new regional arrangement in Asia that affirms the significance of one's own state, and reinforcement of national pride in the way the international community evolves. For South Korea, the Sunshine Policy held out the most hope for centrality, but hosting the Group of Twenty in the fall of 2010 also provided some sense of satisfaction. For Japan, permanent membership in the UN Security Council would have met recent aspirations, superseding aspirations to gain a large voice in the Group of Seven when that organization was at its peak. In the case of China, aspirations are much higher. With recognition already as one of the permanent five members of the Security Council and recent talk of a Group of Two with the United States on the most serious global problems, China seeks to transform the international system in ways that would satisfy its self-esteem steeped in historical memory combining the glory of Sinocentrism and the humiliation of marginalization.

East Asian national identities prioritize dyads perceived through the prism of past victimization and aspirations. They are replete with symbols, which are invoked to arouse the public into a more intense expression of national identity. International relations studies need to recognize the power of these symbols, their foundation in national identity, and their significance in the evolution of bilateral relations. Without addressing historical grievances in the context of national identities, prospects are dim for resolving the major sources of conflict in East Asia, including long-suppressed criticisms of the United States.

U.S. REASONING ON NATIONAL IDENTITY GAPS IN EAST ASIA

The United States threatens other countries' national identities in ways that Westerners often fail to appreciate. It not only exports an omnipresent political identity centered on democracy and human rights and a pervasive economic identity associated with the free market and the global economy, but it is also the source of cultural diffusion that relegates a nation's own traditions to museums and exotic fare of scant interest to younger generations. Its claims to universal values and to be a model of international applicability are said to empower the people in any nation to express their own will, but national elites are inevitably fearful of what will determine the popular will and are insistent that they must shape it in defiance of perceived U.S. standards. In Japan, progressives rejected many of these standards as self-serving in the United States' quest for world domination, while many conservatives viewed them as obstacles to reclaiming pride in Japan's prewar and wartime history. In South Korea, there were also progressives who faulted the United States' identity for standing in the way of reunification, while many conservatives were biding their time to reassert a distinctive Korean identity as an alternative to the outside world. Most important, Chinese Communist elites viewed the export of U.S. values shaping national identity as a mortal threat to the legitimacy of their rule and the type of country they envisioned. The national identity gap was large in Japan and South Korea, despite their acceptance of democracy and some universal values, but it was a chasm in China, where the defense of the national identity against threats emanating, above all, from the United States became an obsession after a series of shocks in 1989.

The temporal dimension exposes the extreme lengths to which East Asian states will go to distance themselves from the United States. South Korea has the least incentive, but its progressives led the way in criticizing U.S. behavior during the Cold War and starting as far back as the perceived imperialist bargain with Japan (Korea for the Phillipines) in 1907. Rejection of the prior glowing review of U.S. historical ties paved the way for anti-Americanism starting in the late 1990s. Conservative Japanese have increasingly revealed their dissatisfaction with verdicts on Pearl Harbor, the atomic bombings of Japan, the Tokyo Tribunal, and the San Francisco Peace Treaty. Only by confronting these long-hidden differences do they expect to put Japan's national identity on a sound footing. Of course, reclaiming the past is most urgent in China, which is defending the superiority of an alternative approach to international relations from premodern times but is also renewing justifications about the history of Chinese Communism. One example is China's reaffirmation, after some hesitation, of the Korean War as a just, defensive struggle against imperialism. This outlook complements the increased condemnation since 2009 of U.S. policy toward North Korea linked to anticommunism.

The U.S. narrative poses the development of the free world and free market as a result of victory over fascism in World War II and the struggle against Communism in the Cold War. Japanese conservatives are prone to qualify the meaning of World War II, the South Korean progressives waver on the aftermath of the war, and Communists in China are launching a frontal assault on the entire history of the era by downplaying the U.S. role in the fight against fascism and criticizing it in the struggle not only with Chinese Communism but also with Soviet Communism. Japan and South Korea have sufficient sources of pride to avoid a crisis in national identity from remaining in the United States' shadow, but the leaders of China have calculated that the legitimacy of their regime requires an unbridgeable divide between the identity sought for their country and that which is attributed to its main rival.

On the ideological dimension, Japan and South Korea have no privileged belief system. The separation of religion and politics holds, and the waning impact of Marxism on progressives has removed that worldview from public attention. In contrast, China's leaders are unwilling to drop ideology from their construction of national identity. Deng made that clear in enunciating the four cardinal principles in 1979. Despite his vaunted pragmatism, he presided over repeated struggles to repel exposés of ideological failure and attempts to revamp the ideological foundation of Communist Party rule. Observers noted the upsurge in patriotic education in the 1990s and the growing assertiveness of what was deemed nationalism in the 2000s, but they often overlooked the role ideology plays in the ascendant national identity. It is not the Maoist version of Communism and it no longer in most publications is buttressed by quotations from Karl Marx and his disciples, but the sharp contrasts drawn with the United States, which is accused of letting ideology drive its foreign policies, serve as a reminder that a sharp ideological gap exists. It is China that rejects putting Sino-U.S. relations on a plane where each would be driven only by national interests and would grope to widen the scope of shared interests. Instead, making the gap existential due to an ideological chasm serves China's national identity ambitions.

Ronald Reagan and George W. Bush took office representing fervent movements to transform the United States' national identity. In keeping with their domestic base, each criticized the previous Democratic president for weakness in engaging China. If Bill Clinton also made softness toward China an issue in his first campaign, his base kept its primary focus on trade rather than on transforming U.S. national identity or even Chinese national identity. The China issue came and went, never gaining a central place in the intensifying identity quest. It served China's plans, however, to charge that the United States was demonizing it with the goal of regime change. This proved useful in the 1990s campaign for patriotic education. Even as Clinton shifted to narrowing the identity gap, downplaying the U.S. critique was limited, especially after the

1997–98 exchange of summits. The groundwork was set for deepening the critique at a time of China's choosing, not due to provocations.

Americans take pride in the transformation of Japan and South Korea's identities, beginning with the military occupation of those countries. In the 1980s, there were also high expectations that China's identity would be gradually transformed under the impact of U.S. support for China's integration into the world economy and global community. Evaluating U.S. expectations against identity responses is one way to understand this region. No country matters more for the identities of these East Asian states than the United States; so its place in dyadic national identity gaps is of special significance.

On each of the dimensions, I observe a contrast between U.S. predictions and what occurred. On the ideological dimension, expectations centered on a continuous replacement of ideological themes with pragmatism. As for the temporal dimension, the assumption prevailed that divergent thinking would diminish; shared identity in the Cold War and then in post–Cold War globalization would bring identities closer. But the opposite occurred. For the sectoral dimension, there was no anticipation that China would welcome a spike in cultural, economic, or political identity, let alone a rise in all three in tandem and in conflict with universal values and free market principles. Democratization seemed to hold hope for convergence in social structure amid a rising recognition of similarities, but China's rejection of it was but one step in widening the divide. On the horizontal dimension, there was also optimism that concerns about hegemonism would diminish in favor of shared thinking about global challenges and regionalism. In 2009, this turned to pessimism. The notion that national identities would lose their intensity—no longer serving as a driving force in relations with the United States or thinking about the West—proved erroneous.

Instead of the above-noted trends, our findings show that after a period when a certain narrowing of national identity gaps occurred, the opposite trend appeared. In Japan during the late 1980s and 1990s, a spike in national identity based on confidence and then a shift in identity linked to loss of confidence called converging trends into question. In South Korea, a decade of ups and downs (from the mid-1990s to the mid-2000s) associated with bursts of confidence and then of doubt defied these expectations. Mostly, Chinese national identity serves as a reproof to U.S. thinking, mainly starting in 2010.

Convergence has been one of the most fundamental assumptions of social scientists since the end of World War II, and it has often driven thinking about international relations, particularly in the United States. The nature of convergence may appear differently, depending on the observer's academic orientation and political leanings. At one extreme, rational choice proponents, notably market-focused economists and democracy-obsessed political scientists, take it as a given that the pursuit of efficiency propels states toward a high degree of convergence with the existing U.S. or, more broadly, Western model. At the other extreme, area specialists with a deep awareness of cultural and structural differences may accept a qualified version of convergence, in which change is partial and two-way because the United States is also reforming in response to practices that prove more effective in global competition. In essence, discussions about convergence center on how to narrow identity gaps, even if they skirt this theme by focusing specifically on structural differences. If the two political extremes find convergence anathema because it contradicts their preferences, others take an interest in it when facing the challenge of a rival power.

Convergence is a way to conceptualize and manage foreign policy. Because it has held the lead position in international relations since 1945, the United States has often found the idea of convergence appealing. It raises hope of lowering costs in maintaining security and forging a coalition of like-minded nations. In the abstract, convergence assumptions apply to many types of states; but in terms of their salience for international relations, they have acquired most significance for discussion about a few states that test U.S. leadership. The history of the past half century reveals a succession of debates about convergence.

Although the U.S. debates over convergence merit attention, the responses to U.S. initiatives are of interest as one reflects on national identity gaps. The goal of convergence causes much greater anxiety in East Asian states because of the fear that their national identities could be in jeopardy. If few in the United States worried that U.S. identity could be undermined by cross-pollination through reform and mutual borrowing, East Asians with narrower notions of the essential elements of their identities were prone to approve borrowing extensively, as long as they saw strong measures to prevent convergence. As part of their debates, they viewed the notion of convergence with the United States and the West as dangerous. It is the response to reducing the national identity gap by means of convergence that exposes the intensity of national identity consciousness in these nations.

The East Asia states were important in U.S. designs for convergence—beginning with Japan from the 1960s to the 1980s as the most modernized non-Western country; continuing with South Korea as a model of modernization and, after 1987, of democratization most beholden to the United States; and ending with China from the 1980s to the 2000s, as the test case for U.S. goodwill toward a Communist rival enabling its globalization and reform. In each case expectations for convergence were raised, reflecting U.S. identity. Responses to U.S. efforts to reduce the identity gap, however, were not well anticipated, showing how states found narrowing the existing gap problematic and responded with efforts to reinforce it.

Americans have never reached a consensus on how to respond to those countries deemed most problematic for U.S. national identity. At one extreme is condemnation of the other state as unworthy of all but minimal cooperation. It must be demonized to avoid contamination at home and the infection of other countries. At the opposite extreme is commendation of the other state as an example worthy of some degree of emulation, but this approach rarely gains many adherents. Two other ways of responding are more nuanced: seeking convergence in anticipation of finding common ground because the other state is amenable to reform; and settling for coexistence because it provides for mutual benefit. These alternatives have different implications for U.S. identity, allowing groups with different identity orientations to gravitate to the option that satisfies their objectives.

Alarm—as after the September, 11, 2001, terrorist attacks against the United States and after its economy unraveled seven years later—creates fertile soil for widening identity gaps. Pride—as when Japan rode the crest of the bubble economy and when China found itself riding high in the financial crisis of 2008–11—also makes it easy to widen identity gaps. Japan's challenge was short-lived, but China's is far reaching. It draws on millennia of continuous Sinocentrism, three decades of one of the most extreme Communist rejections of the existing world order, and the exhilaration of sudden empowerment without parallel in the world or resolution of charges of humiliation. In Chinese reasoning about the nature of gaps in national identity, one can discern how these forces operate and how international relations studies are challenged by a rising power's perceptions.

THE CHINESE REASONING ON NATIONAL IDENTITY GAPS

National identity (*rentong*) only entered common usage in China during the past decade. Yet the idea of ideological purity in support of the regime had been embedded in dynastic history and was carried to a socialist realist extreme by Mao's Communist views. In the 1980s, the Propaganda Department periodically flexed its muscles, and it was given greater responsibility starting in the 1990s. Although attention has centered on the importance of remunerative incentives and the continued reliance on coercive incentives, the Chinese have redoubled efforts to make normative incentives a primary basis of support. Unlike the jerky campaign approach of the Mao era, where the three types of incentives were applied quite separately—normative appeals losing steam, leading to coercive pressure to achieve unreachable goals, before recourse finally was given to material rewards—a coordinated strategy prioritizes consumer benefits while continuously stressing beliefs in a manner adjusted to the latest concerns without relinquishing the threat of coercive restraints. China's leadership is driven by the objective of "cultural security" (*wehua anquan*) by guiding thought at home in opposition to that abroad.

Chinese leaders were first shocked by the massive June 4, 1989, demonstrations in Tiananmen Square and the response by Western states, and then by the disintegration of the socialist bloc followed by the collapse of the Soviet Union, so they reinforced their mindset about the significance of national identity. This had been a prime concern of Mao Zedong in his campaigns to inculcate thought reform and then his obsession with the threat of revisionism. It was a focus of Deng Xiaoping in the way he handled the evaluation of Mao and then the anti-spiritual pollution campaign of 1984 and also the purge three years later of Communist Party reform thinkers, including Hu Yaobang. Yet only starting in 1992, in the shift away from knee-jerk hostility to reform, does one observe a well-conceived strategy for constructing national identity on the basis of lessons learned. This is a strategy of widening identity gaps with countries deemed threatening to China's identity and narrowing identity gaps with the countries regarded as promising partners for the legitimation of rule by the Chinese Communist Party and the rise of China as the center of a new Asian and global order. An embattled China reinforced this strategy, but only a newly empowered China recently has brought the strategy to fruition.

Chinese sources differentiate two key venues for foreign policy. One is the great power (*daguo*) arena, which is dominated by the United States but also has a lineup of other powers, including Russia, Japan, and India. The other is the neighboring (*zhoubian*) arena, where most states are small powers and a few middle powers, such as South Korea, Indonesia, and Vietnam, draw notice. The goal has been to divide the great powers, reduce the U.S. role in the region, and make each middle power dependent on China and constrained by multilateral organizations from any strong resistance to China's rise. For the two decades after the end of the Cold War, this endeavor required caution in expressing negativity, such as anti-imperialism (*fandi*), which had been the favorite slogan in the 1950s and the 1960s, and also antirevisionism (*fanxiu*), a slogan that had arisen in the 1960s and 1970s but had lost any meaning by the start of the 1980s. Yet, by 2010, sources proclaiming the revival of self-confidence emphasized negativity focused on another target, anti-West (*fanxi*), associated with anti-imperialism. This put surrounding areas in the spotlight as the prime battleground for resistance to the West. If some territorial disputes flared in a manner that suggested a direct struggle based on hard power, there was also an intensified effort to cast issues in terms of soft power, where China's superiority rests in part on the contrast between past Sinocentrism versus imperialism and present noninterference versus hegemonism, the two dichotomies reflecting a perceived deep divide between two civilizations, East and West.

At the core of China's national identity construction, which in the years 2009–11 hit its full stride, has been the image of a beleaguered state and also civilization that confronts its antagonists by exposing the great national identity gap that exists. Such exposés share some things in common, while specifying the distinct differences present in each bilateral disparity. Actual coverage depends to some degree on the state of bilateral relations, but as China has continued its rise, it has found less need to tone down arguments regarding differences or to maintain the fiction that cooperation prevails over competition. On all dimensions, it has widened identity gaps with little likelihood that they will be narrowed.

In the 1980s, Chinese culture was under siege, having been weakened by the strident, antagonistic policies of Communist leaders, culminating in the Cultural Revolution, and appearing vulnerable to the arrival in one feverish burst of both the venerated cultural treasures produced in the rest of the world and the latest trendy fashion setters in various spheres of contemporary culture. After the starvation diet during the Cultural Revolution, this "culture fever" posed considerable risk. This was exposed by the impact of Mikhail Gorbachev's glasnost and by alarm over a threefold assault on the cultural essence of Chinese Communism: (1) studies of comparative socialism in search of the values that led to its inhumane results; (2) interpretations of Confucian tradition, which then implicated Chinese civilization as an underlying cause of the evils of the "twenty lost years"; and (3) fascination with the cultural appeal of the West in all phases of its history as a source of more humanistic values. An intense backlash by China's leaders in the 1980s, which involved purging the entire field of comparative socialism and opening the door to a positive reassessment of Confucianism, did not suffice. After June 4, 1989, and especially starting in 1992, when a more sophisticated approach was developed to face a more perilous challenge, China forged a comprehensive strategy of constructing a proud identity impervious to such challenges.

Leaders consciously orchestrated a strategy that put socialism in the background while combating any effort to weaken its foundation in China. Stressing the country's history before 1949, they further demonized the significant "others" that had damaged Chinese national identity and glorified those, including many previously vilified as class enemies, that had defended it. Most important, scholarship credited China's leadership with a vigorous defense of national dignity in the face of repeated challenges. The main line of the new narrative contrasted China's forward-looking efforts to rise and to take pride in its achievements with the suspicious, self-serving criticisms of its adversaries intent on undermining its rise.

This meant highlighting the uniqueness of Chinese culture. In the fall of 2008, as other elements of national identity were also being given a new emphasis, the case was made for distinctive cultural identity (*Zhongguo wenhua teshulun*). The discussion ranged across writings on history, ethnic minorities, and comparisons with the cultures of other countries, especially the United States and the West. Weakness before 1949 was attributed not only to political factors but also to loss of cultural confidence. Striving to Westernize, when China had the opportunity to revert to Eastern culture (*donghua*), was blamed for this loss. Many authors stress sharp differences between the two cultures. Although, from a historical perspective, they note benefits from Western culture, they keep in the forefront a litany of tragedies supposedly emanating from this source. One clear conclusion is to reject a merging of the two types of culture in favor of siding completely with the Eastern variant, which is equated with Chinese culture. Raising the theory of cultural security (*wenhua anquanlun*), writers aim to protect Chinese culture from an invasion. Interest has grown in learning how to export this by going beyond customary cultural exchanges to find ways to spread Chinese as opposed to Western culture, while denying the often-criticized exporting of values seen in U.S. exchanges.

Cultural uniqueness is credited with many positive results—economic, political, and diplomatic. One assumed quality of Chinese culture is an ability to achieve cultural fusion without any serious cultural clash. To make this case, the Chinese whitewash Manchu and Mongol rule, as if under both sets of alien rulers China's identity faced little challenge from ethnic nationalism or a backlash of Han nationalism. Despite Han supremacism on the Internet and simmering tensions with various ethnic groups, Chinese sources feign an unbroken harmonious tradition, yielding voluntary acceptance of a joint value system.[8]

Convergence is anathema. The main thrust of exceptionalism is directed against domestic elites, who are prone to discard the narrow notions of what makes one's nation distinctive. Communists may insist on the priority struggle against capitalists on behalf of the proletariat, but Communism's history in power or even in opposition has centered more on struggle against reformist elites with cosmopolitan tendencies. Class struggle in the Soviet Union in the 1930s and in China in the 1960s and 1970s was replaced by the demonization of advocates of political and cultural reform that might lead to convergence. If Stalin's 1947 anticosmopolitan campaign and Deng's 1987 expulsion of champions of reform Communism purified elite ranks, more frequently, harassment sufficed as the preferred mechanism for marginalizing those who deigned to advocate political or ideological transformation capable of undermining the tight vertical structure of Chinese society.

In the 1990s and 2000s, the dichotomy of socialism versus capitalism was left for political education courses and a select group of sources seen by many as no more than a holdover from a bygone era. Both official and academic sources avoided the contrast between two blocs reminiscent of the Cold War. Although efforts continued to add the word "socialist" to concepts such as a market economy, the term "capitalist" lost favor as a pejorative label, just as "revisionist" was dropped a decade earlier. If in 1991 and early 1992 ideological stalwarts, who had been emboldened by the shift away from reform in 1989, responded to the collapsing Soviet Union with ideological dichotomies, they were quieted through a deliberate, long-range theoretical strategy, in which national identity occupied a prominent place. The dichotomies returned later as China's confidence grew.

The concept of civilization often serves to diminish the notion of national identity because of the stress on a broader, international context, as in Western civilization. Yet in China's case, it reinforces the national level because of both the absence of an outside source or even serious partner and the weight given to the state as opposed to individual rights, which could serve as an opening to international or regional community identity. Indeed, Chinese sources are prone to prioritize state rights (*guoquan*) over human rights. As they discuss the parallel rise in the people's prosperity (*minfu*) and the state's power (*guoqiang*), they incorporate China's dignity (*Zhongguo zunyan*).[9] Although there is some debate over whether recent events such as the Beijing Olympics or the Shanghai World's Fair are an indicator of the level of China's civilization, the thirst for dignity is manifest.

In the year following the January 2011 Obama-Hu summit, China grew more determined to reinforce its cultural national identity and draw a sharp line with those who would try to apply universal values. Whereas at the time of the summit some thought that China was reconsidering its assertive posture of 2010, national identity gaps were not narrowing. In February 2012, China joined Russia in vetoing a UN Security Council resolution aimed at stopping the Syrian government from continuing to massacre peaceful demonstrators and drive the country toward civil war. For theorists of international relations, this move, along with firmer support of North Korea, should not be construed as a realist response to a threat or potential threat but as a statement about the national identity sought by China's leadership. As in the case of Russia, it can be traced to the legacy of Communism and the insistence of widening the national identity gap with the West.

CONCLUSION

Although realist approaches omit reference to trust or distrust and liberal approaches assume integrationist forces advancing mechanistically, the constructivist approach erects too big a tent to establish how to find the drivers in bilateral relations, which are the core of the international system. Yet modified constructivism, as notably articulated by Anne Clunan, offers a firmer foundation. In agreeing with her stress on strivings for collective esteem through the state under the influence of historical memory, one sees the prospect of international relations that revitalize the popular concept of national identities. This leads to the assumption that the international system is reducible to its building blocks, both dyadic relations between states and the domestic drivers on each side that shape them. The result is to narrow the often-elusive constructivist approach to national identity, which combines an analysis of the gap in national identities that steers a relationship and of the multiple dimensions of the identities of each of the states that contribute to this gap.

The national identity approach repackages and clarifies interconnections among concepts that have long informed the study of international relations. The most obvious linkage is with "nationalism," a term associated with patriotism and emotional sentiment that steers diplomats and public opinion alike to suspend some objective criteria in their dealings with the outside world. When nationalism rises or falls, there is evidence that something deeper is invoked, with different intensity or in a changing manner. Clearly, this concept usefully informs many studies, but its application has been too rough-edged to maximize an advance in scholarship, such as by showing the forces behind nationalism and how they were constructed and evolved.[10] Another linkage is with ideology, which may be imposed from above to subsume national identity, although its content will be gradually eroded by elements of that identity even as it also produces changes in the nation's identity. A third concept is historical memory, which is treated here as a dimension of national identity. Finally, coverage of East Asian states often points to the concept of face, arguing that if a state is not treated in a manner deemed fitting to its status, then its leaders may take umbrage. One associates this with the intensity of national identity, another of its dimensions, and the way particular symbols become markers triggering a response. Scholarship on international relations in East Asia is filled with references to nationalism, historical memory, and face. The national identity approach brings these themes together in a coherent manner.

Through this approach, one draws attention to three sets of distinctions. First, the study of a country's identity is usefully seen as a composite of six dimensions, which are specified in the earlier project's results, as described in detail in the companion volume to the present study.[11] Second, national identities are expressed through dyadic relations that are influenced by a national identity gap, and the size of the gap between two states is subject to estimation. Third, such gaps are activated through a sequence of events characterized by a spike in national identity and specific targeting of how changes in relations with a significant "other" will produce a rise in national esteem or overcome a recent drop in that esteem. Regimes intent on widening the gap play a major role in shaping international relations, often in opposition to those eager to narrow the gap.

One implication of this approach is that an avoidance of sensitive issues may serve a temporary purpose, preventing a spike in national identity, but it is unlikely to resolve the underlying problem of historical memories, whether active or latent, poised for future arousal. In the years 1989–92, a misunderstanding of Russian national identity led policymakers to shortsighted decisions. Other cases of miscalculation can be seen in the Bush administration's approaches to South Korea and Japan, which contributed to the election of Roh Moo-hyun and, perhaps, also to the eventual victory of the Democratic Party of Japan. Another test looms. Sino-U.S. relations are at a crossroads. There is a need for closer scrutiny of Chinese national identity and of the gap that exists in national identity within the United States. An analysis of U.S. national identity deserves to be added to this picture. If contested identities complicate analysis using the national identity framework, it still can steer scholarship in directions that have been left relatively unexplored in the field.

NOTES

1   Gilbert Rozman, *The Chinese Debate about Soviet Socialism, 1978–1985* (Princeton, N.J.: Princeton University Press, 1987); Lorenz M. Luthi, *The Sino-Soviet Split: Cold War in the Communist World* (Princeton, N.J.: Princeton University Press, 2008); Thomas P. Bernstein and Hua-Yu Li, eds., *China Learns from the Soviet Union, 1949–Present* (Lanham, Md.: Lexington Books, 2010).

2   David Steinberg, *Korean Attitudes toward the United States: Changing Dynamics* (Armonk, N.Y.: M. E. Sharpe, 2004); Gilbert Rozman, *South Korea's National*

Identity Sensitivity: Evolution, Manifestations, Prospects, KEI Academic Paper Series (Washington, D.C.: Korea Economic Institute, 2009), 1–9; Leif Eric-Easley, Tetsuo Kotani, and Aki Mori, "Electing a New Japanese Security Policy: Examining Foreign Policy Visions within the Democratic Party of Japan," *Asia Policy*, no. 9 (January 2010): 45–66.

3   Jae Ho Chung, "China's 'Soft' Clash with South Korea: The History War and Beyond," *Asian Survey* 49, no. 3 (May–June 2009): 468–83; Gilbert Rozman, ed., *U.S. Leadership, History, and Bilateral Relations in Northeast Asia* (Cambridge: Cambridge University Press, 2010).

4   Gilbert Rozman, *Chinese Strategic Thought toward Asia* (New York: Palgrave, 2009).

5   Anne L. Clunan, *The Social Construction of Russia's Resurgence: Aspirations, Identity, and Security Interests* (Baltimore: Johns Hopkins University Press, 2009), 8–21.

6   Ibid., 40–41.

7   Ibid., 95.

8   James Leibold, "More Than a Category: Han Supremacism on the Chinese Internet," *China Quarterly*, no. 203 (September 2010): 539–59.

9   Editorial Bureau, "Zhongguo sunyan," *Guoji xianqu daobao* in Xinhuawang, January 3, 2011.

10   Allen Carlson, "A Flawed Perspective: The Limitations Inherent within the Study of Chinese Nationalism," *Nations and Nationalism* 15, no. 1 (2009): 20–35.

11   Gilbert Rozman, ed., *East Asian National Identities: Common Roots and Chinese Exceptionalism* (Washington, D.C., and Stanford, Calif.: Woodrow Wilson Center Press and Stanford University Press, 2011).

CHAPTER 7

CHINESE NATIONAL IDENTITY AND EAST ASIAN NATIONAL IDENTITY GAPS

Gilbert Rozman

Chinese coverage aimed at widening or narrowing national identity gaps across Asia has concentrated on four targets: (1) Japan, (2) South Korea, (3) the Association of Southeast Asian Nations (ASEAN), and (4) Islamic civilization. In the first two cases and the third, to some extent, China has widened the gap, while it has sought to narrow the gap with Islamic states as part of Eastern civilization, which is sharply contrasted with Western civilization. Given a continued widening of its gap with India also, the popular image in the 1990s and 2000s of China building trust with its neighbors and pursuing regionalism must be rethought. If soft power relies on narrowing identity gaps, then China is sacrificing it, not for hard power, but for a predilection for widening gaps as a means of achieving national identity aims that are prioritized.

With socialist identity uncertain after the Mao Zedong era, two types of identity were presented to Chinese leaders as offering a path to modernity and modernization. If most attention centered on the Western model, there was another model found in East Asia that also elicited widespread interest. Whether labeled the Japanese model, the South Korean model, Confucian capitalism, or Asian values, modernization in East Asia loomed as an alternative to Westernization not only for a set of policies but also for its identity implications. If Chinese spokespersons never clearly embraced this ideal, they had faced the challenge for the past three decades of clarifying their national identity to counter other East Asian claims, to boost a shared sense of community, and recently to establish China's leadership over an exclusive course of regionalism. To meet this changing challenge, China has at times narrowed identity gaps, but of late it has sharply widened gaps in the region while suggesting a narrowing ahead based on other states embracing Chinese interpretations along all dimensions, not the other way around.

China rarely takes note of the views or actions of the Chinese side to explain why national identity gaps are wide. Instead, it plays up extreme views on the other side. This has typically been the case for Japan since the mid-1980s.[1] Demonization of revisionist views of history serves as the hook to arouse Chinese emotions, which can extend to other Japanese identity themes. In the South Korean case, a historical hook has also been found, which is associated with charges that a similar revisionist nature exists concerning Korean territorial or civilizational claims.[2] If ASEAN was late to be drawn into this divisive strategy, accusations against the territorial claims of several of its members produce a similar effect. The narrative in each case points to unjust demands supported by excessive emotions rooted in national identity, which, then, arouse public opinion in China and lead to a downward spiral in relations. China is invariably blameless, and the Chinese people merely react to extreme provocations. The other side is the guilty party, which is not legitimately pursuing its national interests but allowing national identity, deeply embedded in its culture and history, to distort its outlook and its diplomacy. Cooperation with the United States is taken as proof that states have sinister intentions. This is how national identity gaps in Asia are treated with increasing frequency.

The Chinese refer to two reference groups—the East Asian region and the global South, both filled with developing countries—to contrast with the West and to serve as vehicles for China to assume leadership. In the East Asian region, China found in 2010 that its support was thin, derived mainly from poor states that are weakly integrated into the international system. In the South, China's strongest support is coming from Africa and the Middle East. In both groups, the critical factor for boosting China's standing are the Islamic states. If China can gain support from Indonesia and Malaysia, both of which seemed more at odds with the United States in the early years of the George W. Bush administration than now, its standing in Southeast Asia will climb. Similarly, if it can win backing from the major Islamic countries in the Middle East and North Africa as well as Pakistan and Iran, its claims vis-à-vis the South will be more convincing. Having excluded India, China's hopes for linking the notion of the BRICS states (i.e., Brazil, Russia, India, China, and South Africa—the world's largest fast-growing economic powers) with the South are best met by Russia, although it is located far to the north.

China brings considerable historical baggage to its views of nearby states. Its "blood alliance" with North Korea shapes its image of South Korea.[3] Memories of the war of liberation at the crux of the Communist Party's legitimacy color China's outlook on Japan. The countries of Southeast Asia are perceived through the prism of Sinocentric China. Because Chinese history has been subject to great distortions under Mao and even afterward, these images are part of a national identity narrative determined less by specific moments in recent bilateral relations, although they matter, than by an overall understanding of what China's place in the region has been and should be.

Given the overwhelming preoccupation with the United States, the strategy of managing national identity gaps was tailored to draw other significant states closer to China—as in the case of Russia. The next priority went to Japan, but the strategy for managing it was complicated by the contradiction between using a widening gap with Japan to intensify China's own identity and welcoming a narrowing gap to split Japan from the United States. Later, the goal of forging an East Asian regional identity also encouraged a narrowing gap in spite of continued interest in deepening the contrast, as China strove for leadership in the region. A lower priority was South Korea, whose differences with the United States widening in 2001-03 offered a promising opportunity, but whose legitimacy as the rightful representative of the Korean people conflicted with China's plans for the resuscitation of North Korea and construction of a regional identity. Narrowing the identity gap with South Korea was more dispensable than with Japan before China's surge of confidence in the years 2009–10. Growing interest centered on ASEAN, whose identity seemed ready to be reshaped after the Asian financial crisis and the decision to form ASEAN + 3. Finally, after the September, 11, 2001, terrorist attacks on the United States and the U.S. declaration of the "war on terrorism," the notion of Islamic civilization entered the picture as a force for China's (*Zhonghua wenming*) intercivilizational contacts in opposition to the West.

Of these cases, only the gap between China and the Islamic world was raised to the level of interactions between two civilizations on a par with interactions with the West, led by the United States. Yet, Sino-Japanese relations garnered considerable treatment, in the sense that China represents the pure Eastern civilization and Japan is depicted as a sort of hybrid case, which imbibed Eastern civilization but then lost its essence before succumbing to Western civilization without fully entering it. The case of South Korea has many parallels, but it is accepted as a fuller embodiment of Eastern civilization, even though its features were distorted by the West. Finally, ASEAN emerges in the civilizational narrative as more amenable to a shared community due its background in Eastern civilization and national experiences with Western imperialism.

Chinese writers often use code words for civilization differences. The stress is on the absence of a foundation for shared cultural values. Sometimes, a disparity is attributed to the other side's interference in internal affairs due to its ambitions to spread universal values. Another stock phrase in contrasts is the assertion that differences stem from diverse political systems, in which China may be listed as having a socialist system or as a market economy with features of a socialist state (*tezheng de shehuizhuyi guojia*). One more recognized source of cultural differences is divisions over history. The upshot of such systemic and deep-seated differences is purportedly a lack of trust and the potential for mass emotions to be politicized. Chinese socialism is blameless, whereas prejudice against it is faulted.

When Chinese coverage of security differences with neighboring states grew more critical in the years 2010–11, it was not just a matter of reacting angrily to policy choices in these states that did not satisfy

China's interests. Rather, China had already been reframing the issues involved as tests of civilizational allegiances. No longer does it suffice to further economic integration with China and rely on the United States for security, acknowledging universal values even as a search proceeds for some shared cultural symbols in order to pursue regionalism. Chinese sources insist on a higher standard for regionalism: deciding between Eastern and Western civilization. This tougher stance applies first of all to the two key U.S. allies, Japan and South Korea.

THE NATIONAL IDENTITY GAP WITH JAPAN

Writings on Japan during the 1980s and the 1990s registered a fluctuating identity gap. If sometimes the gap was deliberately widened, other times it was not. When Japan was pursued as a partner in regionalism in the years 2000–3 and again in 2006–8, there were new efforts to project a gap that could be narrowed. Among the most common themes were (1) Japan is bent on gaining more independence from the United States and, thus, is striving for Asian regionalism in a manner that overlaps with China's interest; (2) the collapse of the Soviet Union led to a weakening of the U.S.-Japanese alliance, and Japan is freer to pursue regionalism; (3) Japan was heavily influenced by Chinese civilization, and, despite adopting Western industrial civilization in the course of modernization, it still respects Eastern civilization, which offers common ground with China; and (4) the United States' determination to retain its hegemony in the region leaves Japan dissatisfied and drives other states to seek more Japanese as well as Chinese cooperation.[4] Yet, as China's aspirations rose, anger at Japan also grew.

Given the historical record, China can easily arouse strong feelings toward Japan. But on various occasions it has become clear that the United States is seen as the more important target—in the years 1989–90, when Japan was the weak link in sanctions; and in 2000, when "smile diplomacy" toward Japan followed a spike in anti-American appeals. Relative restraint toward Japan reflected increased hopes for boosting East Asian regionalism as a shared identity or capitalizing on doubts there about the United States; but when the restraints were dropped, the intensity of the identity gap's widening reached a high pitch. This was seen in the mid-1990s and again in the mid-2000s. What made 2010 different was the overlap of demonization of the United States and Japan. A spike in confidence overwhelmed all previous caution.

Before the downturn in Chinese views of Japan in 2010, there was a mixture of hope over cooperation in the pursuit of an East Asian community through ASEAN + 3, which would gradually evolve from a group of nations with economic ties to a political and security system and finally to a shared identity, and suspicion that Japan would not be accepting of ASEAN's leadership, in contrast to China, and would not be willing to commit to such a community.[5] At times Chinese officials calculated that Japan could shift its foreign policy balance away from the U.S. alliance and toward Asian countries, with China the main beneficiary. But that prospect had been dashed by the fall of 2010. If certain Japan experts take note of the diversity of Japanese society and the importance of a "silent majority," leaving open the possibility of mutual trust, their views are easily overshadowed by the recent outpouring of criticism of an "irredeemable nation."[6]

China failed to explore regionalism with Hatoyama Yukio and Ozawa Ichiro after the Democratic Party of Japan (DPJ) took office in 2009, intent on narrowing the identity gap. Because analysts credited Hatoyama with intensified interest in forging an East Asian community and interpreted Ozawa's call for a "normal Japan" to mean support for a Sino-U.S.-Japan triangle rather than one-sided reliance on the U.S. alliance, the lack of enthusiasm in 2009 deserves an explanation. If the DPJ's takeover had occurred earlier, there might have been a different reaction. Yet by 2009 the prospect that Japan would prioritize Sino-Japanese relations and agree to the exclusion, at least partially, of the United States from regionalism did not meet heightened expectations at the moment of a national identity spike. As in the case of the Liberal Democratic Party, the DPJ sought to make the East Asian Summit, not ASEAN + 3, the basis of regionalism. It too was reluctant to proceed from functional and open regionalism to institutional and closed regionalism, in accord with China's way of thinking. Downgrading the alliance from its primary place in foreign relations to a parallel presence with an East Asian community did not meet China's surging aspirations.[7] Thus, the DPJ's shift was not seen as breaking away from Japan's ideological fetters,[8] but as an opportunity to press for more.

In a span of two months in late 2010, the Chinese blamed Japan for deteriorating relations; blamed the West for awarding the Nobel Peace Prize to Liu Xiaobo, as if it was attacking Chinese national identity; blamed South Korea and the United States for failing to respond to North Korean aggression with new talks instead of military exercises; and intensified their criticism of civilizational divides that are destabilizing Asia. If in the winter of 2010–11, in connection with Hu Jintao's visit to Washington, the tone improved somewhat, the autumn rhetoric lingered as a turning point. Japan was in the forefront for the vehemence with which it was criticized and for its pivotal role in China's linkage of great powers, neighboring countries, and East Asian regionalism. It was accused of inciting public opinion against a fictitious "China threat," of acting with malice in causing the boat accident (see below) and the arrests that followed, and of failing to recognize the danger of arousing Chinese public opinion and a China that is now strong enough to defend its interests. Moreover, this incident is viewed as part of an overall right-wing shift that alienates China and harms regional cooperation.[9] Closer Japanese ties with India, South Korea, and the United States anger the Chinese, who now convey a sense of betrayal by Japan and South Korea for their shift toward the United States, especially in 2010. Instead of Japan seeking equality with the United States and a return to Asia, as in the 1990s, and the removal of U.S. bases from Okinawa, which was a theme in 2009, the Chinese now claimed to see a pattern of encirclement.[10]

According to Chinese sources, the issue of sovereignty over the Diaoyu/Senkaku Islands is not a complicated matter of competing jurisdictional claims due to contrasting legal interpretations. Rather, it stands as a fundamental test of Japan's true intentions toward putting its history of imperialism behind it and pursuing international relations on the basis of mutual trust. The dispute in September 2010 is attributed to unprecedented actions by the Japanese, first by detaining a Chinese fishing boat, and then using the pretext that the boat had rammed Japanese cruisers to hold the crew for a time and the captain longer. These illegal actions, according to Chinese sources, signify a great change in Japan's strategy,[11] revealing it as a hard-line state unwilling to accept the status quo and ready to destabilize the region. Allegedly, this helped the Kan Naoto Cabinet to boost domestic support and strengthen the U.S. alliance.

Although Japan was to a degree influenced by Chinese culture, the stress in this instance is placed on the sharp contrast of the two cultures. Viewing postwar Japan through the lens of historical apologies rather than its commitment to peace, sources distort its identity at the same time as they simplify China's peaceful development as consistent with new assertiveness, which rejects letting a conflict such as this end in the absence of a Japanese apology and sharp change of course. Finding "anti-China" tendencies on the rise in Japan and attributing this to Chinese laxity at a time of concentration on reform and openness, many ignore China's own identity. They warn that the overall bilateral relationship would be put at risk and that public opinion, which is already antagonistic to Japan, would be unforgiving.[12] Japanese sources called for restraint, with politicians avoiding "brave talk" and even taking steps to acknowledge China's views in order not to humiliate it.[13] The Chinese made this a test of national identity, as if anything short of total victory would mean capitulation, not to a pragmatic Japan but to a reviving imperialist aggressor. Even after the crisis, these Chinese views remained.

Another Chinese interpretation is that Japan's handling of the island dispute is linked to its containment of China in "neighboring seas" (*linghai*), not excluding Taiwan. As Japan reorients its military toward the southwest and conducts military exercises there, it contradicts the goal of a "peaceful sea" and arouses tensions that will threaten efforts by the Chinese government to constrain public opinion, which is inclined to react more negatively. In this view, only if Japan refrains from acts to show that it is "maintaining sovereignty" can this dispute be managed.[14] Familiar themes reappear of an overly ambitious Japan bent on accelerating its march to becoming a political great power, gaining a greater voice, and forging the political means to become a military great power.[15] The Diaoyu/Senkaku Islands loom as a future military outpost to block Taiwan's northern ports and air routes, while also posing a serious threat to parts of the Southeast China mainland. Not only does Japan intend to grab natural resources to which it is not entitled, it is preparing to contain China in line with the United States' plans to extend its military from Okinawa to these islands and control the Taiwan Strait. China's behavior in 2010 contributed to a downward spiral; as Japan grew more alarmed, some right-wing voices called for joining forces with Taiwan, and Chinese national identity boosters highlighted these reactions as proof that China had to harden its position toward Japan. After much talk in the years 2006–8 of a thaw or a warming of Sino-Japanese relations, the verdict was that they were again below freezing.[16]

Demonization of Japan took on new twists in 2010. After decades of seeking ways to split it from the United States, China lost all patience. The real problem was not Japan's militaristic history but its Western identity, leading it to join with its ally in Cold War thinking and making aggressive moves in East Asia. There is no recognition of the role of realism in these actions. Instead, China finds a receptive audience for suggestions that Japanese national identity is continuously at fault. In line with this thinking, the various security challenges are lumped together. Missile defense, triangular alliance ties with South Korea, reference to China as a hypothetical enemy, repositioning of Japanese forces in the southwest, and even assertiveness on the dispute with Russia over the Northern Kuril Islands (Northern Territories) lingering from World War II are on the list. If the Diaoyu/Senkaku Islands dispute was at the top of the list in the fall of 2010, it soon was engulfed in warnings that regarded the threat from Japan's support for U.S.–South Korean military exercises as even more serious than the threat from North Korea that these exercises were supposedly targeting.[17]

For the Chinese people, relations with Japan are highly sensitive, poised to turn sharply downward with one wrong step. Yet it is acceptable to demonize Japan not only for its half century of repeated aggression but also for an earlier culture that enabled this and for the postwar culture and politics that fail to express appropriate regret. If leaders earlier cautioned the public to keep these emotions under control in order to advance bilateral ties in the national interest, they have no compunction about stirring the emotions, also deemed in the national interest, and using them as a card for unbalanced relations, where Japan should accept China's assertiveness as it adheres to its own passivity. Among Chinese Netizens, there is a widespread feeling that Japan is vulnerable to Chinese economic measures—boycotting Japanese goods, avoiding tourism, and prohibiting the export of rare earth metals. Warnings appear that Japan is in economic peril for allowing bilateral relations to slump. It is seen as needing China more than China needs it. Some recall the days after the normalization of relations between the two countries, when the Japanese came to China repeating that the Japanese people had been victims of militarism just as the Chinese were, giving China reason to anticipate continued deference from a nation that was intolerant of assertiveness from its leaders. When the Japanese grew concerned about China's military buildup and aggressive tone, the Chinese found their reaction an intolerable breach of the basis of normalization.[18] Having failed to resist Japan successfully in its period of expansionism, the Chinese are insistent on not being meek this time. Arguing that dealing with Japan from a position of resentment is a natural outcome of wartime memories, the Chinese fail to note top-down efforts to keep these memories alive and construct national identity in direct opposition to today's Japan.

Coverage of United States–Japan relations reveals that China's manipulation of identity gaps is a propagandistic effort to steer states into its orbit or turn them against each other. When Hatoyama took office, observers insisted that the search for a normal identity requires Japan to merge with Asia and insist on full equality with the United States and that the Futenma base dispute exposes a shaky alliance as U.S. influence declines. Explaining later why Japan has defied expectations that once the DPJ took power it would seek independence from the United States and advance the goal of becoming a normal country, the Chinese stress broken promises due to a dysfunctional political system and intractable economic problems. Yet most emphasis is given to the drift back to Liberal Democratic Party foreign policies under U.S. pressure, utilizing the pretext of the sinking of the *Cheonan*. As Japan's alliance with the United States and ties to South Korea strengthen, there is a negative effect on Sino-Japanese relations. Instead of addressing equality with the United States and the Futenma base issue as its symbol, Japan is distracted by maritime disputes with China as it falls back into instability.[19]

On the one hand, Chinese sources deny Japan the right to become a political great power, arguing that this theme surfaced in the 1980s in an unhealthy manner. The fact that Japan's leaders raised it is considered a sign of inadequate reflection on history and, even more deeply, of a presumption that cultural understanding in Asia is possible without a fundamental shift of course by Japan. Opposing Japan's quest while insisting that it was dangerously linked to a drive to become a military great power, China was widening the national identity gap with Japan. On the other hand, Chinese sources appeal to a shared Eastern civilization as a basis for a joint mission to draw closer together.[20] This appeal preceded China's embrace of regionalism and reflected its rising aspirations in the mid-1990s to capitalize on post–Cold War divisions in U.S.-Japanese relations consistent with the goal of multipolarity. Yet the appeal has faded since the Chinese have become convinced that a common ground on identity would fail to meet China's own identity imperatives. Instead, they are widening this gap.

It is not clear what the limits are of reassertion of maritime sovereignty and spheres of influence. Neighbors have reason for concern. This has been an issue in Russia, despite agreements with China in the post–Cold War period that resolve all differences. It is a concern in Japan, although awareness is weak that Okinawa (the Ryukuus) is seen in China as having about five hundred years of close ties to China before it was annexed by Japan in 1871. Although the Chinese charge that Japan is very ambitious, has a political need to become a military great power, and has plans that pose a threat to China, they keep the extent of their own ambitions along similar lines in the shadows.[21]

Whereas leaders had been careful earlier about acknowledging China's rise, dropping the term "rise" and adding the adjective "peaceful," now there is no such hesitation. It is taken as a fact that Japan and others must accept, even to the point of agreeing to its leadership in the region and rejecting U.S. "Cold War" reasoning on matters such as Taiwan, the Korean Peninsula, and the South China Sea. Especially, Japan is asked to accept the verdict on its history and the implications for the East China

Sea. A few years ago, there was ambiguity in discussions of the international system or the linkage between it and regionalism. No longer is the need to reshape this system in doubt, accompanied by greater specificity about the significance of the emerging East Asian community beyond economics and of forging a multilateral framework in place of U.S. alliances as the only way to guarantee regional security.[22] In all these matters, Japan is treated as a secondary state, not world class, which, given the way things are changing, would wisely avoid siding with the United States. Its failure to cooperate with China has led to criticism that no longer rests principally on its historical transgressions

After its defeat, Japan repeatedly viewed Southeast Asia as its main prospect for asserting itself as a political great power. According to one source, "cutting into" the region took various forms, from riding the bandwagon of anticommunism under Yoshida Shigeru to the "three diplomatic principles" of Kishi, to the Fukuda Doctrine, to agreement on new organizations such as the ASEAN Regional Forum and ASEAN + 3. The "arc of freedom and prosperity" was emphasized in the region, as was enlisting the support of states such as Vietnam, Cambodia, and Laos for Japan's position on the citizens abducted by North Korea. In opposing China on how to define the East Asian community, Japan continues to display values that are centered on the nefarious goal of asserting its leadership in Asia, we are told. Although Hatoyama raised the priority of putting Asia at the center and balancing U.S. and Chinese relations, he did not move far enough to win praise from China for a change of course.[23] This chronology of the shortsightedness of Japan downplays mutual interests in favor of national identity.

One finds a preference for cultural explanations of Japan's foreign policies. In contrast to Western and Japanese emphasis on postwar pacifism, Chinese sources point to deeper longings, which starting in the 1980s were embodied in the goal of Japan becoming a "normal" country. This is seen as requiring constitutional reform and also becoming a political or even a military great power in place of postwar symbols of a peaceful state. Leaders are using a pervasive and rising crisis consciousness to transform Japan's role in international society. Notions of Asianism and the East Asian community are part of this quest, but the objective is to utilize bilateral U.S.-Japanese relations to shape regionalism. A fragile domestic culture distorts Asianism in this way, denying a genuine East Asian community for a region led by Japan and replacing past internationalism in favor of alliance-centered global identity.[24]

Japan is depicted as the United States' running dog and as a state ambitious for military ascendancy in Asia—despite the limitations mandated by Article 9 in its Constitution. It refuses to accept losing leadership in Asia. Western values stand in the way of acceptance of the East Asian community. In the early months of Hatoyama's leadership, the Chinese warned against optimism because he was vague on whether the United States should be in Asia or not. This standard overrode any exploration of how China might work with him to find common ground.[25] With Kan's leadership, Chinese attacks against Japan, including Japan's policy of drawing closer to South Korea, had intensified. This policy was regarded as dangerous, an expression of Cold War thinking targeted against China and North Korea. Kan and Foreign Minister Maehara Seiji were vilified even more than Barack Obama and Hillary Clinton for extremist views, which, although not directly linked to historical revisionism, were placed in the same category of far-right, anti-Chinese thinking. Arguing that Tokyo and Seoul are very dependent on China for trade, writers warn them that they have more to lose if the region descends into a cold war. After all, Japan is vulnerable due to its history and South Korea due to the presence of North Korea. The alternative for both is to join with Beijing against Washington, which is the real instigator.[26] This is the message firmly embedded in China's recent publications that are critical of its neighbors' identities.

Explaining what drives Japan's betrayal of China, these authors insist that the reasons identified in Japan are only pretexts. They point instead to irrationality or political maneuvering. One example is the charge that the Japanese are responding with shock because in 2010 China surpassed their country in gross domestic product. Also mentioned is the presence of a crisis mentality over domestic problems. Another comment is that for the fourth time (Kishi, Sato, Koizumi, and Kan), Japan has set back bilateral relations, a pattern that suggests an inability to adjust to the world order. Pressed by the United States, Japan yields for reasons rooted in the abnormalities of the ties between them.[27] Never mentioned is China's behavior or Sino-Japanese problems that China should help to address.

Although Japan was influenced by Chinese culture and cultural similarities had been cited by Chinese leaders and analysts, the verdict in 2010 was that the two countries had completely different cultural systems.[28] If some may attribute this conclusion to the sense in China that the history issue has not been resolved, a more convincing factor is its determination to widen the gap to pursue a foreign policy agenda that is unacceptable to Japan. Despite the DPJ keeping the history issue well under control, China's interest in widening the gap reached an unprecedented level. Depicting a drastic change in Japanese foreign policy under Kan, Chinese explain it as Japan losing its nerve and agreeing to submit to U.S. pressure while succumbing to old thinking and pressure from the hawks at home.[29] China is faultless. National interests do not matter. A troubled national identity has again led Japan astray.

THE NATIONAL IDENTITY GAP WITH SOUTH KOREA

If shared traditional culture is a unifying force in building a community, then South Korea should have been China's prime target. The strongest support for the continued positive impact of Confucianism in the 1980s and 1990s could be found in this country, especially among conservatives. Public opinion toward China was positive and was growing more so up to 2004. Yet, just as China grew more excited about East Asian regionalism, including its high expectations in 2004 for advancing plans to establish a community, its callous treatment of the history of Koguryo (see chapter 4) caused South Korea to rally around the argument that history is a divisive force between the two states. China proved then, as it was to prove with Japan and other neighboring states in the following years, that its concept of Eastern civilization is exclusively Chinese.

In its two-sided approach to South Korea, China both widens the identity gap and seeks to narrow it on Chinese terms. It blames both South Korea and North Korea for the breakdown in North-South relations during Lee Myung-bak's term in office. It charges that emotional identity issues are distorting South Korean views of China and threatening relations. The case against South Korea extends back many years, but its principal accusations in the years 2008–10 suggest that the situation keeps worsening. Criticizing extreme nationalism in South Korea became popular. It was supposedly manifest in threats to China's territorial integrity, a sense of superiority on cultural matters, twisted views of history that alienate the Chinese, and policies for international relations that are inconsistent with Seoul's national interests.[30] The Chinese suggest that such a narrow emotionalism is deeply rooted in Korean history. It is manifest in agricultural and other forms of protectionism, and it elicits calls for "buying Korean goods," a sign of extreme economic national identity. Also, it can be observed in textbooks and other displays of ancient maps portraying parts of Chinese territory as Korean. Although divergent Chinese and South Korean narratives about the Koguryo state are a major part of this gap over the past, Chinese sources make clear that the problem is much broader than that. In literature, too, the Chinese find distorted views. Another criticism is leveled against claims about the superiority of Korean culture, which involve exaggerating its independent development to the point of seeing it as a separate civilization of world significance and underestimating the influence of Chinese civilization. One gets the impression that there is a kind of cultural struggle under way between China and South Korea, given that the latter supposedly only in 2005 stopped calling its capital "Hancheng," as it has been known in Chinese, in favor of "Shouer," or "capital," which captures the sound of "Seoul." Many other usages of "Han," representing China, are reportedly rewritten with a homophone without the same implications of a shared culture. Whereas China increasingly claims a unifying Eastern civilization with China at the center, South Korea sees this as a threat and is fast distancing itself, warn Chinese publications angered by the trend.

The Chinese attribute the widening national identity gap to South Korea. They trace it back to humiliation with Japan's annexation, the country's division, and also the U.S. occupation. Also noted is the oversensitivity of a small country. The 1997 financial crisis on the heels of an economic miracle aroused wounded pride. Losing cohesion, South Korea decided that it could only induce patriotism with distorted history. In this analysis of causality, one learns of examples of distortions centered on China, even to the point of disclaimers that Korea was a vassal state of China, which allegedly have aroused the public against China and exerted a very negative influence. Variously, these misplaced feelings are demeaned as "small power resentment" or as "great power psychology," as old consciousness revived or newly constructed alarm based on fear that China's rise will lead to hegemony. Such interpretations omit politics in South Korea, as progressives and conservatives came to power. They omit North Korea, too, as if its actions do not matter. Although there is some mention of the impact of Japan on South Korea's identity, nothing is said about the impact of China's actions.

The gap with South Korea opened abruptly in 2004, when the Koguryo issue was recognized by South Koreans as a challenge to their national identity. It did not grow for a few years as the issue was allowed to hover in the background, and then exploded starting in 2008. South Koreans reacted to provocations, such as the manner in which Chinese marchers conducted themselves at the "sacred torch" parade before the Beijing Olympics. Their views of China deteriorated, as reported in an article by Chinese authors based on focus group interviews in Seoul. They observed that many respondents noted the suppression of minorities, socialism, and hard-line policies of China's leaders as negative images of the Chinese political system. Many also noted the poor quality of Chinese products, remarked on corruption and inequality in the society, and expressed fear that a more powerful China will seek hegemony over their state. Above all, they pointed to a lack of trust in China, which is linked to views of China as a friend of North Korea. These views are attributed to a combination of arrogance and self-doubt along with an unwillingness to accept the growing reality of dependence on China. At no point is China faulted. Rather, the authors fault Korean psychology.[31]

Other sources in 2010 charged that South Koreans had a superiority complex about their culture and sought glory in their history. This thinking amounted to an ideology that was harming Sino–South Korean relations. If past Chinese publications had commented favorably on South Korean emotions toward Japan, now that China is an object of dissatisfaction, the Chinese tone is intensely critical. This perspective arouses readers to think that, for reasons strictly internal to the South, people have become obsessed with ridding their country of elements of Chinese culture, ranging from characters and terms of speech to historical references, even making it appear that Confucianism was not an import from China. If there are external causes, they are found in the psychological burden of the U.S. alliance and U.S. troops stationed in the country. North Korea barely figures in such narratives. Allegedly, when Roh Moo-hyun was in office and national identity was tempered, South Korea followed a moderate policy to the North beneficial for stability and development on the Korean Peninsula, but its shift toward North Korea in tandem with the shift toward China escapes attention.[32]

South Koreans are blamed for North Korea's actions. Lee Myung-bak's policies broke from those of the previous decade, which China considers to have been successful. In this way, the South caused a new "cold war" and escalated problems from the bilateral level to a multilateral one.[33] If the South had kept rewarding the North and disregarded its nuclear buildup, pressure would have been put on the United States and Japan to resume the Six-Party Talks on terms welcomed by China. Crediting North Korea with a more positive attitude because it favors unconditional talks as opposed to South Korea resorting to military pressure and treating the North as the enemy, China shifts the onus away from its ally.[34] Its publications go so far as to credit Pyongyang with embracing the national interest and national identity, while blaming Lee Myung-bak for abandoning the Sunshine Policy, provoking the North, and failing to pursue reunification.[35] Only by accepting China's positive role and returning to the Six-Party Talks would Lee act in accord with the values that China endorses, ignoring human rights and even self-defense.

Chinese express a sense of betrayal that South Koreans ignore their national interests in favor of a Western identity and closer ties to their U.S. ally. Earlier, South Koreans had allegedly recognized the value of equidistance between the United States and China and of the early return of wartime operational command, but in 2010 they tilted the alliance in military exercises aimed at China and other moves.[36] The Chinese pretend that fears of North Korean attacks and China's refusal to criticize them are irrelevant and did not cause Cold War thinking to revive. They ignore the impact of the warmer Sino–North Korean relations, especially in the 2010 celebration of sixty-five years of party-to-party relations marked with commentaries on shared socialism, a shared embrace of the Korean War, and a sense of renewal of the treasured bond between the two[37]—all at a time of North Korean acts of belligerence that were threatening to South Koreans.

Perhaps, the foremost indicator of the aggravation of national identity in China was the response to North Korea's sinking of the *Cheonan* in March 2010. Not only did China refuse to blame the North, it embraced a narrative that echoed the views of its ally, from blaming the United States for the failure of reunification in the late 1940s and creating the conditions for the Korean War to retaining Cold War thinking toward the peninsula after the end of the Cold War and arousing anxiety in the North that justified its behavior over the next two decades. Blaming Lee Myung-bak also, especially for ending the much-lauded policies of Roh Moo-hyun, the Chinese in 2010 issued a steady stream of condemnations of South Korea's worldview.[38] The claim is that, driven by political ideology, South Korea seeks regime change. The gap with China, which is purported to be ready to reconvene the Six-Party Talks, where a ready solution to the crisis is available, could hardly be larger in China's narrative.

China provoked South Korea and Japan and then blamed them both for their response and for their sinister, deep-seated motives. Instead of sympathizing with their plight after the *Cheonan* attack revealed North Korea's aggressive strategy, it abetted the North in its inclination to blame others and aroused suspicions about China's own intentions. Similarly, the vitriolic tone of China's rhetoric on the boat-ramming incident in September raised alarm about its motives, and not only with Japan. As tensions mounted and alliances were reinforced, China blamed these responses on Cold War thinking and referred to historic transgressions as if Japan was destined to demonize China and would not be able to solidify ties with South Korea.[39] The only solution would be resumption of the

Six-Party Talks, which were now depicted as an alternative to alliances as a means to bring stability to Northeast Asia. At the root of China's reconceptualization was a rejection of the security arrangements and values that had maintained stability in the region, to the extent of seeking advantage from North Korean bellicosity. Calls for Seoul to take the strategic high road, while refraining from any public clash and accentuating healthy relations with China, are tantamount to asking South Korea to be deferential, stifling concern about Chinese affronts to its national identity. The tone is even more arrogant than that toward Japan.

How does China reconcile its claim to be the champion of regional peace and multilateralism with its call for transformation and a new regional order? The only way to do this is to blame others, who are striving to maintain it, for disrupting the order, while making excuses for those that are really threatening the status quo and whose behavior is useful for raising the prospect of desired changes. Thus, blaming South Korea and rationalizing North Korea's behavior with calls for sincerity from both sides is China's expedient choice, even as the North behaves belligerently.[40]

At times, different views of the Korean nuclear crisis and of South Korea have appeared in China. To recall them, however, is to overlook the pattern of increasing demonization. Recent scholarship and popular articles dealing with various dimensions of national identity are reflected in the sources that inform the coverage recounted above. Whether one reads area studies journals, international relations journals, or the major newspapers, there is no appreciable difference in how South Korea or the North/South divide are covered once national identity is of concern. Naturally, serious scholarship eschews the most sensitive themes in a factual approach.

THE NATIONAL IDENTITY CHALLENGE WITH ASEAN

Although the Chinese acknowledge the diversity of Southeast Asia, they have held high hopes that this region would be in the forefront in their quest for shared identity. If China remained aloof from the

Asian values enthusiasm before the Asian financial crisis, its opposition to Western values and its anti-American thrust had obvious appeal. In retrospect, at least, the Malaysian prime minister Mohamad Mahathir became a heroic figure, even if during the first half of the 1990s his "Look East" policy made Japan a model. Three forces in the region had special appeal to the Chinese. First, the overseas Chinese were recognized as remaining part of Chinese civilization with prospects for supporting the economic and cultural benefits of a regional community. Second, the enduring legacy of anticolonialism is considered fertile soil for anti-Western views, and thus sympathetic to China's push finally to sweep away the vestiges of humiliation at the hands of outsiders. Finally, the large Islamic populations in two critical states, Indonesia and Malaysia—which after 9/11 and, especially, the Iraq invasion had reason to become more anti-American—are viewed not as threats to support rights for the Uighur minority in China but as antagonists of the United States and the West. Despite the disparate or even contradictory nature of this prospective coalition, Chinese aspirations for soft power were rising.

The Asian financial crisis created an opening, the formation of ASEAN + 3 raised expectations, and in 2004 China's leaders were prepared for the upgrading of this body into the East Asian Summit, with China serving as an early host and then beginning to assume a leadership role. But the Chinese were blindsided by the decision in ASEAN to expand the summit in a manner that diluted its significance for regional identity, with India's inclusion as well as that of Australia and New Zealand. When Mahathir resigned and the United States regained its footing while China's own soft power proved to be weaker than anticipated, the case for civilizational agreement was fading. Mahathir emerges in the Chinese chronology as a farsighted thinker whose ideas for regionalism were hijacked by Japan, Singapore, and others in 2005 with an expanded East Asian Summit. Despite increased financial cooperation on a regional level, the United States' push to dilute the notion of regionalism and gain leadership at the expense of China posed a serious challenge.[41] Yet in the years 2009–10 China renewed its effort to make the East Asian community a reality through ASEAN + 3, despite

Japan's opposition and strong indications that the majority of states in Southeast Asia preferred to expand the East Asian Summit and give it the major role. The first meeting of the enlarged body with the United States and Russia was held in 2011.

In 2010, the Chinese saw U.S. involvement in the South China Sea dispute over sovereignty as a perpetuation of Cold War U.S. containment of the Soviet Union, which had shifted to containment of China. Anticommunism made this a link in the overall strategy for the Asia-Pacific region. Using the "war against terrorism" and maintenance of navigational security as pretexts, U.S. support had grown for states in the region. Closer security ties with Vietnam and the Philippines were now allegedly aimed at China's rise, refusing to recognize China's complete sovereignty over the sea. Even when Obama adopted a low-key posture, this did not stand in the way of Chinese blaming him for provoking a new wave of the "China maritime threat theory."[42] Eventually, with the encouragement of states in the region, Obama raised the profile of his response, only to arouse shriller Chinese accusations against U.S. motives.

China seeks integration with Southeast Asia and leadership in regionalism. On the one hand, it has pointed to differences within Southeast Asia as justifying its course of cooperation without interference in each other's internal affairs. On the other, it complains of the slow pace of integration. ASEAN has let China down, both in turning toward a different model of regionalism than China had preferred and in haltingly moving toward integration conducive to China's leadership. When the Chinese are not blaming Washington or Tokyo for pressuring states, they are increasingly openly accusing ASEAN member states of either internal political problems that get in the way of regionalism or of raising divisive issues, such as human rights, that are counterproductive to regionalism. The impression is conveyed that if leaders—Mahathir in Malaysia and Suharto in Indonesia—had remained in power, regionalism was poised to advance faster.[43] As in the case of South Korea's leadership change in 2008, China faults democratic processes and prefers economic integration without regard to other conditions. It does not matter that North Korea or other states did not offer reassurance or win the trust of the partners that grew wary of integration.

The Chinese have been reluctant to suggest that differences with ASEAN member states constitute a national identity gap. The very diversity of Southeast Asia plays into the argument that a stress on values, as by the United States, is inimical to cooperation. Yet, as frustration built over ASEAN's expansion of the East Asian Summit, there was grudging recognition of the seriousness of differences with China, especially related to sovereignty in the South China Sea. Instead of treating this narrowly as a matter of divergent national interests or simply repeating charges that the United States and Japan were stirring up trouble in order to contain China, the Chinese started to blame the people of the region for their attitudes toward sovereignty. In 2010, this came with calls for China to stop being passive and to assert its full sovereignty.[44]

The Chinese claim cultural affinity with Southeast Asia, noting the presence of many overseas Chinese, similarities in modern history, and China's great pull in the region.[45] Yet they charge that the United States' return to the region poses a problem in this "backyard" and arena of China's traditional "sphere of influence." In the midst of this debate on how to respond to changes in 2010, China's response was to insist on sticking to the existing course and counting on cultural affinity. Pretending that the Southeast Asian states were already by early 2011 rejecting the United States' bad influence and meddling, the Chinese express optimism without supporting specifics.[46] The impression prevails that, given the hesitancy of ASEAN and South Korea, China can proceed with economic integration with selected states that will lead toward its preferred regionalism at some future time. Transportation projects are critical to this approach—turning Chinese support for a transportation corridor through the Greater Mekong subregion into an economic corridor and then something more, and developing a corridor to Rason on the North Korean coast as a step toward economic integration with potential political consequences. The fallback position is to pursue close economic ties, leading to leverage and, later, cultural integration.

Southeast Asia is at the crossroads of Confucianism and Islam in Chinese calculations. It also became the principal battleground between Chinese and U.S. soft power.[47] Disparaging the U.S. belief in a "God-given mission" to spread democracy, some point to the appeal of Asian values in Singapore and Malaysia or to the image of Indonesia as a weak state as reproof of the United States' attempts to spread its model to the Muslim world. They also suggest that China enjoys an edge because its model represents stability, development, and regional integration. The appeal of harmony outweighs that of individualism, whereas sovereignty trumps the war against terrorism. If the United States approaches the region from a Cold War alliance orientation, China gains an edge with the area's Confucian cultural legacy and its new soft power stress on multilateral institutionalization reaching beyond economic integration. Yet such optimism obscured China's weakening position in the region in 2010. Even projections of renewed anti-Americanism in Islamic states, spreading eventually to Southeast Asia, did not seem to offer any hope. As Chinese assertive moves in the South China Sea again aroused a backlash in the region in 2011, China's soft power was eroding.

THE CIVILIZATIONAL GAP WITH ISLAMIC CIVILIZATION

Recognizing the hiatus between Western and Islamic civilizations, which was growing in the late twentieth century and then widened much more after the 9/11 attacks and the United States' declared war on terrorism, Chinese sources developed a contrasting narrative of civilizational compatibility between China and the Islamic world. This sanitized China's history of dealing with Islamic minorities, highlighting trust with the Hui population and ignoring tensions with the Uighurs in Northwest China. Also, it whitewashed Islamic civilization without any interest in accounting for the forces of terrorism steeped in fundamentalist Islam or the reactions to repression by many in the Islamic communities of Xinjiang and elsewhere. Instead, an image emerges of the Chinese historically welcoming Muslims, who, in turn, embrace Chinese civilization while retaining the essential elements of their own. Without reference to the antiethnic and antireligious campaigns of the Mao era, except to mention in passing that all minorities suffered along with the rest of the Chinese population in the decade of the Cultural Revolution, the Chinese paint a picture of tolerance, harmony, and mutual complementarity in the course of modernization, generating patriotic attitudes.[48] This picture supports contrasts between China's success in intercultural ties within the range of Eastern civilization and Western failure, seen as due to arrogance about imposing Western values on others in ways that threaten their civilizations.[49]

One popular theme in writing on the successful adaptation of Muslims to life in China is the traditional receptivity of Chinese civilization to foreign religions. In the case of Buddhism as well as Islam, adherents of the arriving religions absorbed much that was beneficial for their existence; they experienced Sinification, as in their use of the Chinese language, or through the efforts of Muslim scholars interpreted the Koran under the influence of Confucianism.[50] A clinching argument is the discovery of harmony as a theme in the Hui culture. Chinese authors grope to identify various things that Islamic and Confucian civilization have in common,[51] although the quality of such comparisons stretches the reader's credulity. After all, this politically inspired writing proceeded against the backdrop of tense relations with the Muslim people of Xinjiang, which was handled by coercion to make them shift to education in the Chinese language and abandon their claims for cultural as well as political rights. Such far-fetched assertions of similarities in the years 2009–10 were orchestrated in provinces with large Muslim minorities, such as Gansu and Qinghai. Top-down construction of national identity was most obvious away from China's intellectual centers, but it appears to have emanated from specific directives also transmitted to central centers of research.

With the explosion of grassroots demonstrations against Arab autocrats in early 2011, the Chinese argument that universal values are a Western concoction rejected by both Islamic and Chinese civilization seemed doubtful. Censorship left many Chinese unclear about the causes of the demonstrations and the nature of the demands for political reform. If the outcome of these convulsions was to be more anti-Americanism after leaders such as Hosni Mubarak in Egypt were blamed for being puppets of the United States, then China might welcome an opportunity to align more closely with the new regimes and echo those charges as further evidence of U.S. interference. This, however, would be at odds with past charges that the real U.S. transgression was pressuring states to adopt the Western values of democracy and human rights. Abrupt shifts in the focus of the identity contrast with the United States would not be anything new. The important point is to draw a sharp contrast.

The image conveyed in many Chinese publications is that the United States demonizes Islamic civilization, arrogantly seeking to control Islamic states and to transform their values. In contrast, China is positively inclined to Islamic civilization and accepts Islamic states as they are, treating them equally. One 2005 source refers to Islam as the United States' "new Bolshevism," replacing fascism and later Communism as the ideological target in a Western tradition dating at least from the Crusades.[52] This assumes that all these were artificial enemies that proved convenient for U.S. politics.

Although notions of the global South broadly cover Latin America, Africa, and much of Asia, the Islamic states have an indispensable role in this concept. Given the refusal of China to rely on India and the uncertainty of Brazil and South Africa as middle-power partners, attention to the South is heavily weighted toward the Islamic states. If improved U.S.-Pakistani relations starting in 2001 and U.S.-Indonesian relations thereafter narrowed China's options, there was no sign of wavering. When tensions rose in the U.S.-Pakistani relationship, as in 2011, China's reasoning was reaffirmed. Similar to the role of North Korea as an alleged victim of U.S. policies and prejudices, Muslim sympathizers of terrorism were often absolved of blame in this one-sided narrative.

In February 2011, President Mubarak was ousted by demonstrators in Egypt, complicating the impact of narrowing the identity gap with Islamic states. First, the parallels with the Tiananmen Square demonstrations in 1989 raised questions about why the Egyptian people could change the system and be ready for democracy, despite China's insistence that democracy is not a universal value and thus it had to crush the quest for representation at home. Second, there was cautious hope that the fall of a U.S. ally could unleash resistance to U.S. foreign policy with a potential for closer Sino-Islamic cooperation. This requires that a combative Islamic national identity take priority over the secular identity associated with civil society in civilizational analysis.

The early 2011 mass demonstrations in Egypt and elsewhere in the Islamic world produced new accusations against the United States amid expressions of confidence that China would benefit from closer cooperation across civilizations. As long-repressed Islamic groups gain a voice, the United States will face the headache of choosing between stability and human rights. Its hypocrisy will be exposed as its interference draws more negative attention. The Chinese argue that these are not "color revolutions" to fear. Instead, they highlight opposition to U.S. hegemonism as well as the existing order that suppresses the will of the masses. The outcome is likely to be growing solidarity that can lead to a flowering of Islamic civilization in opposition to the West and, presumably, in cooperation with China, which shares this opposition.[53] With Iran leading the struggle against the West and Pakistan linked to China despite ambivalent ties toward the United States, the prospect of Egypt reviving as a center of Islamic cooperation whets China's appetite for an axis of anti-American Islam.

With the United States claiming support for democratization as opposition movements massed against repressive regimes, the Chinese responded that nations in the Middle East have national identities that have not been swayed by the Internet advocacy of U.S. values when the gap with the West remains very large.[54] On trial is Western civilization steeped in racism and imperialism, and Muslim populations will not forget this. Yet in 2011 the drama over Libya left the Chinese in a quandary as China's failure to veto a UN Security Council resolution opened the door to NATO intervention, which drew sharp criticism in China. By early 2012, the focus had turned to the Syrian bloodbath to keep President Bashar Assad in power, which the Security Council failed to address owing to vetoes by Russia and China. It was becoming more difficult to portray the West as the villain and China as the real supporter of the oppressed Muslim peoples of the world. The strained civilizational arguments about East versus West were not holding up well in this complicated environment.

CONCLUSION

China approaches national identity through such themes as culture, civilization, Cold War thinking, ideology, values, and soft power. With varied wording, these themes reveal an obsession with the ideas that influence international relations. This is not rigorous academic analysis, but concerted propagandistic messaging to put China in the most positive light and blame the West as the source of world problems, from imperialism to hegemonism. The impression is conveyed of China as an innocent victim that has suffered and continues to suffer humiliation. Although China's rise is not complete with economic and military power, the critical test is seen to be cultural power, reflected in the victory of its spiritual civilization—a victory not just for one country but for all who have suffered from racism along with colonialism and a loss of cultural autonomy. The true scourge of twentieth-century history was not Communism but the civilization of the West. This scourge continues. The Chinese depict Iran and North Korea as states that have been provoked by the United States and are striving to protect themselves, including with nuclear weapons, because they are endangered, as China has been. Moves to deny Islamic states an authentic voice are associated with the containment of China. They are deemed to be just one more part of the prolonged effort to co-opt Japan and South Korea into the West, undermining their natural linkages to Eastern civilization, and to pit the ASEAN member states against China, obstructing their reconnection through regionalism.

Chinese approaches to national identity gaps in Asia go forward as part of this grand narrative. The impression long prevailed that China normalized relations with Japan in the 1970s, with South Korea in 1992, and with many Southeast Asian states during the course of the 1990s, creating momentum for improved ties. Yet in 2010 a different image appeared—of China not yet normalized in relations with the United States' allies and resentful of the Southeast Asian states for their audacity in welcoming the United States into the East Asian Summit and also in resisting China's claims to sovereignty over the South China Sea. At a time of optimism about China's "peaceful development" and rapidly expanding regional ties, China alienated its neighbors, compounding the problem by blaming them. Instead of building a sense of community by narrowing identity gaps, it brazenly widened them as a sign of its overconfidence about anti-Americanism, its unrestrained optimism about its economic clout, and its obliviousness about the negative legacy of a history of Sinocentrism, Communist revolutionary expansionism, and autocracy.

Many authors predict that the West and non-West will be in balance during the pivotal next decade, as China is identified as both a world great power (*shijie daguo*) and a developing-state great power within the now ascendant East. Yet most tenuous in forecasts of how China will successfully navigate this transition is the identification of states that will support China's leadership of the struggle against the West. Only Russia is often listed, with hints of uncertainty about its course over the decade. The Islamic states and states that are poorly integrated into the world order and are intent on building nuclear weapons appear to be the other partners.[55] Without explaining what holds the non-West together, the Chinese indulge in wishful thinking. The manipulation of identity gaps in Asia reveals the extremes to which this wishful thinking is proceeding. If China's foreign policy was more cautious in 2011 than in 2010, with more awareness that the power gap with the United States will take time to close, there was no significant backtracking on how to depict national identity gaps. Expedient policy adjustments do not change the momentum of official Chinese thinking regarding civilizational differences.

NOTES

1   Gilbert Rozman, "China's Changing Images of Japan 1989–2001: The Struggle to Balance Partnership and Rivalry," *International Relations of the Asia-Pacific* 2, no. 1 (Winter 2002): 95–129.
2   Gilbert Rozman, ed., *U.S. Leadership, History, and Bilateral Relations in Northeast Asia* (Cambridge: Cambridge University Press, 2011).
3   Wang Yizhou, "'Dongya gongtongti' gainian bianzhi," *Xiandai guoji guanxi*, spec. ed. (2010): 86.
4   Feng Zhaokui et. al., *Zhanhou Riben waijiao 1945–1995* (Beijing: Zhongguo shehuikexue chubanshe, 1996), 7–32.
5   Wang Lianhe, "Dongya gongtongti: Gouxiang, jiyu, tiaozhan," *Shijie jingji yu zhengzhi*, no. 2 (2006): 76–81.
6   Ibid.
7   Song Junying, "Dongya hezuo de xintaishi ji Zhongguo de zhanlue xuanze," *Taipingyang xuebao*, no. 5 (2010): 43–44.
8   Liu Jiangyong, "Tongxiang Dongya gongtongti zhi lu: Hezuo yu chuangxin," *Waijiao pinglun*, no. 2 (2010): 57–60.
9   Editorial, *Huanqiu shibao*, September 8, 2010.

10 Peng Guangqian, "Meiri junyan shiji mingan duihua shishi hangmu ezha,'" *Renminwang*, December 7, 2010.

11 "Shei tiaoqile Zhongri jian jei zhechang Diaoyudao wenti de yanzhong fengbo?" *Huanqiu shibao*, September 24, 2010; "Weishenme Diaoyudao fengbo buneng jiuci huashang juhao?" *Huanqiu shibao*, September 27, 2010.

12 *Huanqiu ribao*, September 13, 2010, editorial.

13 Kazuhiko Togo, "'Ryodo mondai nai' no saiko," *Asahi shimbun*, September 30, 2010.

14 "Sheping: 'Zhuang,' Riben dangqu de gaowei dongzuo," *Huanqiu shibao*, September 8, 2010.

15 "Diaoyudao zhengduan de lailong qumai," *Huanqiu shibao*, September 9, 2010.

16 "Renqing Riben," *Guoji xianqu daobao*, September 23, 2010.

17 "Zhuanjia: Meirihan gouzhu xinjunshi tongmeng," *Renminwang*, December 3, 2010.

18 "Renqing Riben."

19 Zhang Yaohua, "Riben zhengtan dongdang dui qi neizheng he waijiao de yingxiang," *Guoji wenti yanjiu*, no. 6 (2010): 63–69.

20 Feng Zhaokui et. al., *Zhanhou Riben waijiao* (Beijing: Zhongguo shehuikexue chubanshe, 1996), 32.

21 "Diaoyudao zhengduan de lailong qumai."

22 Han Li, "Zhongguo jueqi yu Dongbeiya de anquan zhanlue xuanze," *Yanbian dangxiao xuebao*, no. 10 (2010): 67–69.

23 Kang Degui, "Riben dui Dongnanya de zhengzhi 'qieru,'" *Riben xuekan*, no. 4 (2010): 32–43.

24 Ba Dianjun, "Cong wenhua shijiao touxi Riben waijiao zhengce de zhanlue xuanze," *Riben xuekan*, no. 4 (2010): 93–106.

25 Wei Ling, "Guifan, zhidu, gongtongti: Dongya hezuo de jiagou yu fangxiang," *Waijiao pinglun*, no. 2 (2010): 67–81.

26 "Rihan lianshou 'zhendui Zhongchao' shi weixian niantou," *Huanqiu shibao*, November 25, 2010.

27 Feng Zhaokui, "Fazhan yu shijie chaoliuxiang yizhide Zhongri guanxi," *Riben xuekan*, no. 6 (2010): 3–16.

28 "Riben shehui guanyu yong 'ruorou qiangshi' sikao wenti," *Huanqiu shibao*, September 30, 2010.

29 Wu Jinan, "Riben Minzhudang waijiao zhengce tiaozheng de dongyin ji zhanwang," *Guoji guancha*, no. 6 (2010): 1–8.

30 Wang Sheng, "Shixi dangdai Hanguo minzuzhuyi," *Xiandai guoji guanxi*, no. 2 (2010): 36–41.

31 Wang Xiaoling and Dong Xiangrong, "Hanguoren xinmuzhong de Zhongguo xingxiang," *Dangdai Yatai*, no. 2 (2010): 109–32.

32 Guo Rui and Ling Shengli, "Minzuzhuyi yu Hanguo waijiao zhengce," *Shijie jingji yu zhengzhi luntan*, no. 3 (2010): 150–59.

33 Shi Yongming, "Tiananhao' shijian yu guoji weiji guanli," *Heping yu fazhan*, no. 5 (2010): 45–51.

34 Wang Linchang, "Chaoxian he Hanguo weihe tanbulong," *Huanqiu shibao*, February 14, 2011.

35 "Huoshan koushang de Lee Myung-bak," *Shidai zhoubao*, January 6, 2011.

36 "Zhuanjia: Meirihan gouzhu xinjunshi tongmeng," *Renminwang*, December 3, 2010.

37 *People's Daily*, October 12, 2010.

38 Shi Yongming, "'Tiananhao' shijian yu guoji weiji guanli," 45–51.

39 "'Rihan jiemeng' juefei kongxue laifeng," *Guoji xianqu daobao*, rep. in Xinhuawang, January 14, 2011.

40 Ding Gang, "Chaoxian bandao de chengyi yao yidianyidian jilei," *Renmin ribao*, February 10, 2010.

41 Wang Yuzhu, "Yazhou quyu hezuo de lujing jingzheng ji Zhongguo de zhanlue xuanze," *Dangdai Yatai*, no. 4 (2010): 73–87.

42 Wang Chuanjian, "Meiguo de Nanzhongguohai zhengce: lishi yu xianshi," *Waijiao pinglun*, no. 6 (2009): 87–99.

43 Wei Hong and Xing Laishun, "Guonei zhengzhi yu Dongmeng yitihua jincheng," *Dangdai Yatai*, no. 2 (2010): 43–57.

44 Shao Jianping and Li Chenyang, "Dongmeng guojia chuli haiyu zhengduan de fangshi jiqi dui jiejue Nanhai zhuchuan zhengduan de qishi," *Dangdai Yatai*, no. 4 (2010): 144–56.

45 Wang Xin, "Meiguo jiaru Dongya fenghui zhihou de Zhongguo Dongnanya waijiao zhengce de jidian sikao," *Heilongjiang shizhi*, no. 19 (2010): 94–95.

46 "Meiguo Dongya zhanlue tiaozheng," *Dongfangwang*, February 17, 2011.

47 Tan Xiao and Liu Bingxiang, "Zhongmei zai Dongnanya diqu de 'ruanshili' bijiao," *Dongnanya zongheng*, no. 10 (2010): 3–8.

48 Ma Kelin and Yang Rong, "Cong zongjiao yu falude guanxi kan Yisilanfa wenhua dui Huizu de yingxiang," *Gansu shehui kexue*, no. 5 (2009): 270–73; Ding Jun, "Zhongguo Yisilanjiao 'aiguo aijiao' de lilun yu shijian," *Xibei minzu daxue xuebao* (zhexue shehui kexue ban), no. 1 (2010): 1–9.

49 Shan Jinfeng, "Ziwo de 'taxing': Lun Huizu wenhua de jianrongxing," *Qinghai minzu daxue xuebao*, no. 7 (2010): 69.

50 Ma Mingliang, "Yisilanjiao de Zhongguohua yu 'yiru guanjing,'" *Alabo shijie yanjiu*, no. 5 (2009): 53–60.

51 Zhang Xiaonan, "Yisilanjiao 'Zhongdao' guan yu Rujia zhongyong sixiang zhi bijiao," *Guangxi shehuizhuyi xueyuan xuebao*, no. 1 (2010): 82.

52 Gao Zugui, "Meiguo zai 'dongdanghu' de zhanlue liyi fenxi," *Meiguo yanjiu*, no. 3 (2005): 82–98.

53 "Meiguo zai Aiji de mudi bushi minzhu," *Huanqiu shibao*, February 17, 2011.

54 "Mei waijiao zai 'wang' zhong xianru ziwuo hunluan," *Wenhuibao*, February 17, 2011.

55 Jin Canrong and Liu Shiqiang, "Weilai shinian de shijie yu Zhongguo: Guoji zhengzhi shijiao," *Xiandai guoji guanxi*, spec. ed. (2010): 26–31, 40.

CHAPTER 8

CHINESE NATIONAL IDENTITY AND THE SINO-U.S. CIVILIZATIONAL GAP

Gilbert Rozman

U.S. leaders and diplomats generally welcome convergence between a rising power and the United States in national identity. Although influential voices sought to widen a fundamental divide under the shadow of the right-wing witch hunt of Senator Joseph McCarthy in the Eisenhower era and of neoconservatives in the Ronald Reagan and George W. Bush eras, most political leaders and foreign policy experts have seen convergence as in the interest of the United States. They were eager for Nikita Khrushchev's reforms to succeed to lessen the danger of nuclear war and to sustain the process of the USSR's de-Stalinization that could lead to market reforms and democratization. They encouraged Japan to build on its foundation of democracy and a free market to normalize its society and economy as it rid itself of the cultural legacy that had led to World War II and had kept alive calls for historical revisionism.

When China's turn came to challenge the United States' global leadership, hopes again concentrated on signs of convergence. An intense desire to narrow the national identity gap with the country deemed the foremost rival is premised on the following reasoning: that the narrower the identity gap, the greater the chance for peace and mutual trust; that the more progress toward narrowing the gap, the more likely that social science theory on shared human nature and modernization will be confirmed; and that the closer the partner's identity, the more productive negotiations will be to resolve differences. In contrast, U.S. rivals fear convergence. In the Chinese case, the wider the national identity gap, the greater the benefit, because the Chinese Communist Party's legitimacy will be better promoted, China's citizens will be more likely to criticize their country's rival for global power, and China will position itself in the international soft power competition for early gains. The coverage of the United States with China in recent years, notably from 2009, strives to enlarge this identity divide.

U.S. officials have long sought ways to narrow the national identity gap with China. During the 1970s and 1980s, they struggled to transform the joint criticism of Soviet foreign policy into an agreement on principles for the international system rooted in national identity, not just China's Five Principles of Coexistence. After the shock to bilateral relations in 1989 brought on by the Tiananmen Square repression, U.S. leaders criticized China over human rights but also strove to rebuild mutual trust in what was expected to be a postcommunist world. This overture expanded in Bill Clinton's second term. In 2005, the notion of "responsible stakeholder" was the basis for another overture for reducing the distance between the two states. No U.S. leader took office more determined to find common ground with China than Barack Obama in 2009. Yet a very different calculus existed in the Chinese leadership. Only by widening the national identity gap with the West, and especially with the United States, would the Chinese Communist Party reinforce its grip on power and claims to legitimacy. Indeed, the argument spread that the threat from acceding to U.S. overtures and narrowing the national identity gap extended to the very survival of Chinese civilization. In the years 2009–11, instead of praising Obama's new outreach, Chinese sources pondered a rising civilizational threat. Obama's idealism and support for multilateralism are seen as more threatening than Bush's wars.[1]

For at least a quarter century, China's interest in drawing a sharp divide was tempered by awareness of its need to reassure its foreign investors and keep its economy zooming ahead. On the surface, the

Chinese repeated the favored slogan that cooperation prevails over competition. At the same time, they insisted that this does not mean convergence, and they kept up a steady stream of accusations against U.S. hegemonism and foreign policy in general. This meant walking a tightrope to avoid open demonization. Yet, as confidence grew, restraints were dropped. What burst forth in 2010 was not an aberration or a response to a political struggle over the composition of the new leadership team to come in 2012 but a clarification of a national identity that had been somewhat shielded from view and had been obsessed with the United States as the "other."

In the 1990s, drawing a contrast with the United States proved challenging because China's rise was still uncertain and memories of the Soviet Communist failure cast a shadow on some types of claims to superiority. The main contrast centered on political identity, as the Chinese accused the United States of insisting on unipolarity to impose its system and values on others. Rather than proclaiming the superiority of China, it associated China with other states that were justly seeking multipolarity and developing states that were resistant to the U.S. model. Particularly, the United States' treatment of Russia figured prominently in this demonization of China's rival. But the accusations of this period were rather tame compared with what would follow. The Chinese hesitated because they realized that they could exert influence as other states saw an opening to distance themselves somewhat from the remaining superpower and were exploring new opportunities for Asian regionalism.

In the period 2001–7, the Chinese national identity narrative was transformed into claims of Chinese superiority on many dimensions, with China representing the rise of Asia and Asian regionalism, and the United States proving to be more vulnerable to demonization. Relative success economically and in boosting both soft and hard power lifted China's confidence. The Bush administration's unpopular policies had aroused anti-Americanism, making China's case easier. During these years, the Chinese had their greatest success in making the case for a sharp identity contrast. Again, the main thrust was a negative portrayal of the United States, but the positive image of China was spreading. As successful as China was in rallying national pride and boosting soft power, its gains were prone to exaggeration. Anti-Americanism was already on the decline before the end of the Bush administration. China's position in Asia was far from secure; it had raised suspicions in Japan, South Korea, India, and elsewhere in the region. Moreover, images of rising pride within China prove difficult to verify because the leadership encourages the voices of its enthusiasts and silences those with strong dissenting opinions. Various modest exclamations, as presented by moderate academics and officials, about China's "peaceful development" and positive relations with each great power did a lot to obscure the sharp thrust of others, who were intent on widening the national identity gap through demonization of the United States and all other great powers (apart from Russia) while glorifying a mixture of Chinese traditional culture and renewed socialism as essential to China's future

The most effective evocation of a national identity gap came in the charge that U.S. policies were directed against China's rise, not because of its authoritarian system but due to such factors as Cold War thinking that had been transferred to China from the Soviet Union and inherent opposition to an Asian challenger. Denial of the Olympics to Beijing was interpreted as evidence that U.S. identity was incompatible with Chinese identity. While making few claims to its own superiority, China kept the spotlight on U.S. blemishes. In this perspective, the United States had unsavory motives in abetting Taiwan's quest for de jure independence, weighing denial of freer trade, and demeaning what leaders claimed to be Chinese culture.

The period 2009–10 witnessed a quantum leap in Chinese national identity differentiation. As pride on each of the six dimensions of national identity intensified in China, criticisms of the United States accelerated as well. Beginning as buildup to the Beijing Olympics and response to the U.S. loss of face in the world financial crisis, the polarization of identity rhetoric kept growing in the first years of the Obama administration even as circumstances turned less favorable. The fall of 2009 saw a ratcheting up of both rhetoric and confrontational moves. Continued rapid economic growth and military modernization fueled optimism, in spite of evidence that China's soft power was being damaged and its national identity discourse was overreaching. If in early 2011 there were signs of caution, the momentum of this spike has not abated.

The spread of national identity "fever" is often manipulated by a group in the leadership, transmitted to the public in a manner that arouses them to clamor for more, and then used as a brake on others in the leadership or as a way to shape the transition to new leaders. Although Deng Xiaoping's designation of Hu Jintao as the leader from his generation made it difficult to head off his rise to the top post, there was no end to the struggle between factions to control the agenda and to name Hu's successor and the rest of the lineup of the next Political Standing Committee. As the jockeying intensified in the years 2009–10, Hu's handling of U.S. relations was fraught with increased sensitivity. If he appeared weak in the face of the perceived divergence in national identities, his position would weaken and the succession to Xi Jinping and others outside his faction could take a decisive turn. Thus, Hu had to walk a fine line between achieving success in his January 2011 summit with Obama based on carefully scripted compromises and standing firm in defense of China's own goals and identity.

Soft power draws more attention than hard power in Chinese discussions of threats to security. The Soviet collapse resulted, in large part, from the contagion of ideas from the West, readers have been told. Ousted Chinese leaders and purged intellectuals are depicted as succumbing to "bourgeois spiritual pollution," which in 1989 was blamed both for the demonstrations in Tiananmen Square that were brutally suppressed on June 4 and for the overall strategy of the United States toward China and other socialist countries. Even when Chinese national power rose dramatically and the regime succeeded in mobilizing mass support through appeals to symbols of national identity, there was no letup in the obsession with the threat posed by "universal values" and Western civilization. By 2010, China could assert its own positive narrative covering all six dimensions. As its identity spiked on all the dimensions, it championed an irreducible gap as a basis for intensified competition with the United States in reshaping the global order.

All the dimensions of national identity figure in the mobilization by the Chinese leadership, especially its powerful Propaganda

Department, to convey the Sino–U.S. gap as vast and unbridgeable. This is the case despite the conflicting goal of gaining recognition from summits and other meetings with U.S. leaders that China is a global power in equal standing to the United States, if not itself a superpower. Similarly, the Soviet Union and Japan, in their time, had sought such acknowledgment. This ambivalence between questioning the status of the United States and beseeching it to confirm the status of your country as its foremost counterpart produces both anomalies and inconsistencies. When one's own national identity spikes and expectations are at their highest, the contrast is likely to be drawn most pointedly. But, precisely at that point, interest in a confirmation of national power and identity also keeps intensifying.

China's differentiation from the United States does not stop at two national identities. More general concepts are invoked. If socialism versus capitalism faded as a point of general reference after the early 1990s, it is reappearing. "East versus West" is now a commonplace dichotomy, as is the integration of an East Asian community confronting an alien presence from the West. In each case, a natural process appears to be obstructed by antagonistic values: Anticommunism led to both the Korean and Vietnam wars; Cold War thinking survives in attitudes toward regionalism and the Six-Party Talks; and hegemonic thinking embedded in Western ethnocentrism inheres in the fear of the natural flowering of China's leadership and civilization.[2] China emerges in such dichotomies as a representative of a wider world, drawing together in a tectonic struggle against the reigning civilization in recent world history without having to compromise its own national identity in order to exercise its leadership.

National identity, of course, is not equivalent to strategic policymaking. China's policies may become less assertive even when the identity rhetoric is not tempered. Officials in charge of bilateral relations may accentuate cooperation. Academic experts may downplay the sources of tension. Yet if such caution is not buttressed by corresponding interpretations of the various dimensions of national identity, one would be remiss to ignore the restraining force of identity. It can, in the short run, be an independent factor, but predictions of long-term policy would best not overlook how the cumulative national identity rhetoric shapes both public and official thinking.

THE IDEOLOGICAL DIMENSION

After three decades of downplaying ideology for external consumption while continuing to insist that it matters for political education and retention of socialism, Chinese spokespersons grew more assertive about ideology. Following Mao Zedong's abuse of ideology and criticism of the Soviet failure to reform due to rigid ideology, Chinese leaders naturally were wary of claiming an ideological edge over the United States as a capitalist state trumpeting an ideology centered on freedom. In the 1990s, after China was put further on the defensive, the ideological response centered on making the U.S. worldview the focus of criticism. Whether the United States was under the sway of Cold War ideological thinking against Communism, now concentrated only on China, or it was the heir to imperialist thinking that denied China any right to rise from dependency, it drew a barrage of charges for its approach to international affairs. It was accused of bullying its allies, such as Japan, to deny them equal relations, and vindictively repressing its current and former adversaries—that is, the Soviet Union—to extend its dominance. Taken for ideological reasons, U.S. actions were hegemonic. As U.S. policymakers debated how to deal with China in the decade after 1989, there was considerable receptivity to these accusations inside China. Other nations were also concerned about the new pressure for reducing trade and financial barriers, and they perceived an ideological element in U.S. policies as well. Indeed, great powers as diverse as Russia, India, and Japan were all inclined to accept portions of the same argument as they sought more leverage in a unipolar world. As long as the focus was fixed on the way the United States presented itself, China could find support for a big ideological gap.

George W. Bush's neoconservative ideological rhetoric and agenda opened the door for a more assertive Chinese ideological push. Even as China's leaders were inclined to find accommodations in addressing international problems, such as the North Korean nuclear crisis, they reinforced criticisms demonizing U.S. intentions.[3] Deepening the ideological case against the United States, China was emboldened to broach its own ideological themes. The concept of "harmony" straddled Confucian ideals and socialist legacies, once class conflict had been omitted. In its domestic variant, calling for a "harmonious society," the contrast with the rancor in U.S. politics was unmistakable. Moreover, in its international variant, a "harmonious world," China sought to capitalize on global discontent with Bush's foreign policies, which were tainted with unilateralism and pressure tactics. The ideological element in national identity gained momentum even after Bush shifted direction internationally. Yet it lacked clear references to socialism as distinct from capitalism, and it only gradually embraced China's traditional civilization in opposition to the history of Western civilization.

Only starting in 2008 did thoughts about trumpeting ideology truly escape from the shadow of the 1980s and 1990s. This was manifest in China's increased boldness in asserting Communist ideology, glorification of Confucian traditional thought, and even less restraint in demonizing U.S. ideology, dismissing Obama's shift in rhetoric.[4] China's resumption of the ideological struggle differed in many respects from Mao's extremist antirevisionist ideology of class struggle and anti-imperialism. It contrasted in its support for a globalized world economy. It marginalized dissenters while leaving them some scope to make their cases indirectly, as long as no frontal challenge was mounted against core principles. Yet the main objective was similar: to highlight the sharpest possible differences and to reinforce the uniqueness of China's system.

One of the shorthand ways of shifting the blame for failing to compromise on problems is to cite vestiges of the Cold War. Rather than posing constructive ideas to manage the North Korean nuclear issue, the Taiwan Strait standoff, and the legacy of U.S. alliances in East Asia, many refer to them as vestiges that undermine a shared sense of security.[5] They criticize the ideological prisms that present North Korea as a Communist dictatorship and China as a socialist state, as if these are the causes of national identity widening rather than symptoms of a failure to promote political reform while invoking ideology in Pyongyang and

Beijing. Instead of acknowledging China's ideological drift, the Chinese insist that U.S. officials retain an outdated ideology.

This U.S. ideology is antisocialist. It needlessly injects values into issues that could be handled with trust and pragmatism. It responds to forces of integration and multilateralism with containment, which is meant to turn other states against China, and with unilateralism.[6]

Chinese sources criticize the United States as ideological for its appeal to human rights and democratization as a smokescreen for narrow national interests, its Cold War mentality in boosting alliances and containing China, and its economic ideas that drove the world into the global financial and economic crisis that began in 2008. Other countries are urged to distance themselves from similar ideological conceptions, thereby improving their ties with China. Despite treating the giants of socialism as fundamental to China's thinking, the Chinese insist that they are the ones without an ideology. There are acknowledgments of Marxist-Leninist and Maoist thought and of Deng Xiaoping theory (Ma), recognition that traditional Confucian culture (Zhong) is of rising influence, and even an occasional mention of the role of Western ideas (Xi), notably among youth.[7] Referring to the world financial crisis as the failure of the Western capitalist model, the Chinese assert that international society is now reconsidering the merits of different models of development and of values.[8] China's rise is thus being embellished with ideological meaning.

In the 1980s, Chinese leaders stood firm against ideological convergence, as was occurring under Mikhail Gorbachev in the USSR. In the 1990s, they reasserted an ideology masked as resistance to an opposing ideology. During the 2000s, they intensified their critique of the other ideology while building the case for their own ideology. Finally, as the decade ended and the 2010s began, they asserted their own ideological amalgam. In its boldest form, it renews the struggle between socialism and capitalism, amplifies the struggle against Western imperialism, and resuscitates China's past civilization in sharp contrast to Western civilization as the basis for future Eastern superiority.

Narrowly contrasting China's continuing priority on peace and development with its past belief in war and revolution, the Chinese pretend that this is an ideological focus that excludes threatening developments. Yet recent warnings that instability caused by other states is making it hard for China to stick to this course alert us to the shallowness of China's claims. At the same time, there is a revival of simplistic claims that socialist countries could not start a war as a means to rise or even seek hegemony, as the United States does.[9] Memories of China's critique of the Soviet Union are ignored amid insistence that China has learned the lessons of its fall. In contrast, Obama's reference to a "Sputnik moment" in his 2011 State of the Union Address is interpreted as a Cold War association of China with the Soviet challenge, exaggerating threat perceptions when China is way behind and is committed to peace and development.[10]

There is reason to conclude that the ideological dimension takes precedence in Chinese thinking. Even those who argue that U.S. power and determination must not be underestimated and that China should for the next five to ten years recommit itself to pursuing common interests do not contradict the thesis that different civilizations and ideologies destine the only two world-class powers to clash over which will be number one.[11] No mention is made of narrowing the identity gap, because China has rejected such change and Chinese sources register no doubt that the United States will stick to its course.

THE TEMPORAL DIMENSION

Self-perceptions of Chinese history looked grim in 1980. The claim that Mao was 70 percent good and 30 percent bad aroused ridicule amid revelations of the horrors unleashed in the Cultural Revolution. The best hope for deflecting criticism was to shift the blame to the Confucian traditions that had favored autocracy while stifling individualism. Emphasis on borrowing from the capitalist states created the impression that China's future depended on convergence—not a basis for confidence. The United States was favored over the Soviet Union, which blurred pride in the Cold War struggle against U.S. imperialism, whereas integration into the United States–led community of states did not suggest that China offered a superior model for future competition.

242

In the 1980s, China readjusted its temporal outlook. It reconsidered Mao-era condemnations of its Confucian heritage, reinforced restrictions on criticisms of the Mao era apart from brief, formulaic remarks, and slowly intensified complaints against the United States for being no less responsible than the Soviet Union for the harm it was doing to China and the international system it was forging to channel China's rise through "spiritual pollution" or "bourgeois peaceful evolution." In this sweeping historical reconstruction, the Chinese resumed contrasting their past with that of the United States and the West. Taiwan was the most potent symbol of damage from U.S. national identity, but the broader themes of imperialism and interference in China's internal affairs pointed to a wide gap dangerous to China's identity, even if during the 1980s there was considerable confusion about what exactly that was.

Given these reconsiderations, by 2010 China had turned history into a simplistic narrative that sharpened its divide with the United States. Veneration of its own past clearly distinguishes China from the West, which had been depicted by some as superior for its Enlightenment and Industrial Revolution. Insistence that China's record under Mao warrants primarily praise reconceptualizes the Cold War as U.S. anticommunism striving to hold down China and to oppose the Soviet Union, as in the Korean War, whose aim is interpreted as seeking to overthrow the Chinese regime.[12] Finally, belittling the cooperative atmosphere of the 1990s and 2000s also serves the purpose of widening the gap with the United States. Without putting the spotlight on this recent period, the case would be less obvious for transforming the international system and exposing why the United States must be unseated as the world's lone superpower.

By 2010, there was virtually no limit to the praise given to China's Confucian past: a model of harmony; the center of a peaceful, stable international system; and a source of inspiration for national and regional development in today's world. More than the Mao era, this period had become the focus of claims of past superiority. The old litany of accusations against its feudal backwardness had dropped from sight. In contrast, the history of the West was often targeted for criticism as a period of rampant contentiousness and intolerance.

Almost mysteriously, the West had somehow launched the Industrial Revolution and spread its values around the world, but such steps are not praised as an indication of cultural superiority in today's China. The glorifying of China's premodern history is accompanied by a demeaning of the premodern West.

Juxtaposing China's century of humiliation and Western imperialism leads to a condemnation of China's victimizers and a general denunciation of the course of Western history, which is replete with wars and cultural arrogance. Although mention is made of the achievements of modernization from which other states borrowed, the record of aggression and injustice suffices to discredit the West as a model. And this contrast is sharpened by attributing China's problems largely to the way it was treated by the Western states. This identity divide has been noted with the greatest consistency.

Another shift came with insistence that the Communist record under Mao warrants praise, with only minimal mention of its shortcomings. Again, foreign policy serves best to draw the desired contrast. Although the contrast is less stark for the period beginning with the normalization of Sino-U.S. relations, even the 1970s and 1980s are interpreted in a more negative light as part of the determination to differentiate identities. The Chinese have grown assertive in presenting the entire history of the Cold War as a struggle with the United States, which abused their country at every turn, while China never erred in its conduct and always suffered at U.S. hands. The common cause of the period 1972–89 fades in significance, while China's insistence on equidistance between the superpowers by 1982 is deemed the proper response to new affronts. Given this dichotomous logic, there are no grounds for narrowing the national identity gap in covering the Cold War era.[13] Containment is the common thread.

The Cold War divide was confused when China prioritized criticism of the Soviet Union and then, under Deng Xiaoping's leadership, stressed a U.S. partnership as well as the benefits of economic cooperation and borrowing for modernization. Although the Chinese repudiated the "twenty lost years" after Mao's radicalization, they gave less notice to the Sino-U.S. rivalry during three-quarters of this period. Yet reassessing Sino-Soviet history has made it easier to reemphasize differences with the United States. China's place in the Cold War against the United States and the misguided U.S. anticommunism resurfaced in the agenda to demonize China's main rival. This is part of a narrative about how for 170 years, starting with the Opium War, China was never able to escape external pressure, the threat of war, and containment. It was always behind in military modernization, and it faced states that repeatedly abused their power.[14]

Publications on the post–Cold War period paint China as the object of pressure and containment by the United States. Whether squeezing it with sanctions, rallying states to contain it, or trying to trick it into abandoning its values and identity, the United States has emerged as more an antagonist than a partner. Given this situation and images of intensifying U.S. efforts to block China's rise, recent writings make it clear that the confrontation is intensifying and cannot be resolved by moderation on China's part.[15] The danger is that China could be co-opted into a West-centric order at a time when it should recognize that it is poised to lead the developing states in forging a different order, to which the United States must acquiesce.[16] This impression that the U.S. side is weighed down by forces deeply embedded in history holds that this adversary continues to exacerbate problems in bilateral relations without the prospect of changing direction. The dichotomous narrative is filled with pessimistic thinking.

The most stunning reversal is the image in 2010 that the two post–Cold War decades, as well as the prior two decades after Sino-U.S. relations had improved, are really an extension of the Cold War.[17] Viewing Northeast Asia and Sino-U.S. relations through the prism of the Korean War and the U.S. alliance systems, China demonized U.S. behavior as ideological, especially in its continued hostility toward North Korea. Only by normalizing relations with North Korea as well as accepting China's approach to the incorporation of Taiwan into China while conceding on maritime territorial disputes would Washington acknowledge the end of the Cold War and China's rightful return. However, a panicky United States—fearful of loss of hegemony and the monopoly of Western civilization—is instead striving to form an Asian NATO and lighting fires that oblige a China committed to peace and development to respond, however reluctantly. The notion of Obama as the "first Pacific president" or the United States' continuation of its traditional leadership role were twisted to mean more Cold War–style containment of China.

By the years 2009–10, China's notion of each historical period stood in stark contrast to U.S. national identity. Not only does the United States receive no credit for struggling against European colonialism and welcoming the rights secured through the French Revolution, it is treated as just another imperialist power swayed by a civilization of conflict rather than harmony. Veneration of its own history distinguished China from the West, which, in contrast to claims of superiority due to the Enlightenment as well as the Industrial Revolution, was now chastised as inherently flawed. Especially clear in the sharp contrast between two civilizations that drove history for millennia are the claims that under the influence of Confucianism and supportive of the Tianxia outlook that all peoples are together under Heaven, China coexisted harmoniously with other civilizations to the degree that it even formed a large umbrella under which they comfortably persisted while Western civilization strove to eradicate the others. Rewriting history in praise of Confucianism and in search of harmony preoccupied Chinese identity boosters as attacks on the West traced the roots of imperialism.

Because U.S. thinking supposedly has not really changed since the Cold War, as it has continued to contain North Korea and China and also Russia, the recent period now appears as a continuation rather than a new era. Only by accepting "equal" relations and ending its infringement on China's core interests will the United States really justify a different verdict, we learn.[18] If accusations against U.S. hegemonism throughout these twenty years are a mainstay, many examples of Sino-U.S. cooperation that had been cited as positive fall under the new shadow of accusations against nefarious U.S. motives. History is a means to make a contrast, which now must be reinforced.

THE SECTORAL DIMENSION

After its cultural self-annihilation peaked in the Cultural Revolution decade, China appeared vulnerable to an onrush of Western and even East Asian culture. As reform initiatives were being launched to overcome the dismal state of the Chinese economy, economic pride also had scant foundation. Although China gained political identity from its recognition as a partner of the United States and as a state seeking equidistance in the strategic triangle with the Soviet Union, it was slow to raise its overall sectoral identity before the 1990s. Each of these elements received higher priority under the strategy set by Deng and developed by Jiang Zemin starting in 1992. Instead of "cultural fever" drawing the Chinese to various foreign cultural magnets, a concerted effort began to boost pride in Chinese culture. With double-digit economic growth becoming habitual, economic national identity soared, gaining further momentum after the bursting of the U.S. high-technology bubble starting in 2000 and the housing bubble starting in 2008. Political identity became a persistent priority, although the concept of the "Beijing Consensus" was not directly embraced.[19] China was no longer vulnerable to U.S. pretensions, so it put forth its own pretensions as the country with the strongest case for sectoral identity, notably after 2008 when its rhetoric cast aside previous cautions.

Economic national identity experienced the most dramatic transformation in the 1990s and 2000s, rising sharply again starting in 2008, when China not only emerged in much better shape than the United States and its allies but also expressed optimism that its model of development would both sustain its rise to first in the world in total gross domestic product and prove superior in the coming stage of competition among nations. This was attributed increasingly to the role of the state and even to contrasts between flawed elements of capitalism in the United States and elsewhere and reformed socialism in China.[20] If the Soviet Union in the 1960s and Japan in the 1980s were triumphal over the superiority of their economic models at times when they were rapidly gaining on the United States, China's triumphalism was the most pronounced. Disparaging the economic model of the West became part of the narrative trumpeting China's state-driven, newly recentralized system supposedly opposed to protectionism.

Chinese sources are intent on refuting long-standing claims for the merits of the U.S. international role in providing public goods, including economic ones. They insist that the hegemonic power gained economic advantage at the expense of other states. Its actions, driving up oil prices during the Iraq War or recklessly handling financial transactions before the world financial crisis hit, proved destabilizing. As its share of the global economy shrinks, they argue, conditions are developing to end its hegemony.[21] With China in the lead, developing countries have become the driving force for world economic growth, reducing the U.S. role. Given this reasoning, these sources dismiss the standard argument that the United States is the indispensable global source of stability and economic prosperity. Their prevailing assumption is not only that China will be first economically but also that its model will prove superior.

Cultural national identity draws an even sharper contrast with the United States. In 2010, the glorification of Chinese culture, historically and at present, knew few bounds. As opposed to the class struggle rhetoric of past Communism, which identified a positive message only when the masses turned to conflict, the central thesis became the celebration of harmony across history. Not only were internal ethnic minorities embraced by Confucian-inspired elites and masses, but conflict within China was minimized in an unparalleled record of stability. Rule by non-Han minorities had only proven the merits of Han openness to outsiders, affirming the harmonious character of politics and society. The Communist Party's rule supports this tradition, drawing praise as further evidence of China's success in maintaining harmony, as if the Maoist era had never happened. Although little is written about the disharmony of American life, the impact of American culture abroad is criticized for its intolerance and disruptive consequences for other societies. Raising the clash between Chinese civilization and Western civilization to the level of a long-term struggle over the shape of international society, Chinese sources touching on comparisons put cultural identity at the forefront.[22]

The world financial crisis offered proof to the Chinese not only that the model of U.S. and capitalist economics is flawed but also that there is a crisis of cultural values in the West. This comes amid a perceived renaissance of Chinese culture. In this narrative, the hegemony of Western culture is roundly criticized as resulting in cultural colonization, even exacting a price on states that pursued modernization. If China had remained passive, it now can more actively counter Western hegemonism in this sphere as the fragmentation of global culture proceeds.[23]

Political national identity has also been boosted, but it remains somewhat in the shadows. The Chinese insist that they do not seek to export their political system and have balked at openly endorsing the "Beijing Consensus," a concept attributed to the West. Yet, in rejecting the superiority of democracy or the "Washington Consensus," they leave no doubt about their preferences. Portraying their model as different, they stress a distinct political identity, even if its nature is somewhat obscured. Most important, it serves to distance China from the United States, through insistence that the U.S. model is a bad fit for China and warnings that the model is also unsuitable for other countries. At the very least, the U.S. political model is under a cloud, through its contrast to China's noninterference in internal affairs.

THE VERTICAL DIMENSION

China's leaders put a contrast in the vertical dimension at the core of their identity claims. Instead of reverting to Communist ideology to support this, they draw on Confucian ideals, emphasizing family and state cohesion as opposed to the individualism found in the West. Yet this claim poses problems. After all, for a century Chinese critics, including Marxists, blamed Confucian social relations for a lack of development away from so-called feudalism. Even now there are cautionary discussions of dependent personalities that lack the creativity needed for the next stage of global competition. Inherently, the Chinese claim to a different model rests mostly on the state's role rather than collectives within society, or even the family. This case is not convincing, except for claims to faster economic growth, and it faces rebuttals by those who stress corruption, arbitrary decisionmaking, and the stifling effect of the state's various forms of control. Only simplistic dichotomies at a time of economic contrasts with the West have allowed China to overcome incredulity about its vertical claims, centering on the state's leadership even at the expense of market forces.[24] As repression intensifies to maintain the illusion of harmony and order, the assertions of Chinese superiority are unlikely to escape growing doubts.

The clash between Communism and capitalism has been downplayed in favor of a clash between Eastern and Western civilizations. In this narrative, China's past draws praise for harmony as various ethnicities prospered together and stability prevailed, a 180-degree shift from its earlier pride in peasant rebellions and a past full of an instability that was seen as necessary for progress. In contrast, today's preferred image of Western civilization is that it caused countless clashes with outsiders and stressed individualism, resulting in more conflict. All this is supported with reference to specific examples, including the status of Muslim minorities in premodern China.[25]

Recent Chinese sources acknowledge a Chinese model (*Zhongguo moshi*) as a distinct path of development with diverse elements. Never doubting its political distinctiveness, they now insist on its economic exceptionalism and add claims for cultural and social uniqueness. If references to its Confucian roots have become commonplace, they do not displace assertions that it also reflects socialism. For instance, one source on the Chinese model attributes its cultural character to a mixture of Confucian culture and Marxist ideology.[26] Drawing a contrast with the Western order, which is seen as having peaked in the Cold War, it insists that their values are more accepting of diverse cultures, equality, and cooperation. All these themes fit into the narrative about harmony, especially between the individual and society, but the claims lack academic rigor. There is no direct comparison, examples are poorly defined, and contrasts are presented to illustrate propaganda points, not to promote research. Sensitive topics of national identity are typically the province of the Propaganda Department, and journals make no distinction between deductive presentations to illustrate desired contrasts and findings from genuine scholarship.

Instead of Chinese-style personal relations enabling rampant corruption, as was once recognized, recent emphasis has been put on personal connections, sometimes called *guanxi*, serving to boost harmony. The rule of law and the rights of individuals are downplayed in favor of distinctive Chinese cultural traits. Above all, harmony is a convenient excuse for prioritizing order over the pursuit of justice and an acceptance of official policies and decisions over an insistence on redressing grievances.[27] A leap is made in joining social harmony and economic success. China's economic success is trumpeted as proof of both its social system and its political model. In turn, each is now more often linked to the socialist road China is taking, however vague may be the association with any prior notion of socialist thinking on social policies.[28]

Chinese authors take pride in China's development model, considering it scientific and successful. Increasingly, they also castigate the Western democratic model as unable to overcome internal problems. Attributing to it hypocrisy and easy manipulation by narrow interests, they argue that the world financial crisis exposed its serious shortcomings.[29] This sharp contrast is at the core of national identity.

Chinese diatribes against the Nobel Peace Prize being awarded to the imprisoned Liu Xiaobo showcased the vertical dimension. He was accused of rejecting the state, political authority, and the socialist system and of instead advocating a Western-style democratic system. Supposedly, he did not respect China, similar to the "separatist" Nobel Prize winner, the Dalai Lama. Little is said about his opposition to the Chinese Communist Party or its shortcomings. Instead, he is accused of disdaining Chinese culture and of supporting full Westernization. This logic is inherently authoritarian, while also insisting on a dichotomy between global norms founded on universal values and China's national identity, which disguises socialist identity as traditional.[30]

GILBERT ROZMAN

THE HORIZONTAL DIMENSION

Since Deng Xiaoping launched his reforms in 1978, China has faced the challenge of redefining itself. In Mao's final decade, it presented itself as socialist verging on Communist, in contrast to the revisionist Soviet Union, and as anti-imperialist with close ties to developing countries, in contrast to the United States. In 1979, the term "revisionism" was dropped from China's lexicon just as normalization, accompanied by economic integration with the United States and its allies, left a hole in China's national identity rhetoric. The 1980s were filled with stops and starts linked to Deng's limits on reconsidering socialism and even anti-imperialism in the approved worldview. In the 1990s, socialism was downplayed, even if was deemed essential to identity, as antihegemonism was upgraded in the struggle against U.S. global leadership. Although the emphasis shifted in the 2000s to China's tradition and pride in its latest success, the international component of identity grew more diverse. By 2010, China was positioning itself at multiple crossroads within the community of nations.

China had been part of the dichotomy between West and East during the Cold War before it muddied this concept by making the Soviet Union its primary antagonist. In 2010, Chinese sources were trumpeting the dichotomy of North versus South, building on past association with developing countries and increased confidence in their rise, especially in economic integration with China and through emerging middle powers. Likewise, by repeating claims that Asia is rising to be the center of the world in this century, they draw a contrast with the old center in the West, above all the United States. In this sense, they rejuvenate the divide between East and West. These two geographical dichotomies are replete with references to U.S. hegemonism and the struggle to dislodge it. Although some Chinese confuse the issue in asserting the rise of the Asia-Pacific region in place of the Euro-Atlantic region, this is omitted in discourse on national identity. Similarly, China's embrace of "globalization" is often qualified as the meaning of this term is narrowed, and its support for regionalism is asserted only to the degree that the East Asian region is closed to others, notably the United States. A

U.S. presence in regionalism is seen as inconceivable because it would bring hegemony, arrogance toward others, and an incompatible civilization.[31] In the world financial crisis, the socialist-versus-capitalist dichotomy was also creeping back into Chinese rhetoric. A strategy of treating the United States as the "other" is served by all these divides.

Situated at multiple crossroads, China is part of the South, Asia, East Asia, the East, the developing world, the rising powers, the anti-imperialist states, the anti-non-economic globalization states, and the socialist states. All these identities are relevant to widening gaps, particularly with the United States. Given the emphasis put in prior years on China's peaceful development, its support for a harmonious world, and its embrace of multilateralism and cooperation above competition, these identity themes could cause confusion. They reflect a duality of China lying low and biding its time without directly challenging the world order and U.S. leadership, and of China rising up to assert its rightful identity, which long had to be shielded due to insufficient power. In 2010, the shift was accelerated amid debate over the continued relevance of Deng's cautions. Not of its accord, supposedly, China is being forced to move away from these past ideals.

The world order is in flux. The United States strives for an orderly transition, eying China's cooperation as critical to this goal, while China stresses replacement of the old order with grave doubts that this will come through the cooperation of the United States. If it can draw together the rising middle powers, tap into the volatility of the Middle East, and capitalize on the rise of Asia, China would drive the reordering of the international community. In contrast to the United States' hesitation to acknowledge a quick reordering, China is inclined to exaggerate how and when this shift will occur. Yet the main focus of new attention is East Asia, where the U.S. role has recently been denigrated and China's rise has been celebrated. Regionalism is lauded at the expense of globalization.

East Asia excludes South Asia and West (Southwest) Asia, the South Pacific, and, of course, North America. It is defined by geography and culture, fortifying its exclusive identity. Culture includes a racial component, a Confucian component, and shared values as well as patterns of interpersonal relations, which lead to distinctive approaches to international relations. Although Japan is recognized as within the region and as a possible partner, its notion of the East Asian community arouses suspicion because it idealistically blurs the line between regionalism and globalization.[32] However, the main contrast is drawn with the United States, which is accused of striving to force its leadership and values on a region that has been coalescing well without it.

Treating East Asia as historically and culturally coherent and judging U.S. policy as an outsider's intervention, writers insist that the U.S. desire for a democratic Asia-Pacific community is aimed at imposing an alien approach while containing China's rise.[33] The possibility of finding common ground, even in dealing with conflict-ridden situations, is often dismissed. The convergence in values is not taken seriously. Instead, the identity gap is widened to suggest an irreconcilable contest for regional supremacy.

George W. Bush's challenge to Chinese national identity centered on the global community. At the regional level, he was seen as neglecting Southeast Asia, leaving China scope for forging an East Asian community. On North Korea, he relied on the Six-Party Talks, which supposedly put China in the driver's seat. Although his initiatives toward India, Afghanistan, and Central Asia drew a rebuke, they were considered secondary to the general trend of the United States leaving Asia. Meanwhile, his campaign for transforming the global community proved so counterproductive that China was able to make extensive inroads without growing very concerned. Anti-Americanism flourished with little effort by China, as it grew confident about regionalism. Because the center of globalization was shifting to Asia and the United States was losing the soft power war, China could be relaxed in its response to Bush. Without saying it in so many words, the Chinese left no doubt that 9/11 had been a godsend for their state.

Barack Obama posed a different challenge with his audacious return to Asia. This was immediately recognized in Chinese publications, which criticized him and his secretary of state, Hillary Clinton, directly and portrayed a struggle between civilizations. Instead of stressing antiterrorism and antiproliferation, he was seen as being on the guard against

China and opposing an integration process that was not under U.S. control.[34] One factor was that the Six-Party Talks had largely lost their benefit in relaxing U.S. concerns about China and in dividing Japan and South Korea in their responses to U.S. regional policy. The Chinese neglect to mention their country's responsibility for this situation, amid increasing wariness about serving as a "responsible stakeholder," which is equated with serving U.S. interests.

Many Chinese sources depict a natural course of regionalism independent of globalization that is both a fresh start after an abnormal interlude in Asian history and a resumption of earlier regional relations—cultural, economic, and political. They suggest that the United States under Obama is disrupting this process in many ways. It is playing on the contradiction between economic integration and security uncertainty to inhibit the former. Alliances and the hub-and-spokes security system do not correspond to the needs of an economically integrated region, they insist. Also, Obama is pressing for a free trade agreement for the Asia-Pacific region—the Trans-Pacific Partnership—in hopes of circumventing what is seen as the natural regionalism. Of concern, he inserts values into the pursuit of regionalism, drawing on Western traditions without considering Eastern ones. In this light, writers leave the strong impression that there are only two alternatives: a U.S. plan to control the region with itself at the center versus an exclusive regionalism that rejects outsiders such as the United States. This kind of dichotomous logic is typical of the identity gap widening being practiced by China. In this depiction, the United States is bent on preventing regionalism, which inevitably puts China at the center, not because of anything China is doing but due to its own flawed national character (*guojiaxing*).[35] Opposition to boosting the East Asian Summit as a threat to the integration of East Asia has been linked to criticisms of the Western bias of the international system.[36]

Chinese sources increasingly pit regionalism against internationalization. By doing so, they seek to exclude the United States as a hegemonic power that intrudes where it is not wanted. In the case of the South China Sea, they insist that the natural course is for bilateral talks to go forward between China and bordering Southeast Asian states.

Not only the United States, in its 2009–11 "return," but also India and Japan are accused of attempting to internationalize the disputes about this waterway. If Southeast Asian states welcome U.S. involvement in pursuit of a balance of power, the United States is motivated by the containment of China. In contrast to images of East Asian regionalism as a positive force for China's power and identity, such warnings treat internationalism as a negative force to reinforce U.S. power and an outmoded system of security relations that interferes with China's aspirations.[37] As the United States is declining, the Chinese contend, it is playing up its security role as if that keeps it at the center. It suppresses regionalism and presses for more internationalism as a basis for hegemonism, especially under Obama's push to strengthen alliances and form a parallel trans-Pacific community to the existing trans-Atlantic community. In objecting to this reorganization of Asia, China offers its own blueprint, supported by criticisms of U.S. motives and appeals to civilizational ties rooted in history.

Writers reject internationalism because it is an affirmation of the existing interstate system. They reify the notion of a hegemonic power resisting a rising power, as if the only factor is the defensive alarm of the former to see its status usurped. While noting that there were previous spikes in Sino-U.S. tension in the years 1995–96, 1999, and 2001, they suggest that today's clash is different. Instead of one narrow issue, this time the full range of differences are involved; divergent social systems, ideologies, and civilizations face each other. If, when confronting the Soviet Union, the United States resorted to containment, and if, in facing competition from Japan, it applied economic pressure to achieve political goals, China has positioned itself to be able to counter such pressure, after drawing lessons from the Soviet Union's fall.[38]

The Chinese generally leave the impression that the motivation behind U.S. containment is not anticommunism but hostility to the rise of a rival. This hostility appears to be rooted in U.S. values and fear about the West's cultural monopoly being broken. It is essential for the Chinese to downplay association with any hint of the negative history of socialism or any sign that U.S. fears could be linked to conduct based in socialism. Thus, an innocent China that has given no reason for offense and whose values pose no danger for peace and justice is unduly targeted. Yet this line of reasoning clashes with other criticisms of the United States as still under the sway of anticommunism.

Writers attribute to other countries, especially the United States, hostile intentions in identifying it as an "enemy" or "threat." No matter how often they are reassured about the United States' interest in finding common interests, they twist whatever data they can muster into arguments for why China is being contained or demonized. The propensity of U.S. leaders to refer to "rogue states," the "axis of evil," and the "war on terror" serves to frighten people and boost the defense budget, following a history of constructing threats in the West to bolster state authority.[39] There is no recognition of interactive policies and statements. China is never faulted for arousing concern.

As the case of the South China Sea reveals, China sees the U.S. presence in the region as hegemonic and illegitimate. Arguing that America is there to check China's rise, analysts equate its military presence and interest in preventing any one state from gaining control over sea lanes as an improper intrusion. Recognizing that the sea is deemed the "Mediterranean Sea of Asia" and that "any state that controls it controls all of East Asia," writers still reject the interest in maintaining freedom of navigation and preventing one state from taking control, which Americans cite.[40] They often ignore the concerns of other Asian states that China would seize control, acting as if only the United States is arousing them. Behind this reasoning is the notion that Asia is for the Asians and that the U.S. presence is just another manifestation of imperialism. There is an assumption that China does not seek unequal relations, let alone hegemony. As a result, Asians should accept it rather than the United States as the leading state. No mention is made of past sponsorship of revolutionary forces or of reasons why Chinese policies still arouse distrust. National identity presumes a benign history and the absence of concern about Chinese pressure, as in the way it responds to visits to other countries by the Dalai Lama.

The Chinese have taken to defining East Asia as a unit historically and culturally coherent and to judging U.S. policy as an outsider's input that either serves regionalism of this exclusive type or does not.[41] They insist that the U.S. desire for a democratic Asia-Pacific community is aimed at imposing an alien approach while containing China's rise. The possibility of finding common ground, notably in dealing with conflict-ridden situations, is dismissed. Convergence in values is not taken seriously. Instead, the identity gap is widened to suggest an irreconcilable contest for supremacy.

More cautious Chinese analysis proposes a two-track approach, refraining from excluding the United States and threatening its interests, while striving to limit its role by reinforcing the leading role of the Association of Southeast Asian Nations (ASEAN) and also countering U.S. ambitions for an "East Asian democratic, free trade system" with support for Asian values. In early 2009, China had already reached agreement in principle with the ASEAN member states, Japan, and South Korea on currency swaps to address the financial crisis together, and three-way Sino–Japan–South Korean cooperation was advancing to the point that leadership in East Asian integration would shift to include second-stage cooperation from ASEAN, opening the way for China to play a more active role in some areas. Yet concern was rising that Obama would stir up divisions not only over security but also over values, causing rifts in a region rife with religious and cultural differences. China's hope for integration could be jeopardized by this U.S. "return" after it had supposedly ignored ASEAN.[42] If some analysts warned that a dual track would be needed, given the potential of the U.S. strategy, the direction chosen was more confrontational. In contrast to such cautions, boosters of an assertive Chinese identity saw an opening.

With the expansion of the East Asian Summit to include the United States as well as Russia, China debated the proper response. It had conceived of the Asia-Pacific Economic Cooperation forum as led by the United States and ASEAN + 3 as led by small countries in ASEAN in transition to increasing Chinese leadership. Unlike Europe, where Germany and France played a leadership role in integration, China did not see Japan as a partner in this fashion. But now there is a new challenge from an organization led by small states, which the United States is determined to use to strengthen its political, economic, and military influence in the region. It is no longer clear that small states will stay in charge. These new circumstances lead the Chinese to predict the alienation of states and new trouble, but they see no alternative to remaining active.[43] A refusal to see promise in the expanded East Asian Summit is a sign that China does not envision narrowing its differences with the United States or accepting an inclusive form of regionalism, but is seeking ways to sharpen the difference between Chinese-led Asian regionalism and the U.S. order.

Three disputes on China's borders have become interlinked in the rhetoric about U.S. containment and the internationalization of matters that should be regional. The North Korean nuclear crisis, the East China Sea territorial dispute, and the rift over the South China Sea are treated as examples of containment and U.S. efforts to split China from other countries. All serve as examples of sovereignty—China voices indisputable sovereignty over critical parts of the two seas, and it does not criticize North Korea militancy toward South Korea because that would be interfering in Korean affairs. U.S. efforts to broaden involvement in these issues—drawing states such as India and Japan into the South China Sea dispute and striving to bring North Korea before the UN Security Council for its attacks on the South—are depicted as interference in regional matters.[44] Long having supported Russian reestablishment of a sphere of influence in the former Soviet Union, China increasingly sees a parallel in U.S. hegemonic behavior to limit both its influence and the rise of regionalism.

Many Chinese treat the transition to the second decade of this century much as Americans treated the transition to the final decade of the past century. The world is in great flux. The old order is disappearing. China can look forward to new prospects for shaping a world order to its liking. Although optimism about economic superiority figured in both sets of expectations, the military dimension is also in evidence. The United States' earlier thinking rested on confidence in its military superiority. China's outlook draws on expectations that there will be a change in the balance, especially as new technologies are introduced. The Americans saw their model as the winner, and the Chinese highlight their model and values. They also attribute fear of it and the accompanying China-threat discourse to Westerners who are unwilling to accept China's rapid rise. Rather than avoid raising the sensitivities of those who are steeped in past racism and who are now determined to contain China, China must speak out and press for major changes, many argue. However, in 2011 there was a backlash against optimism of this sort, postponing the timing of the transition without attacking the assumptions behind it.

THE INTENSITY DIMENSION

China was criticized in the United States after its brutal crackdown on the peaceful demonstrators in Tiananmen Square in June 1989 shocked viewers who had been impressed by the public's aspirations. Brief revulsion followed other exposés of the way China handled prominent human rights issues or ethnic protests or of how the Chinese public was aroused against the United States following the accidental bombing of China's Belgrade embassy in 1999 and the accidental EP-3 airplane collision in 2001. Yet advocates of strong reactions to abuses of this sort were frustrated by the priority U.S. political leaders and business and international experts place on cooperation in pursuit of both geopolitical and economic objectives. At each point a downward spiral appeared possible, the U.S. side exercised self-control, and, before 2010, the Chinese recognized the value of cooperation to prevent an identity gap escalation.

U.S. restraint was most problematic under George W. Bush, when members of his administration were tempted to prioritize the challenge from China. Yet the terrorist attacks on the United States on September 11, 2001, refocused attention, raising the strategic imperative of improved bilateral relations. In 2010, the danger of a vicious cycle was rising, as Americans were more pessimistic about their own country and were more alarmed about China's precipitous rise and, even more, its assertive behavior. With the election to Congress in 2010 of many conservative Republicans, who are loathe to compromise and inclined to demonize liberals and even moderates in the United States as well as the international community, the danger was rising of a widening national identity gap that would also be welcomed on the U.S.

side. The seriousness of the issues dividing the two countries means that if they are left to fester and China continues to treat them as cause for demonization, the United States may be tempted to do the same.

The case for U.S. military containment against an innocent China rested on three incidents in 2010: the *Cheonan* sinking in the Yellow Sea, the fishing boat incident in the East China Sea, and the sovereignty dispute in the South China Sea. From the United States' perspective, China's behavior was egregious and its neighbors were angered enough to seek support. Although Washington preferred to enlist Beijing's help in toning down the rhetoric in each instance, the Chinese response was to transfer the blame to the United States, to insist that China was being demonized as part of a deliberate containment strategy, and to grow more assertive in its challenge.[45]

The intensity of China's identity spike does not bode well for narrowing the identity gap. If the many foreign policy setbacks China suffered in 2010 added a note of caution, as did China's decision to treat the Hu-Obama summit as a success, there was no sign that the Chinese narrative had changed appreciably in early 2011. With the exception of North Korea and Iran, foreign policy challenges that are potentially explosive for Sino-U.S. relations are under China's direct control. Just by cooling the intensity of its appeals to national identity, it is in a position to limit any widening in the national identity gap. Given Obama's interest in doing more, China also has an opportunity to start narrowing the gap, if it so desires.

The more intense the national identity, the more assertive the foreign policy is likely to be. One restraining factor for China has been Deng Xiaoping's stricture for it to bide its time and not show its hand, "*taoguang yanghui*." In 2010, however, an ever-increasing number of influential voices argued for relaxing this limitation or doing away with it. They cited China's rising power, the altered global environment, and the provocative acts of Obama, such as selling arms to Taiwan and meeting with the Dalai Lama. Many in China, noting that *taoguang yanghui* was only meant to be temporary, argued that conditions had changed and that national identity could now be brought openly to the surface. Others warned that Deng's logic has lasting merit and that there are too many unknowns to proceed rashly in international relations.[46] The debate centered more on realism versus identity than on what should be China's national identity.

At the time of Hu's visit to Washington, it became essential to state that China wants cooperation rather than confrontation with the United States. Yet the nature of the desired bilateral relationship suggests little trust and poor prospects for both sides working together to resolve problems. After all, it appears to many Chinese that the attack on 9/11, the North Korean nuclear challenge, and other threats are what induced U.S. leaders to postpone the containment of China. This offers China little reassurance, because, in their view, the U.S. mindset remains delusional about maintaining hegemony over an unjust global system. America has never abandoned its Cold War mindset, not even of late, as it grows old and sick along with the rest of the West, while the developing states prosper, Chinese sources repeatedly argue. By resisting America's schemes and flattery to bring China into its fold, they contend that China will build up comprehensive national power to the point where U.S. pressure will be of no avail. This narrative indicates no narrowing of the identity gap, just a temporary extension of *taoguang yanghui*.[47] Although analysts should be on the alert for signs that China's leaders, in a top-down manner, seek a narrowing gap and thus should encourage U.S. officials to respond positively, there should be no room for idealism that simply brushes aside evidence that the gap is failing to narrow or may be widening further as China grows more confident of its relative power.

NOTES

1   Nin Xinchun, "Aobama waijiao; mengjiang yu xianshi," *Heping yu fazhan*, no. 6 (2009): 5–8, 41.

2   Niu Zejing, "Shexi Dongya gongtongti yujingxia Meiguo waijiao zouxiang yu Zhongguo de yingdui zhi ce," *Fazhi yu shehui*, no. 5 (2010): 135–36.

3   Gilbert Rozman, *Strategic Thinking about the Korean Nuclear Crisis: Four Parties Caught between North Korea and the United States*, rev. ed. (New York: Palgrave, 2011).

4   Yin Chengde, "Shilun Aobama waijiao de de yu shi," *Guoji wenti yanjiu*, no. 2 (2010): 1–7.

5   Wang Yizhou, "'Dongya gongtongti' gainian bianzhi," *Xiandai guoji guanxi*, spec. ed. (2010): 86.

6   Zhou Qi, "Renzhi gongtong liyi shi Zhongmei guanxi fazhan de guanjian: Zhongmei jianjiao 30 zhounian huigu," *Shijie jingji yu zhengzhi*, no. 11 (2009): 7–11.

7   Wang Yizhou, "'Dongya gongtongti' gainian bianzhi," 87.

8   "'Sixiang zhibian' xia de dangjin shijie waijiao," *Renmin ribao*, September 2, 2010.

9   Feng Zhaokui, "Fazhan yu shijie chaoliuxiang yizhide Zhongri guanxi," *Riben xuekan*, no. 6 (2010): 5, 12–13.

10 "Hanjian de weijigan congheerlai?" *Anhui Zhongguo qingnianbao*, February 21, 2011; for the text of Obama's address, see http://www.whitehouse.gov/the-press-office/2011/01/25/remarks-president-state-union-address.

11 Yuan Peng, "Dui Zhongmei guanxi weilai fazhan de zhanlue sikao," *Xiandai guoji guanxi*, spec. ed. (2010): 65–70, 83.

12 Zhou Qi, "Renzhi gongtong liyi shi Zhongmei guanxi fazhan de guanjian."

13 Ibid.

14 Xia Xingyou, "Zhongguo bixu nadao yizhang bubei qiling de ruchangjuan," *Guangming ribao*, January 28, 2011.

15 Yuan Peng, "Dui Zhongmei guanxi weilai fazhan de zhanlue sikao."

16 Tang Yanlin, "Meiguo dui Zhongguo jueqi de renzhi duice ji Zhongguo de yingdui," *Shijie jingji yu zhengzhi*, no. 3 (2010): 30–45.

17 Jin Lihua, "Dongbeiya wenti de lishi kaocha yu qishi," *Hebei jingmao daxue xuebao*, September 2010, 24–28.

18 Xu Hui, "Zhongmei junshi huxin weihe nanyi jianli?" *Waijiao pinglun*, no. 2 (2010): 22–29.

19 See Joshua Cooper Ramo, *The Beijing Consensus* (London: Foreign Policy Centre, 2004), 3.

20 Dong Huaiping, "'Wenhua zijue' yu Zhongguo zhengzhi shengtai kechixu fazhan guannian de goujian," *Zhejiang xuekan*, no. 4 (2009): 229–35.

21 Bao Jianyun, "Meiguo weihu haishi pohuaile shijie jingji de wending?" *Shijie jingji yu zhengzhi*, no. 5 (2009): 17–27.

22 Cao Yuan, "Qianxi wenhua zhuquan yu qingshaonian guojia minzu yishi," *Anyang shifan xueyuan xuebao*, 2009, 129–32.

23 Wang Yuechuan, "Houdongfangzhuyi yu Zhongguo wenhua shenfen," *Lilun yu chuangzuo*, no. 3 (2010): 4–9.

24 Lei Xingchang, "Zhongxifang 'wenhua' chayi bijiao fenxi," *Kexue, jingji, shehui*, no. 1 (2010): 173–76.

25 James Leibold, "More Than a Category: Han Supremacism on the Chinese Internet," *China Quarterly*, no. 203 (September 2010): 539–59.

26 Yu Yingli, "Congxin jiedu 'Zhongguo moshi': Gainian yu yingxiang," *Xiandai guoji guanxi*, no. 6 (2010): 25–32.

27 Dong Huaiping, "'Wenhua zijue' yu Zhongguo zhengzhi shengtai kechixu fazhan guannian de goujian."

28 "Cong zhengzhi zhidu kan Zhongguo weishenme zong hui chenggong?"
Available at www.xinhua net.com.

29 Song Xiaochuan, "Xifang minzhu moshi de neizai quexian yu shijianzhong de
wudao," *Zhongguo shehui kexue bao*, February 16, 2011.

30 "Nuobeier Hepingjiang shi Xifang gei Liu Xiaobo de zhengzhi kaoshang,"
Xinhuawang, October 15, 2010.

31 Li Dongyi, "Dongya quyuhua ruhe chuli yu Meiguo de guanxi:Yu Ouzhou
quyuhua de duibi fenxi," *Waijiao pinglun*, no. 2 (2010): 90–92.

32 Wang Yizhou, 'Dongya gongtongti' gainian bianshi," 84–88.

33 Zhang Xiaoming, "Meiguo shi Dongya quyu hezuo de tuidongzhe haishi
zuaizhe," *Shijie jingji yu zhengzhi*, no. 7 (2010): 4–13.

34 Wang Yiwei, "Meiguo Yatai zhixuguan de xin bianhua jiqi mianlin de taozhan,"
Guoji guancha, no. 3 (2009): 1.

35 Ibid., 6.

36 Li Wei, "Dang guoji fenghui biancheng 'qingdanguan,'" *Guancha pinglun*,
November 22, 2010, 17.

37 Ju Hailong and Ge Hongliang, "Meiguo 'chongfan' Dongnanya dui Nanhai
anquan xingshi de yingxiang," *Shijie jingji yu zhengzhi luntan*, no. 1 (2010): 87–97.

38 Yuan Peng, "Zhongmei guanxi xiang he chuqu?" *Waijiao pinglun*, no. 2 (2010):
1–7.

39 Liu Yongtao, "Jiangou anquan 'weixie': Meiguo zhanlue de zhengzhi xuanze,"
Shijie jingji yu zhengzhi, no. 6 (2010): 118–28.

40 Wang Quanjian, "Meiguo de Nanzhonghai zhengce: lishi yu xianshi," *Waijiao
pinglun*, no. 6 (2009): 87–91.

41 Zhang Xiaoming, "Meiguo shi Dongya quyu hezuo de tuidongzhe haishi
zuaizhe."

42 Chen Yiping, "Gaibian yu yanxu: Aobama zhengfu de Dongya zhengce yu
Dongya yitihua," *Dongnanya yanjiu*, no. 5 (2009): 31–43.

43 Wang Zhong, "Huanqiu Liaowang: Dongya fenghui renao guohou gengying
sikao weilai," *Renminwang*, October 29, 2010.

44 Xie Xiaojun, "Meiguo chashou Nanhai, yiyu hewei?" *Shishi shuping*, 2010,
10–11.

45 Hanxu Dong, "Yong rouxing celue yingdui geng qiangda de Meijun," *Huanqiu
shibao*, February 15, 2011.

46 Wang Zaibang, "Lun chuangzaoxing de jianchi taoguang yanghui, yousuo
zuowei de tujing fenxi," *Xiandai guoji guanxi*, spec. ed. (2010): 48–53.

47 "Xinshiji shinian yu Zhongguo waijiao dazhanlue," *Xinhuawang*, January 28,
2011.

CONTRIBUTORS

See-Won Byun is a Ph.D. student at George Washington University and Kelly Fellow of the Pacific Forum at the Center for Strategic and International Studies.

Cheol Hee Park is professor and associate dean of the Graduate School of International Studies at Seoul National University. In 2011, he published a book in Korean, *The LDP Regime and Changes in the Postwar System.*

Gilbert Rozman is the Musgrave Professor of Sociology at Princeton University. He has recently published a revised, updated version of *Chinese Strategic Thought toward Asia* and coedited *China's Foreign Policy: Who Makes It and How Is It Made?*

Scott Snyder is senior fellow for Korea Studies and director of the Program on U.S.-Korea Policy at the Council on Foreign Relations. He is the author of *China's Rise and the Two Koreas: Politics, Economics, Security* and editor of *The U.S. and ROK Alliance: Meeting New Security Challenges.*

Kazuhiko Togo is director of the Institute for World Affairs and professor of international politics at Kyoto Sangyo University. Previously, he was Japanese ambassador to the Netherlands and director-general of the European and Oceanian Department of Japan's Ministry of Foreign Affairs.

Ming Wan is professor of government and politics at George Mason University, on leave at Keio University in 2010–12. His two recent books are *The Political Economy of East Asia: Striving for Wealth and Power* and *Sino-Japanese Relations: Interaction, Logic, and Transformation*.

Yongnian Zheng is professor and director of the East Asian Institute at the National University of Singapore. He is the editor of *China: An International Journal*, and the editor of the China Policy Series, which is published by Routledge.

INDEX

human rights, 188, 241; and China, 78,
116, 167, 219, 223–28, 235, 260;
and Japan, 26, 80; versus state rights
(*guoquan*), 199
humanism, 196
Huntington, Samuel, 66
Hu Yaobang, 76–77, 89, 195

ideological dimension, 96–100, 156–60,
181–82, 190–91, 200, 239–42
Ilin, Ivan, 31–32
incentives, 194
India, 67, 140, 209, 227, 239, 254; and
China, 195, 203, 205, 236; and
regionalism, 10, 222, 256; and U.S.
ties, 254, 259
Indian Ocean, 135
individualism, 21, 30, 225, 242, 249–51
Indonesia, 34, 195, 205, 222–24, 227
intellectual property rights, 118
intensity dimension, 121, 156, 170–72,
179–81, 186–87, 191–93, 200
inter-Korean ties: declaration of 2007,
108, 113; summit of 2000, 110
internationalism: and China, 8, 118, 128,
162, 187, 242, 253–56; and Japan, 70,
78–80, 167, 186, 215
International Monetary Fund, 146
international relations theory, 128–33,
137, 141, 147–48, 172–78, 181–88,
192–94, 199–200
international system, 140–45, 199;
historically, 67, 69, 194; and
regionalism, 214; transformation of,
128, 187, 243; and West-centric order,
234, 245, 255, 262
Internet: control of, 9; nationalism, 12,
81, 116, 198, 212, 228
Iran, 37–39, 205, 228–29, 261; nuclear
program of, 19, 41; and Persia, 140
Iraq War, 37–38, 222, 248
Ishihara Shintaro, 54

Islamic World, 182; and China, 203,
205–6, 222–30; and Japan, 5–6, 15,
17–19, 34–41; and South Korea, 7

Japan, and colonialism, 36, 45, 49, 56,
99–100, 162–63, 171, 176, 180, 205,
217; and revival of imperialism, 210;
as a bridge, 5, 19, 27–28, 78, 184; as
normal, 16, 33, 52–53, 72, 175, 186,
208, 212–14; as a peaceful country, 74,
209; as a political and military great
power, 72, 210, 213–15; as a teacher,
74–75, 78, 222; bubble economy of,
22, 179, 186, 194, 247; communal
values of, 4; defense buildup, 83, 209;
names for, 68, neoconservatives or
revisionists of, 46, 53–54, 60, 157,
182, 187, 204, 215, 233; shock of
falling behind China, 215, weakness
toward China, 12, 212
Japan-Russia relations, 5, 12, 28–34, 174,
211
Japan's Ministry of Foreign Affairs,
bashing of, 12
Java, 135
Jiang Zemin, 81, 247
Johnston, Alistair Iain, 142

Kaifu Toshiki, 79
Kanji cultural sphere, 164
Kan Naoto, 58, 83, 210, 215–16
Katakura Kunio, 34, 38
Kato Junpei, 17, 34–42
Kazakov, Alexander (Sasha), 31–32
Khrushchev, Nikita, 174, 233
Khubilai, 136
Kim Dae-jung, 55, 113, 164, 174–75
Kim Il-sung, 99, 110, 112
Kim Jong-il, 88, 111, 113
Kim Jung-un, 13, 88
Kishi Nobusuke, 5, 35, 74, 215; three
pillars of, 18, 214